Comments from readers of the Windows version of this book...

"I am more than halfway through the lessons, and I am really learning about many of the advanced features of Excel. And it is fun.

The book is organized so that each lesson fits on two facing pages with an excellent sample file that you work with. Lessons in each section build on the ones before, you get a sense of accomplishment as you finish each lesson and move on.

I thought I was an accomplished Excel user, but I now realize I had only scratched the surface of what Excel can do.

I have purchased quite a few books on Excel over the years, but this will be the only one in which I will have read every page.

I recommend this book for anyone who wants to think of themselves as an Excel power user".
– A reader from the USA

"If you are an Excel intermediate level user, then I can recommend, thoroughly, that you purchase this book. It is extremely well written and the exercises provided will, indubitably, help you consolidate your knowledge and expertise.

I am writing this review as an IT trainer with 30 years' experience, though recently retired, who has bought and attempted to read through the many volumes of Excel that are available. For me this is the best...great stuff.

I might be sticking my neck out here but buy this volume and you probably will not need, or want to, attend an actual course!"
– A reader from the United Kingdom

"OK this book is a no brainer. Mr Smart makes learning Excel simple and efficient.

His website has tons of additional material and the practice Excel worksheets are the best tool because you apply each lesson as you go. This makes learning easier and retention much greater.

I have four children and my 10 and 13-year-old are now sharing this book with me along with the Essential Skills book.

Thank you!"
– A reader from the USA

"This is the best software book I have ever purchased.

I taught Excel to 11-16 year olds for years, I now get 'how do I' questions from staff in industry on Excel all the time as I know my Excel. I cannot believe how much I have learnt from this book in a couple of days, and there's so much still to take in".
– A reader from the United Kingdom

"Great book. Love how it is set up in sessions (approx. 90 mins each). Also, the layout is such that if you know how to do a particular bit, you can ignore it and just go into the next step".
– A reader from the United Kingdom

"A very well thought out resource. I can say only good words about this book:

It's very practical
It's concise and at the same time very well explained
It saves your time and money

It's a fantastic book and I recommend it everybody who wants study Excel's advanced features".
– *A reader from the USA*

"The design of this book means I can quickly progress through areas I understand or read the detail on topics I am not sure of. The support materials available to practice with are varied and relevant to business.".
– *A reader from the USA*

"Easy to read. Short concise chapters. Covered all that I required. I would recommend this book to anyone who wants to learn more detailed Excel".
– *A reader from the USA*

"Great book to use for teaching and those with beginner's skills. Easy to follow great examples. Each chapter tends keeps you interested in the subject".
– *A reader from the USA*

"We were looking for a book to cover the next step beyond basic Excel and this is it. Other books were too field/profession specific but this one can be used by anyone".
– *A reader from the USA*

"As Ever Mike Smart leads you through Excel in simple progressive steps and you are amazed by how much you have learnt. Would recommend to anyone who has to use Excel.

Must be one of the best resources for learning it".
– *A reader from the United Kingdom*

"I have a vast library of Excel manuals. But for learning Excel quickly, the Smart Method is excellent.

Each page is a lesson. You ramp up in skill and knowledge at a deliberate pace. The writing is clear as well as the diagrams. The font is a perfect size.

If you are new to this version of Excel or want to improve upon your current skill set, then give this manual a try. I am sure you will find it extremely useful".
- *A reader from the USA*

Who Is This Book for?

If you can already use all of Excel's essential features but want to raise your skills to true Expert level, you've found the right book.

This book isn't for absolute beginners. If you're just starting out with *Excel 2016 for Mac*, you should buy our *Essential Skills* book to learn all of Excel's most important features.

This book will give you advanced Excel skills that are rarely mastered by the average user. By the end of the book you'll be a true Excel expert, able to use all of the power available from the world's most powerful business tool. Your Excel skills will be greater and broader than almost all other Excel users in the workplace.

This book is for *Excel 2016 for Mac* users who:

■ Are already comfortable with Excel 2016 for Mac's basic features (ideally by completing all of the lessons in our *Essential Skills* course).

■ Want to use *all* of Excel 2016 for Mac's more powerful and complex features.

Use of this book as courseware

This book is also the official courseware for The Smart Method's *Excel 2016 for Mac OS X Expert Skills* course.

Smart Method courses have been taken by a varied cross-section of the world's leading companies. We've had fantastic feedback from the vast number of professionals we've empowered with advanced Excel skills.

This book is also suitable for use by other training organizations, teachers, schools, colleges and universities to provide structured, objective-led, and highly effective classroom courses.

This book is not suitable for learning *Excel 2016 for Windows*

You could be forgiven for thinking that the (confusingly named) *Excel 2016 for Windows* (suitable only for Windows desktop and laptop computers) was "just the same" as *Excel 2016 for Mac*. Unfortunately, this is not the case. The *Excel 2016 for Windows* version has an enhanced feature set and a radically different user interface to the *Excel 2016 for Mac* version.

We've produced a special version of this book suitable for Windows users:

Learn Excel 2016 Expert Skills (for Windows) with The Smart Method
ISBN: 978-1-909253-09-4

Learn Excel 2016 for Mac OS X Expert Skills with The Smart Method

Mike Smart

Published by:

The Smart Method® Ltd
Burleigh Manor
Peel Road
Douglas, IOM,
Great Britain
IM1 5EP

Tel: +44 (0)845 458 3282 Fax: +44 (0)845 458 3281

E-mail: sales@ExcelCentral.com
Web: http:// ExcelCentral.com (this book's dedicated web site)

FIRST EDITION

International Standard Book Number (ISBN13): 978-1-909253-12-4

1 2 4 6 8 10 9 7 5 3

Author's Acknowledgements

O would some Power, the gift to give us, To see ourselves as others see us!

Robert Burns, Scottish poet (1759-1796)

Many people will read this book. Some will be confronting advanced concepts, such as pivot tables and macros, for the very first time. Others will be seasoned professionals with an IT background. Readers will include students, office workers, accountants, administrators, doctors, scientists, engineers, bankers and many other professions.

The book aims to communicate how to use Excel's advanced features in a way that is comprehensible to all.

I couldn't have written the original version of this book without the help of many pairs of eyes. I have been extremely lucky to have had this help, throughout the writing process, from a wonderful group of international readers who kindly agreed to test drive the course prior to going to print.

I'm very grateful to Nate Barber (from San Antonio, Texas, USA). Nate was already a seasoned Excel power user and provided some wonderful technical insights. He also highlighted many cases where my British English didn't quite make the journey across the Atlantic. His feedback really helped me to improve the book in so many ways.

Many thanks are also due to Valérie Rousseau (from Quebec, Canada). Valérie spotted an embarrassing number of grammatical errors in my writing, and managed to discover errors that had been missed by all other reviewers.

Huge thanks also go out to Mark Casey (from London, England). Mark provided clear and concise feedback that caused me to completely re-write some of the lessons. His excellent command of the written word enabled me to eloquently re-phrase some of my clumsier sentences.

I'd like to show great appreciation to Lorna Henderson (from Auckland, New Zealand). Lorna provided fantastically detailed feedback, resulting in hundreds of improvements to the book. There's hardly a page in the book that has not benefited from her suggestions and comments.

Many thanks also to Heidi Hembree (from Maryville, Tennessee, USA). Heidi highlighted many areas where I hadn't communicated concepts as well as I should have. Her feedback had a significant impact upon every session.

I'm also extremely grateful to Rosalind Johnson (from Pantymwyn, Wales). Rosalind's useful suggestions helped me to improve the readability of many lessons.

Thanks are also due to Jennifer Lashely (from London, England). Jennifer highlighted many potential pitfalls when working through the lessons that I was then able to eliminate from the final copy.

Special thanks are also due to Simon Smart (my son) who took time out of his own busy software development schedule to undertake a very comprehensive technical proof read.

Huge thanks also to Sue Ferrario (from Douglas, Great Britain) who tirelessly completed the final proofread of the book prior to going to print.

I'd also like to thank the many others that have helped to shape the content of this book that I have not mentioned by name. Your contributions were greatly appreciated.

Contents

Session Two: Data Integrity, Subtotals and Validations   71

Session Three: Advanced Functions   105

Session Four: Using Names and the Formula Auditing Tools   159

Session Five: What If Analysis and Security   193

Session Six: Working with Hyperlinks, Other Applications and Workgroups   221

Session Seven: Forms and Macros   247

Session Eight: Pivot Tables

Appendix A: Differences between the Windows and Mac versions of Excel 2016   335

Appendix B: Skills Covered in the Essential Skills Course   343

Index   349

Introduction

Welcome to *Learn Excel 2016 for Mac OS X Expert Skills with The Smart Method*®. This book has been designed to enable students to master Excel 2016 for Mac advanced skills by self-study. The book is equally useful as courseware in order to deliver classroom courses.

Smart Method® publications are continually evolving as we discover better ways of explaining or teaching the concepts presented.

Feedback

At The Smart Method® we love feedback – both positive and negative. If you have any suggestions for improvements to future versions of this book, or if you find content or typographical errors, the author would always love to hear from you.

You can make suggestions for improvements to this book on our support forums at:

http://forums.excelcentral.com

Future editions will always incorporate your feedback so that there are never any known errors at time of publication.

If you have any difficulty understanding or completing a lesson, or if you feel that anything could have been more clearly explained, we'd also love to hear from you. We've made hundreds of detail improvements to our books based upon reader's feedback and continue to chase the impossible goal of 100% perfection.

Downloading the sample files

In order to use this book, it is necessary to download sample files from the Internet. The sample files are available from:

http://ExcelCentral.com

Type the above URL into your web browser and you'll see the link to the sample files at the top of the home page.

Problem resolution

If you encounter any problem downloading or using the sample files, you'll find detailed help in our support forum at:

http://ExcelCentral.com (click *Support* on the top menu).

You can also post a support request there if necessary and we'll do everything possible to quickly resolve the problem.

Typographical Conventions Used in This Book

This guide consistently uses typographical conventions to differentiate parts of the text.

When you see this	Here's what it means
Click *Line Color* on the left-hand bar and then click *No line.*	Italics are used to refer to text that appears in a worksheet cell, an Excel dialog, on the ribbon, or elsewhere within the Excel application. Italics may sometimes also be used for emphasis or distinction.
Click: ▲→File→Open... 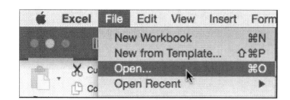	Move the cursor to the Menu Bar at the top of the screen. Click the File menu and click the Open... option from the drop-down list.
Click: Home→Underline. 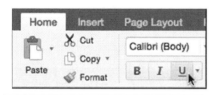	Click on the ribbon's *Home* tab and then click the *Underline* button (that's the left-hand side of the button, not the drop-down arrow next to it).
Click: Home→ Underline Drop Down→Double Underline. 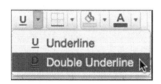	Click on the ribbon's *Home* tab and then look for the *Font* group. Click the drop-down arrow next to the Underline button (that's the right-hand side of the button) within this group and then choose *Double Underline* from the drop-down list.
Click: ▲→Excel→Preferences→ Formulas and Lists→Custom Lists→ Import	This is a more involved example. 1. Move the cursor to the Menu Bar at the top of the screen. 2. Click the *Excel* menu and click *Preferences* from the dropdown list. The *Excel Preferences* dialog appears. 3. Find the *Formulas and Lists* group in the dialog and click the *Custom Lists* button. Another dialog pops up. 4. Click the *Import* button.
Type: **European Sales** into the cell.	Whenever you are supposed to actually type something on the keyboard it is shown in bold faced text.

Press <Cmd> + <Z>.	You should hold down the **Cmd (⌘)** key and then press the **Z** key.
∑ AutoSum ▾	When a lesson tells you to click a button, an image of the relevant button will often be shown either in the page margin or within the text itself.
note In Excel 2016 there are a possible 16,585 columns and 1,048,476 rows. This is a great improvement on earlier versions.	If you want to read through the book as quickly as possible, you don't have to read notes. Notes usually expand a little on the information given in the lesson text.
important Do not click the *Delete* button at this point as to do so would erase the entire table.	Whenever something can easily go wrong, or when the subject text is particularly important, you will see the *important* sidebar. You should always read important sidebars.
tip **Moving between tabs using the keyboard** You can also use the **<Cmd>+<PgUp>** and **<Cmd>+<PgDn>** keyboard shortcuts to cycle through all of the tabs in your workbook.	Tips add to the lesson text by showing you shortcuts or time-saving techniques relevant to the lesson. The bold text at the top of the tip box enables you to establish whether the tip is appropriate to your needs without reading all of the text. In this example you may not be interested in keyboard shortcuts so do not need to read further.
anecdote I ran an Excel course for a small company in London a couple of years ago...	Sometimes I add an anecdote gathered over the years from my Excel classes or from other areas of life. If you simply want to learn Excel as quickly as possible you can ignore my anecdotes.
trivia The feature that Excel uses to help you out with function calls first made an appearance in Visual Basic 5 back in 1996 ...	Sometimes I indulge myself by adding a little piece of trivia in the context of the skill being taught. Just like my anecdotes you can ignore these if you want to. They won't help you to learn Excel any better!
The World's Fastest Cars	When there is a sample file (or files) to accompany a lesson, the file name will be shown in a folder icon. You can download the sample files from: *http://ExcelCentral.com*. Detailed instructions are given in: *Lesson 1-5: Apply a simple filter to a range.*

Putting the Smart Method to Work

Excel version and service pack

This edition was written using the first released version of *Microsoft Excel 2016 for Mac*, running under the *Apple OS X El Capitan (10.11)* operating system. You'll discover how to confirm which versions your computer is running in: *Lesson 1-3: Check that your Excel version is up to date.*

Excel 2016 can also run under *Leopard (10.5), Snow Leopard (10.6), Lion (10.7), Mountain Lion (10.8), Mavericks (10.9), Yosemite (10.10)* and any future OS X version. If you're using a different version of OS X this book will be equally relevant, but you may notice small differences in the appearance of some of the screen grabs in the book. This will only occur when describing an operating system (rather than an Excel) feature.

Users of earlier operating system versions should also consider updating their operating system to El Capitan, as Apple offer a free update (or at least they did at the time of writing this book in January 2016).

This book is written purely for Excel 2016 for Mac. If you are using Excel 2004, Excel 2008 or Excel 2011, you need to upgrade to Excel 2016 for Mac to use this book.

Sessions and lessons

The book is arranged into *sessions* and *lessons*. In a *Smart Method* classroom course a session would generally last for between sixty and ninety minutes. Each session would represent a continuous period of interactive instruction followed by a coffee break of ten or fifteen minutes.

When you use this book for self-instruction I'd recommend that you do the same. You'll learn better if you lock yourself away, switch off your telephone and complete the whole session without interruption. The memory process is associative, and we've ensured that each lesson within each session is very closely coupled (contextually) with the others. By learning the whole session in one sitting, you'll store all of that information in the same part of your memory and should find it easier to recall later.

The experience of being able to remember all of the words of a song as soon as somebody has got you "started" with the first line is an example of the memory's associative system of data storage.

We'd also highly recommend that you do take a break between sessions and spend it relaxing rather than catching up on your e-mails. This gives your brain a little idle time to do some data sorting and storage.

Read the book from beginning to end

Many books consist of disassociated self-contained chapters, often all written by different authors. This approach works well for pure reference books (such as encyclopedias). The problem with this approach is that there's no concept of building knowledge upon assumed prior knowledge, so the text is either confusing or unduly verbose as instructions for the same skill are repeated in many parts of the book.

This book is more effective as a learning tool because it takes a holistic approach. You will learn Excel in the same way you would be taught during one of our *Smart Method* classroom courses.

In our classroom courses it's often the case that a delegate turns up late. One golden rule is that we can't begin until everybody is present, as each hands-on lesson builds upon skills taught in the previous lesson.

I strongly recommend that you read the book from beginning to end in the order that it is written. Because of the unique presentational style, you'll hardly waste any time reading about things that you already know and even the most advanced Excel user will find some nugget of extremely useful information in every session.

How this book avoids wasting your time

> Nobody has things just as he would like them. The thing to do is to make a success with what material I have.
>
> *Dr. Frank Crane (1861–1928), American clergyman and journalist*

The only material available to me in teaching you Excel is the written word and sample files. I'd rather have you sitting next to me in a classroom, but Frank Crane would have told me to stop complaining and use the tools I have in the most effective way.

Over the years I have read many hundreds of computer text books and most of my time was wasted. The big problem with most books is that I have to wade through thousands of words just to learn one important technique. If I don't read everything I might miss that one essential insight.

This book utilizes some of the tried and tested techniques developed after teaching vast numbers of people to learn Excel during many years of delivering *Smart Method* classroom courses.

As you'll see in this section, many presentational methods are used to help you to avoid reading about things you already know how to do, or things that are of little interest to you.

Why our classroom courses work so well

In *Smart Method* classroom courses we have a 100% success rate training delegates to *Essential Skills* level in one day (the subject matter of our *Essential Skills* book) and to *Expert* level in a further single day (the subject matter of this book).

One of the reasons we can teach so much in a single day is that we don't waste time teaching skills that the delegates already know. Class sizes are small (six maximum) and the instructor stands behind the delegates monitoring their screens. The instructor will say "Open the sample file *Sales* that you'll find in the *Samples* folder on the C drive". If everybody does this, no time is wasted explaining how. If anybody has difficulty, more information is given until all delegates demonstrate success.

Another key to learning effectively is to only teach the best way to accomplish a task. For example, you can save a workbook by clicking the *Save* button on the *Quick Access Toolbar* or you can press the **<Ctrl>+<S>** keys on the keyboard. Because clicking the *Save* button is the easiest, fastest and most intuitive method we only teach this in the classroom. We do mention the alternatives in the book, but only in a sidebar.

How this book mimics our classroom technique

Here's a lesson step:

note You can also use the **<Ctrl>+<S>** keyboard shortcut to save your work.	**1 Save the workbook.** When you are editing a workbook the changes you make are only held in the computer's memory. If there is a power cut or your computer crashes, you will lose any work that has been done since the last save. For this reason, you should get into the habit of regularly saving your work. Click the *Save button* on the *Quick Access Toolbar* at the top left of the screen.

If you already know how to save a workbook read only the line: *Save the workbook* and just do it. Don't waste your time reading anything else.

Read the smaller print only when you don't already know how to do something.

If you're in a hurry to learn only the essentials, as fast as possible, don't bother with the sidebars either unless they are labeled **important**.

Read the sidebars only when you want to know everything and have the time and interest.

Avoiding repetition

> 2   Convert the table into a range.
>
> This was covered in: *Lesson 1-12: Format a table using table styles and convert a table into a range.*

A goal of this book (and our classroom courses) is not to waste your time by explaining any skill twice.

In a classroom course, a delegate will sometimes forget something that has already been covered earlier in the day. The instructor must then try to get the student to remember and drop little hints reminding them about how they completed the task earlier.

This isn't possible in a book, so I've made extensive use of cross references in the text pointing you back to the lesson in which the relevant skill was learned. The cross references also help when you use this book as a reference work but have forgotten the more basic skills needed to complete each step.

Use of American English

American English (rather than British English) spelling has been used throughout. This is because the Excel help system and screen elements all use American English spelling, making the use of British English confusing.

Examples of differences are the British English spelling: *Colour* and *Dialogue* as opposed to the American English spelling: *Color* and *Dialog*.

Because this book is used all over the world, much care has been taken to avoid any country-specific terminology. In most of the English speaking world, apart from North America, the symbol # is referred to as the **hash sign**. I use the term *hash* throughout this book.

First page of a session

1. The first page begins with a quotation, often from an era before the age of the computer, that is particularly pertinent to the session material. As well as being fun, this helps us to remember that all of the real-world problems we solve with technology have been around for a long time.

3. The session objectives *formally* state the precise skills that you will learn in the session.

At the end of the session you should re-visit the objectives and not progress to the next session until you can honestly agree that you have achieved them.

In a *Smart Method* course we never progress to the next session until all delegates are completely confident that they have achieved the previous session's objectives.

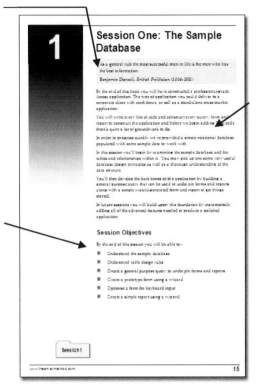

2. In the next few paragraphs we *informally* summarise why the session is important and the benefits that you will get from completing it.

This is important because without motivation adults do not learn. For adults, learning is a means to an end and not an end in itself.

The aim of the introduction is to motivate your retention of the skills that will be taught in the following session by allowing you to preview the relevance of the material that will be presented. This may subconsciously put your brain into "must remember this" mode—assuming, of course, that the introduction convinces you that the skills will be useful to you!

Every lesson is presented on two facing pages

Winston Churchill was well aware of the power of brevity. The discipline of condensing thoughts into one side of a single sheet of A4 paper resulted in the efficient transfer of information.

A tenet of our teaching system is that every lesson is presented on *two* facing sheets of A4. We've had to double Churchill's rule as they didn't have to contend with screen grabs in 1939!

If we can't teach an essential concept in two pages of A4 we know that the subject matter needs to be broken into two smaller lessons.

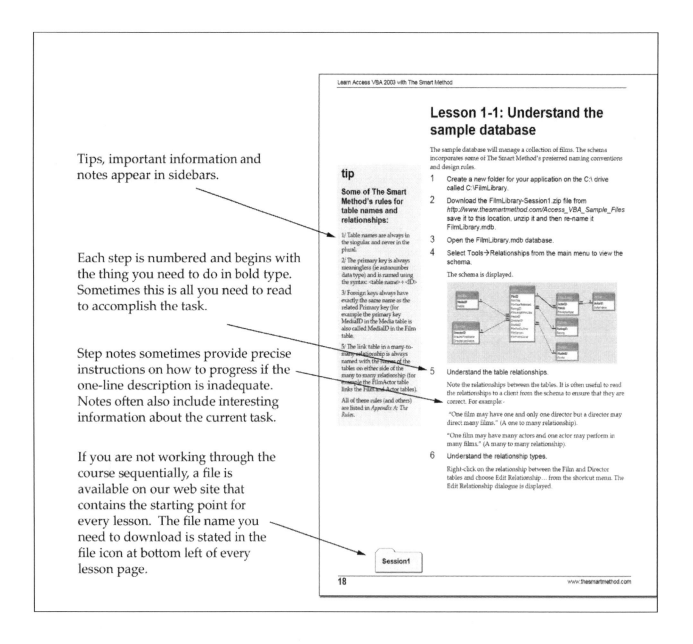

Learning by participation

Tell me, and I will forget. Show me, and I may remember. Involve me, and I will understand.

Confucius, Chinese teacher, editor, politician and philosopher (551–479 BC)

Confucius would probably have agreed that the best way to teach IT skills is hands-on (actively) and not hands-off (passively). This is another of the principal tenets of The Smart Method® teaching method. Research has backed up the assertion that you will learn more material, learn more quickly, and understand more of what you learn if you learn using active, rather than passive methods.

For this reason, pure theory pages are kept to an absolute minimum with most theory woven into the hands-on lessons, either within the text or in sidebars. This echoes the teaching method in Smart Method courses, where snippets of pertinent theory are woven into the lessons themselves so that interest and attention is maintained by hands-on involvement, but all necessary theory is still covered.

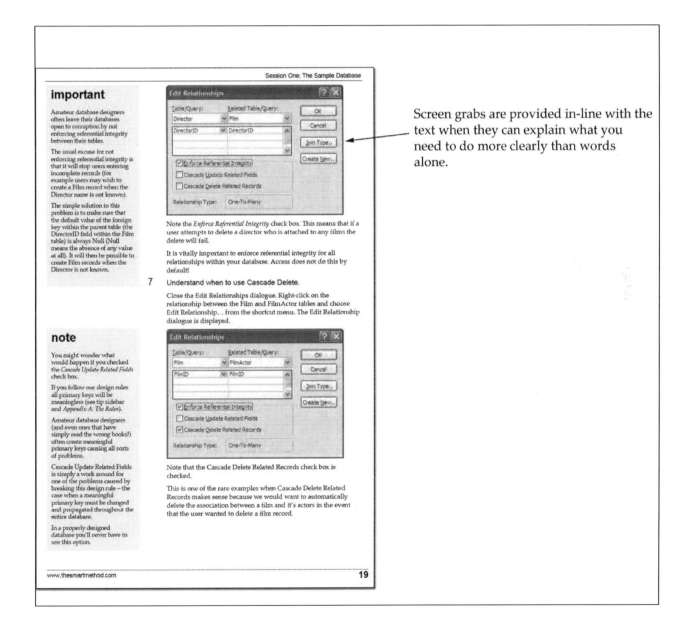

Screen grabs are provided in-line with the text when they can explain what you need to do more clearly than words alone.

Session One: Tables, and Ranges

> As a general rule the most successful man in life is the man who has the best information.
>
> *Benjamin Disraeli, British Politician (1804-1881)*

Excel now has a fantastic *table* feature (introduced for the first time in Excel 2007) making it possible to implement many features previously only available in true relational database products (such as Access, SQL Server and Oracle).

In this session you'll learn all about tables, how they differ from ranges, and how to use them effectively to manage data.

This lesson also introduces *structured table references* that provide a completely new way to reference dynamic table data. This has eliminated the need for the complex workarounds previously required to work with dynamic ranges.

Session Objectives

By the end of this session you will be able to:

- Configure your mouse and display ribbon group names
- Understand update models
- Check that your Excel version is up to date
- Change the Office Theme
- Apply a simple filter to a range
- Apply a top 10 and custom filter to a range
- Apply an advanced filter with multiple OR criteria
- Apply an advanced filter with complex criteria
- Apply an advanced filter with function-driven criteria
- Extract unique records using an advanced filter
- Convert a range into a table and add a total row
- Format a table using table styles and convert a table into a range
- Create a custom table style
- Sort a range or table by rows
- Sort a range by columns
- Sort a range or table by custom list
- Name a table and create an automatic structured table reference
- Create a manual structured table reference
- Use special items in structured table references
- Understand unqualified structured table references

note

If you have a very old mouse

If you have an Apple mouse that was manufactured before 2005, it's possible that it truly has only one button and can't be configured to allow a 'right click'.

If this is the case, I'd strongly recommend purchasing a mouse that has two buttons.

This book will always use the terms 'left click' and 'right click' to indicate which of the mouse buttons you should use.

If you can't attach a two-button mouse, you can simulate a 'right click' by holding down the <Ctrl> key before clicking with the mouse.

Lesson 1-1: Configure your mouse and display ribbon group names

If you're using your Mac with default settings and hardware, it's likely that your mouse appears to only have one button instead of two. This is great for simple programs, but makes it more difficult to use complex business applications like Excel.

It is possible to work with Excel using a single mouse button, but many features are much easier to use if you're able to 'right click' to access a contextual menu.

Even if your mouse only appears to have a single button, it's likely that it can be configured to recognize the difference between a 'left click' and 'right click'. Only very old mice truly only have one button (see sidebar if this is the case).

This lesson will show you how to enable two-button functionality on your mouse.

1   Test your mouse.

Move your mouse pointer down to any of the icons on the Dock at the bottom of the screen and click the right mouse button.

Even if your mouse only seems to have one button, click the mouse with your finger on the right side of the mouse.

If a contextual menu appears as shown above, your mouse is already configured for right clicking and you don't need to do anything else. If no menu appears and a program opens instead, read on to learn how to enable right-clicking.

2   Open the System Preferences dialog.

If it hasn't been removed, you should see the System Preferences icon on the Dock at the bottom of the screen.

If you don't see this icon, you can access System Preferences by going to the Launchpad by either clicking its icon on the Dock or pressing the <F4> key.

Click the System Preferences icon.

The *System Preferences* dialog appears:

3   Open the Mouse settings dialog.

trivia

The history of the Apple mouse

The very first Apple mouse was included with the Apple Lisa system, released in 1983. The Lisa mouse had only one button, setting a standard that Apple followed for over 22 years.

The design of Apple's mice remained very similar to the Lisa Mouse until the Apple Desktop Bus II mouse was released in 1993. This was the first of Apple's mice to use the rounded shape that is used by almost every computer mouse today.

The Apple Desktop Bus mouse was followed by the Apple USB Mouse in 1998. Nicknamed the 'hockey puck' because of its round shape, the USB Mouse was not very well received due to its short cable and tendency to rotate.

In the year 2000, the Apple Pro Mouse was released. The Apple Pro Mouse was Apple's first optical mouse, and the first to use the '0-button' design that has continued in Apple's latest generation.

The Apple Mighty Mouse was released in 2005, and was the first Apple mouse capable of both left and right-click, as well as including a trackball.

The most recent Apple mouse as of 2016 is the Apple Magic Mouse, first released in 2009. The Magic Mouse replaces the trackball with the ability to perform gesture controls on the surface of the mouse itself.

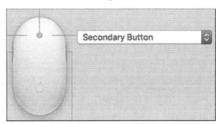

Click the *Mouse* icon in the *System Preferences* dialog (the 4th icon from the left on the second row).

The *Mouse* dialog appears:

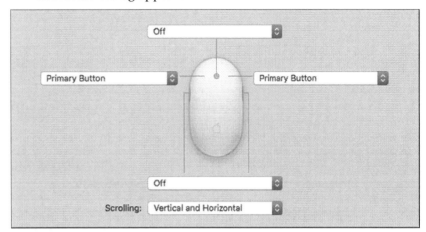

Note that this dialog may look different depending upon the type of mouse you are using.

4 Set the right mouse button to *Secondary Button*.

1. Click the drop-down menu pointing to the right mouse button and click *Secondary Button* from the shortcut menu.

2. Close the *Mouse* dialog by clicking the red *Close* button.

5 Test your mouse again.

Try right-clicking one of the Dock icons again. This time you should find that the contextual menu appears.

6 Display ribbon group names.

Excel 2016 for Mac hides the names of Excel's ribbon groups by default. You will need to configure Excel to display group names in order to follow the instructions in this book.

1. Open Excel (if it isn't open already).

2. Click: ⌘→Excel→Preferences.

   The *Excel Preferences* dialog appears.

3. Click *View*.

4. In the *In Ribbon, Show* group, click *Group Titles*.

5. Close the *Excel Preferences* dialog.

In Ribbon, Show

☐ Developer tab
☑ Group Titles

note

Not all Excel 2016 users will have the same feature set

With Excel's new continuous improvement strategy there may be three different versions of Excel 2016 in use at any one time.

1. Perpetual license users. These users will have access to the feature set that existed when Excel 2016 was first released.

2. Subscription users. These users will have access to all of the features that have been added since Excel 2016 was released.

3. Office Insider users. These users will have early access to new features that will eventually be made available to subscription users.

This situation has the potential to cause some problems. For example, new functions may be added in an update.

If a subscription user sent a workbook containing one of these functions to a perpetual license user, the workbook would not work correctly.

For this reason, it may be useful to restrict yourself to core Excel 2016 features if you need to distribute your workbook to other users.

Lesson 1-2: Understand update models

The move from perpetual licenses to subscriptions

The Perpetual license model

Software used to be purchased in a box at a store and then installed onto a computer using an installation CD. This type of product is often called a perpetual license, boxed copy or one-time purchase.

In this model, a new version was released every few years. The four most recent Office versions for the Mac have been: Office 2004, Office 2008, Office 2011 and Office 2016.

When a new version was released, it would usually have many new features. During the life of the release, no new features would be added and updates would be restricted to bug fixes of the features in the original release.

The Subscription model

In 2011, Microsoft introduced Office 365. This enables users to purchase the right to use Office (and all future versions of Office) for a monthly or annual subscription. At the time of writing (February 2016), the cheapest monthly subscription cost $6.99.

When Excel 2016 was released, Excel 365 subscribers didn't have to make any extra payment to upgrade to the new release. Office 2011 perpetual license holders, in contrast, had to buy the new release.

Office 2016 continuous improvement paradigm

With the *Office 2016* release, Microsoft has changed to a paradigm of continuous improvement. This means that new features (or improvements to existing features) can potentially be incrementally added to the product every month.

Perpetual license holders don't get these improvements. They are locked into the feature set that existed when they purchased their license.

For users of the subscription model, updates are not optional

The new update strategy expects and requires users to continually update their computers. Users that do not keep their software current will not be supported. For most users, updates will be configured to happen automatically. You'll learn how to make sure that your computer is configured to update automatically in: *Lesson 1-3: Check that your Excel version is up to date.*

note

Is Office 2016 the last version of Office?

In May 2015, at Microsoft's Ignite conference, Microsoft announced that Windows 10 would be the last version of Windows.

In the future, Windows 10 will be treated as a service rather than a product, with continuous incremental updates and improvements.

This is the model used by software such as the Google Chrome browser that updates very frequently.

It isn't unreasonable to speculate that the new update strategy for Office 2016 will also remove the need for future major releases of Office.

There is, however, a major difference between Microsoft Office and Windows 10.

Windows 10 users do not have to pay for updates. This means that there's no good reason not to keep their copy of Windows 10 up to date.

Office 2016, on the other hand, has both perpetual license holders and Office 365 subscribers.

My own speculation is that a new version of Office will be released from time to time. This would allow perpetual license holders to catch up with Office 365 subscribers (who will enjoy monthly incremental updates).

Another possibility is that the perpetual licenses will be discontinued at some point in the future.

Whatever the future holds, it is unlikely that there will ever be a need for a major new Office version in the future.

Updates

Perpetual license model

Perpetual license holders don't receive any new features, but still receive security updates.

If you are using the perpetual license version, you may find that you're unable to work with workbooks that were created by users of the subscription model, because they may use features that have been added via updates since the first release of Excel 2016.

Subscription model

Users of the subscription model will receive new features via a monthly update as soon as they are available.

Updates sometimes (but not always) contain new features. If you are a subscription model user, Microsoft only support the current release. In other words, you will be an unsupported user if you do not keep your software updated each month.

Office Insider

This is a special option that's provided for testing purposes. It offers a preview of the next subscription model update.

This enables corporate users to thoroughly test the next release before it is installed on their users' computers.

Lesson 1-3: Check that your Excel version is up to date

Updates

When a new product like Excel 2016 for Mac is first released it often has many bugs (as do all computer programs of any size).

Microsoft is very pro-active at fixing bugs that are found and regularly releases updates.

Updates normally only fix bugs found in the original program, but Microsoft sometimes take things a little further by including new, or at least enhanced, features with their updates.

I had many emails from readers of my earlier Excel books suggesting that some Excel features were missing, or that some of the examples didn't work. In almost every case the reader had switched automatic updates off and was using an out-of-date Excel version.

Automatic Updates

Normally Microsoft Office (including Excel) will look after updates without you having to do anything if Automatic Updates are enabled.

If you don't enable Automatic Updates, there is a danger that you may have an old, buggy, out of date version of Excel installed.

This lesson will show you how to enable Automatic Updates and make sure that you are using the latest (most complete, and most reliable) version of Excel 2016 for Mac.

1   Start Excel and open a new blank workbook (if you have not already done this).

2   Make sure that Automatic Updates are enabled.

    1. If the Menu Bar isn't visible at the top of the screen, move the mouse cursor to the top of the screen to make it appear.

        You should see the following options:

        If you see a different set of options, it means the Excel window isn't selected. Make sure that the Excel window is selected either by clicking on it or by clicking the Microsoft Excel icon on the Dock.

    2. Click: →Help→Check for Updates.

        The Microsoft AutoUpdate dialog appears.

note

The Office Insider program

You might have noticed the tempting option to *Join the Office Insider program* in the *Microsoft AutoUpdate* dialog.

Joining the Office Insider program allows Microsoft to install updates on your computer that have not yet been fully tested. This means that you get early access to new features, but it also greatly increases the chances of encountering bugs in the untested early releases.

Joining the Office Insider program is not a good idea for most users. It is better to wait for the final versions that have been fully tested than to risk the potentially disastrous consequences of downloading untested updates.

3. Make sure that *Automatically* is selected.

3 Check for updates and update to the latest version if necessary.

1. Click the *Check for Updates* button.

   You may be prompted to enter your password to confirm that updates should be allowed.

2. Install any updates that are available.

3. Click the red *Close* button in the top-left corner of the *Microsoft AutoUpdate* window to close it.

4 Click the *Close* button in the top-left corner of the Excel window to close Excel.

Lesson 1-4: Change the Office Theme

Excel 2016 allows you to change the colors of screen elements (such as the menu bar and ribbon) by selecting one of two *themes*. The available themes are called *Colorful,* and *Classic.*

Colorful

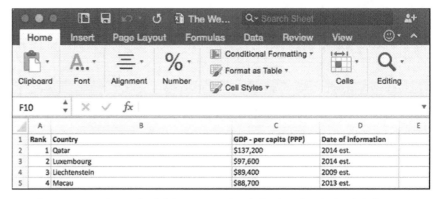

Excel 2016 uses the *Colorful* theme as the default. The Colorful theme makes it clear which of the Office applications you are using as Word, Excel, PowerPoint, Outlook and other Office applications each have their own unique color.

The previous version of Excel for the Mac (Excel 2011) didn't provide the option to change themes and was fixed to the *Classic* color scheme.

Classic

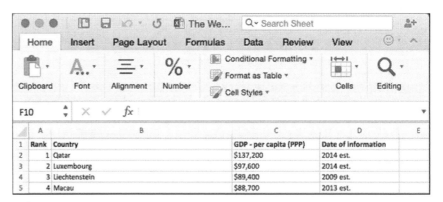

The *Classic* theme doesn't have the unique color scheme for each Office application and instead uses the gray color scheme that was used by Excel 2011 and earlier versions of Excel for the Mac.

1   Open Excel and open a new blank Excel workbook.

2   Change the *Office Theme.*

    1.   Click: ⌘→Excel→Preferences.

© 2016 The Smart Method® Ltd

The *Excel Preferences* dialog appears.

2. Click *General* from the *Authoring* group.

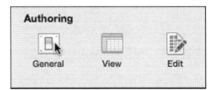

The dialog changes to show the *General* options.

3. In the *Personalize* group, click the *Office theme* dropdown menu and select *Classic*.

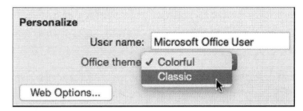

A dialog pops up to inform you that this change will affect all Office applications (see sidebar).

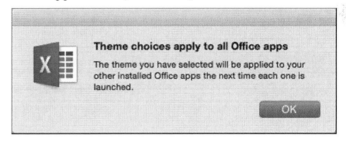

4. Click *OK* to close the dialog.

The color scheme changes immediately.

Experiment with each theme until you discover the one you prefer. All of the screen grabs in this book were done using the *Colorful* theme. If you choose the *Classic* theme, the screen grabs in the book may look slightly different to what you see on your computer screen.

3   Close Excel.

important

Organizing your sample files folder

When you complete a lesson that involves a sample file that is changed, you will be instructed to save the file with a suffix.

By the time you've completed the course you'll have sample files such as:

Sales-1
Sales-2
Sales-3
Sales-4 ... etc

The first file is the sample file that you downloaded and the others (with the number suffix) are interim versions as you complete each lesson.

The sample file set includes the starting sample file and all interim versions.

The interim versions are provided for three reasons:

1. If your work-in-progress becomes unusable (for example after a system crash) you can continue without starting at the beginning again.

2. If a lesson doesn't seem to give the results described, you can view the example to get some clues about what has gone wrong.

3. When you have completed the course you will use this book as a reference. The interim versions allow you to work through any of the lessons in isolation if you need to remind yourself how to use a specific Excel feature.

It is a good idea to place the sample files in a different folder to your saved work. If you don't do this, you'll be over-writing the sample interim files (such as Sales-1, Sales-2 etc) with your own finished work.

Inventory-1

Lesson 1-5: Apply a simple filter to a range

1 Download the sample files (if you haven't already done so).

1. Open your web browser and type in the URL:

   http://ExcelCentral.com

2. Click the *Sample Files* link on the top left of the home page.

3. Download the sample files for *Excel 2016 Expert Skills for Mac* (also see sidebar: *Organizing your sample files folder*).

   Be sure to select the *for Apple Mac* version of the course, as the Windows sample files may not work on a Mac.

2 Move the sample files to your Documents folder.

By default, the sample files will be downloaded to your *Downloads* folder. They will be easier to access and work with if you move them to your *Documents*

1. Open Finder by clicking its icon on the Dock.

2. Click the *Downloads* folder under *Favorites*. ⬇ Downloads

3. Click and drag the downloaded *AllSessions2016Expert* file into the *Documents* folder.

3 Open *Inventory-1* from your sample files folder.

This workbook contains a list showing all goods in stock.

	A	B	C
1	Product Name	Supplier	Category
2	Aniseed Syrup	Exotic Liquids	Condiments
3	Boston Crab Meat	New England Seafood Cannery	Seafood
4	Camembert Pierrot	Gai pâturage	Dairy Products

4 Add a filter to the range.

1. Click anywhere inside the range.

2. Click: Data→Sort & Filter→Filter.

   See the facing page sidebar if you can't see the *Sort & Filter* group on the ribbon.

Notice that small drop-down arrow buttons have appeared in the range header row:

	A	B	C
1	Product Name ▼	Supplier ▼	Category ▼
2	Aniseed Syrup	Exotic Liquids	Condiments
3	Boston Crab Meat	New England Seafood Cannery	Seafood

5 Use the filter to display products in the *Seafood* category.

1. Click the drop-down arrow to the right of *Category* in cell C1.

2. Uncheck the *(Select All)* check box.

3. Check the *Seafood* checkbox.

4. Click the Close button 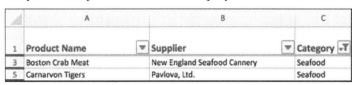 to close the filter dialog.

Only Seafood products are now displayed:

	A	B	C
1	Product Name ▼	Supplier ▼	Category ▼
3	Boston Crab Meat	New England Seafood Cannery	Seafood
5	Carnarvon Tigers	Pavlova, Ltd.	Seafood

Notice that the filter button next to *Category* in cell C1 has changed to show that a filter condition is in effect.

Notice also that the row numbers along the left of the worksheet are no longer sequential.

6   Add a second filter condition to show items in the *Seafood* category with an inventory value greater than 1,000.

1. Click the drop-down arrow to the right of *Value* in cell F1.

2. Click the *Choose One* drop-down menu and select *Greater Than*.

3. Type **1000** into the text box.

Filter

By color: None

Greater Than | 1000

4. Click the Close button to close the filter dialog.

Only rows that are in the *Seafood* category and exceed a value of 1,000 are now shown.

	A	B	C	D	E	F
1	Product Name ▼	Supplier ▼	Category ▼	Unit Price ▼	In Std ▼	Value ▼
3	Boston Crab Meat	New England Seafood Cannery	Seafood	18.40	123	2,263.20
5	Carnarvon Tigers	Pavlova, Ltd.	Seafood	62.50	42	2,625.00
26	Inlagd Sill	Svensk Sjöföda AB	Seafood	19.00	112	2,128.00
51	Röd Kaviar	Svensk Sjöföda AB	Seafood	15.00	101	1,515.00
59	Spegesild	Lyngbysild	Seafood	12.00	95	1,140.00

7   Remove the filter from the range.

1. Click anywhere inside the range.

2. Click: Data→Sort & Filter→Filter.

Notice that the small drop-down handles have disappeared from the range header row and that all rows are now displayed.

8   Use *Filter by selection* to only show rows in the *Dairy Products* category.

1. Right-click any cell in the *Category* column containing the text: *Dairy Products*

2. Click: Filter→By Cell Value from the shortcut menu.

Notice that only rows that are in the *Dairy Products* category are now displayed.

9   Remove the filter from the range.

Lesson 1-6: Apply a top 10 and custom filter to a range

1 Open *Inventory-1* from your sample files folder (if it isn't already open).

2 Add a filter to the range.

Click anywhere inside the range and then click:

Data→Sort & Filter→Filter

3 Apply a top ten filter to identify the ten items that have the most expensive inventory.

    1. Click the drop-down arrow to the right of *Value* in cell F1.

    2. Click the *Choose One* drop-down menu.

    3. Click *Top 10*.

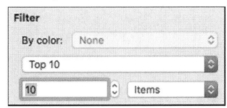

    It is possible to use this dialog to filter to a number other than 10 or to filter to the *Bottom* values (if you wanted to show the items with the least expensive inventory).

    4. Click the Close button ⊠ to close the filter dialog.

    The ten items with the most expensive inventory are shown. Note that they are still sorted alphabetically, in ascending order, by *Product Name*. You'd probably want to sort the rows by value in descending order. Sorting will be covered later, in: *Lesson 1-14: Sort a range or table by rows.*

4 Clear the filter condition from the Value column.

    1. Click the button to the right of *Value* in cell F1.

    2. Click the *Clear Filter* button at the bottom of the filter dialog.

    The filter condition is removed and all items in the list are shown.

5 Use a Between filter to show items that have a value between 1,000 and 3,000.

    1. Click the drop-down arrow to the right of *Value* in cell F1.

    2. Click *Between* from the *Choose One* drop-down menu.

Inventory-1

note

Filtering by color

Excel 2016 also has the ability to filter by cell color.

The *Filter by Color* option only lights up when at least one cell in the column has a background color.

You can then click the filter arrow at the top of the column and choose *By color*. This brings up a fly-out menu listing every color in the column:

A second drop-down menu appears, allowing you to choose two different criteria.

3. Set the filter condition to: is *Greater Than or Equal To 1000* **And** is *Less Than or Equal To 3000*.

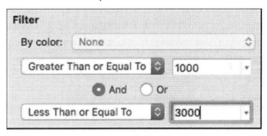

4. Click the Close button to close the filter dialog.

Only products with a value between 1,000 and 3,000 are shown.

6 Remove the filter from the range.

1. Click anywhere inside the range.

2. Click: Data→Sort & Filter→Filter.

Notice that the small drop-down arrows have disappeared from the range header row and that all rows are now displayed.

Lesson 1-7: Apply an advanced filter with multiple OR criteria

note

The criteria can appear anywhere on the worksheet and does not have to be complete

It is quick and convenient to place the criteria above the range to be filtered.

You may, however, place the criteria anywhere in the workbook – even on a different worksheet.

In this example, all of the fields in the range are listed by making a complete duplicate of the range headers. The advanced filter will work just as well if the header list is not complete.

Example:

To filter down to the *Seafood* category you could simply type **Category** into cell J1 and **Seafood** into cell J2 and then set the criteria range to J1:J2.

note

The criteria range can span any number of rows

In this example, a criteria range of four rows is used (A1:F4).

You can use as many rows as you need in your criteria range.

It is crucial that you leave at least one blank row between the criteria range and any other range on the worksheet.

1   Open *Inventory-1* from your sample files folder (if it isn't already open).

2   Create the criteria range.

The criteria range is the area on your worksheet where you define the advanced filter criteria.

1. Insert five blank rows at the top of the worksheet.

2. Copy the range headers from row 6 to row 1.

    Your worksheet should now look like this:

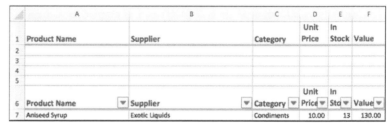

Each of the rows 2-4 can now be used to define the criteria needed for each column in the range.

3   Add filter criteria to show all products in the *Condiments*, *Seafood* and *Confections* categories.

This is an example of a filter with three OR criteria. The filter can be defined as:

Condiments OR Seafood OR Confections.

Add the three filter criteria by typing (or copy and pasting) the three category names into cells C2:C4.

	A	B	C	D	E	F
				Unit	In	
1	Product Name	Supplier	Category	Price	Stock	Value
2			Condiments			
3			Seafood			
4			Confections			

4   Apply the criteria using an advanced filter.

1. Click anywhere in the range to be filtered (any cell in the range A6:F75).

2. Click: Data→Sort & Filter→Advanced.

    The *Advanced Filter* dialog is displayed with the range already defined. Because you clicked within the range in step one, you have saved yourself the trouble of manually selecting the range.

Inventory-1

note

Using wildcards in criteria

Sometimes you will want to filter using a subset of the letters in a text column.

In this case, you can use the wildcard characters – the asterisk (*) and the question mark (?).

The asterisk means that any number of wildcard letters can occur between the letters.

The question mark means that only one wildcard letter can occur between the letters.

Here are some examples:

C*g   Finds **Containing**
           Finds **Citing**
           Finds **Changing**

S?d   Finds **Sid**
           Finds **Sad**
           Finds **Syd**
           Finds **Sud**

note

Text filters are inexact by default

This lesson's example works just fine, but it would have worked just as well if you had entered the filter expression **Cond** instead of **Condiments**.

For the same reason, the filter expression **Dairy** would return the category **Dairy Products**.

Sometimes this isn't what you want and you need an exact match. In this case, you need to enter the filter conditions like this:

="=Seafood"

="=Dairy Products"

Unlike **Con**, The filter condition

="=Con"

... doesn't return the *Condiments* category.

3. Click in the *Criteria range*: text box.

4. Select the range A1:F4 with the mouse.

   The criteria range appears as: A1:F4.

5. Click the *OK* button.

The range is now filtered to display only *Condiments, Seafood* and *Confections*.

6	Product Name	Supplier	Category	Unit Price	In Stock	Value
7	Aniseed Syrup	Exotic Liquids	Condiments	10.00	13	130.00
8	Boston Crab Meat	New England Seafood Cannery	Seafood	18.40	123	2,263.20
10	Carnarvon Tigers	Pavlova, Ltd.	Seafood	62.50	42	2,625.00
14	Chef Anton's Cajun Seasoning	New Orleans Cajun Delights	Condiments	22.00	53	1,166.00
15	Chocolade	Zaanse Snoepfabriek	Confections	12.75	15	191.25

5 **Remove the advanced filter from the range.**

1. Click anywhere inside the range.

2. Click: Data→Sort & Filter→Clear.

   The advanced filter is cleared and all records are displayed.

6 **Save your work as** *Inventory-2*.

Lesson 1-8: Apply an advanced filter with complex criteria

1   Open *Inventory-2* from your sample files folder (if it isn't already open).

2   Create complex advanced filter criteria.

This time you are going to create a filter with both AND and OR criteria. This is an example of a filter that is beyond the scope of a simple filter. Here are the criteria that you are going to apply:

WHERE

Category equals Condiments

OR

(Category equals Seafood AND Value is greater than 2,000)

OR

Value is greater than 3,000

This will list everything in the *Condiments* category.

It will also list products in the *Seafood* category, but only if their value is greater than 2,000.

It will also list all products that have a value greater than 3,000 irrespective of which category they are in.

1. Set the criteria range as follows:

	C	D	E	F
		Unit	In	
1	Category	Price	Stock	Value
2	Condiments			
3	Seafood			>2000
4				>3000

2. Apply the advanced filter using the skills learned in: *Lesson 1-7: Apply an advanced filter with multiple OR criteria.*

If you still had *Inventory-2* open from the previous lesson, the correct cells should already be selected for the advanced filter.

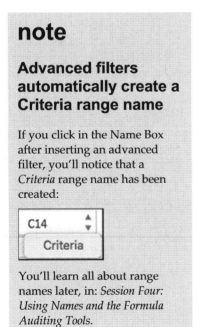

note

Advanced filters automatically create a Criteria range name

If you click in the Name Box after inserting an advanced filter, you'll notice that a *Criteria* range name has been created:

C14

Criteria

You'll learn all about range names later, in: *Session Four: Using Names and the Formula Auditing Tools.*

Inventory-2

Now you can audit the results:

	A	B	C	Unit Price	In Stock	Value
6	Product Name	Supplier	Category			
7	Aniseed Syrup	Exotic Liquids	Condiments	10.00	13	130.00
8	Boston Crab Meat	New England Seafood Cannery	Seafood	18.40	123	2,263.20
10	Carnarvon Tigers	Pavlova, Ltd.	Seafood	62.50	42	2,625.00
14	Chef Anton's Cajun Seasoning	New Orleans Cajun Delights	Condiments	22.00	53	1,166.00
16	Côte de Blaye	Aux joyeux ecclésiastiques	Beverages	263.50	17	4,479.50
21	Genen Shouyu	Mayumi's	Condiments	15.50	39	604.50
24	Grandma's Boysenberry Spread	Grandma Kelly's Homestead	Condiments	25.00	120	3,000.00
27	Gula Malacca	Leka Trading	Condiments	19.45	27	525.15
31	Inlagd Sill	Svensk Sjöföda AB	Seafood	19.00	112	2,128.00
38	Louisiana Fiery Hot Pepper Sauce	New Orleans Cajun Delights	Condiments	21.05	76	1,599.80
39	Louisiana Hot Spiced Okra	New Orleans Cajun Delights	Condiments	17.00	4	68.00
45	Northwoods Cranberry Sauce	Grandma Kelly's Homestead	Condiments	40.00	6	240.00
47	Original Frankfurter grüne Soße	Plutzer Lebensmittelgroßmärkte AG	Condiments	13.00	32	416.00
52	Queso Manchego La Pastora	Cooperativa de Quesos 'Las Cabras'	Dairy Products	38.00	86	3,268.00
53	Raclette Courdavault	Gai pâturage	Dairy Products	55.00	79	4,345.00
61	Sir Rodney's Marmalade	Specialty Biscuits, Ltd.	Confections	81.00	40	3,240.00
63	Sirop d'érable	Forêts d'érables	Condiments	28.50	113	3,220.50
73	Vegie-spread	Pavlova, Ltd.	Condiments	43.90	24	1,053.60

- All eleven *Condiments* products are listed irrespective of their value.

- Only three *Seafood* products are shown – only the items with a value greater than 2,000.

- Items such as *Sir Rodney's Marmalade* are listed, even though they do not appear in the *Condiments* or *Seafood* categories. This is because their value is greater than 3,000.

3 Remove the advanced filter from the range.

1. Click anywhere inside the range.

2. Click: Data→Sort & Filter→Clear. [Clear]

The advanced filter is cleared and all records are displayed.

4 Save your work as *Inventory-3*.

Lesson 1-9: Apply an advanced filter with function-driven criteria

When a company conducts a physical stock check of its inventory, there will always be some errors in the count. Auditors have to verify the accuracy of a stock check. To do this, they extract some random samples in order to establish the likely margin of error.

In this lesson, you'll take the *Inventory* workbook and extract an auditing sample by using an advanced filter in conjunction with a MOD (Modulus or Remainder) function.

Excel's MOD function returns the remainder after a number is divided by a divisor. It is often used in conjunction with the INT (integer) function to convert minutes into hours and minutes. For example, to convert 170 minutes into 2 hours 50 minutes you would use the functions like this:

=INT(170/60)   This returns 2, as the whole number part of 2.83 is 2.

=MOD(170,60)   This returns 50, because 60 only divides evenly into 170 twice (120) leaving 50 over.

You're going to use the MOD function in conjunction with an advanced filter to show one transaction in every five, so that you can sample one in five (20%) of the products to check during the audit.

1   Open *Inventory-3* from your sample files folder (if it isn't already open).

2   Add a column to the left of the range, head it with the text: **No** and fill it with incremental numbers.

	A	B	C
6	No	Product Name	Supplier
7	1	Aniseed Syrup	Exotic Liquids
8	2	Boston Crab Meat	New England Seafood Cannery
9	3	Camembert Pierrot	Gai pâturage
10	4	Carnarvon Tigers	Pavlova, Ltd.

3   Add a MOD function to cell A2 that will return TRUE when the value in cell A7 is divisible by five.

1. Type the following function into cell A2:

    =MOD(A7,5)=0

	A	B
1		Product Name
2	=MOD(A7,5)=0	

2. Press the **<Enter>** key.

    The cell contains the value: *FALSE.*

	A	B
1		Product Name
2	FALSE	

This is because the number in cell A7 (the value: 1) is not evenly divisible by five.

Here's how the MOD function works:

- The value in cell A7 is divided by five and the remainder is returned. In this case the remainder is 1, because the number 1 is not evenly divisible by 5.

- The expression 1=0 is not true, so the cell displays a result of FALSE.

- If cell A7 had contained a value that is evenly divisible by 5 (such as 5 or 10) the MOD function would have returned zero (because the remainder is zero). This would result in the cell displaying a TRUE result, because the expression 0=0 is true.

4   Apply an advanced filter using the *Criteria range* A1:A2.

Notice that you didn't type the word **No** into cell A1 (a copy of the text header appearing in cell A6).

For a function-driven filter, you must leave the cell above the formula blank. This tells the advanced filter to work directly upon the result of the function.

1. Apply an advanced filter in the same way as you did in: *Lesson 1-7: Apply an advanced filter with multiple OR criteria*, using A1:A2 as the *Criteria range*. The *Advanced Filter* dialog should look like this:

2. Click the *OK* button.

6	No	Product Name	Supplier
11	5	Chai	Exotic Liquids
16	10	Côte de Blaye	Aux joyeux ecclésiastiques
21	15	Genen Shouyu	Mayumi's

Note that the numbers in column A now read 5,10,15,20...

The list now contains the 20% sample needed for the audit.

5   Save your work as *Inventory-4*.

note

You'll learn other ways to extract unique records later

Later, in: *Lesson 2-13: Remove duplicate values from a table*, you'll learn a more powerful way to extract unique records using Excel's *Remove Duplicates* feature.

In *Session Eight: Pivot Tables* you'll also discover an extremely fast way to extract unique records using a Pivot Table.

tip

Use this technique to find spelling mistakes

You'll often encounter a cell range that contains spelling mistakes.

For example, a cost center column could contain the common spelling error *Stationary* (not moving) instead of *Stationery* (writing materials). The spell checker won't help you find the errors because both are real words.

You can use the *Unique records only* feature to extract all unique values from the list. You can then A-Z sort the extracted unique list to see if any words appear that have two different spellings.

	I
1	Repairs
2	Stationary
3	Stationery
4	Tools
5	Travel

Sorting will be covered in *Lesson 1-14: Sort a range or table by rows.*

Inventory-4

Lesson 1-10: Extract unique records using an advanced filter

1   Open *Inventory-4* from your sample files folder (if it isn't already open).

2   Click: Data→Sort & Filter→Clear to show all items in the range.

Notice that one supplier often provides multiple products. For example, *Specialty Biscuits, Ltd.* supplies four different products:

A	B	C
54	Scottish Longbreads	Specialty Biscuits, Ltd.
55	Sir Rodney's Marmalade	Specialty Biscuits, Ltd.
56	Sir Rodney's Scones	Specialty Biscuits, Ltd.
61	Teatime Chocolate Biscuits	Specialty Biscuits, Ltd.

In this lesson you'll extract a list of suppliers from the workbook using an advanced filter. The advanced filter's *Unique records only* feature will be used to ensure that each supplier is only listed once.

You will be amazed at how often you'll find this feature useful in your day-to-day business use of Excel.

3   Delete rows 1-5 (the cells that were previously used to define the advanced filter criteria conditions).

After deleting these rows your worksheet should look like this:

	A	B	C
1	No	Product Name	Supplier
2	1	Aniseed Syrup	Exotic Liquids
3	2	Boston Crab Meat	New England Seafood Cannery
4	3	Camembert Pierrot	Gai pâturage
5	4	Carnarvon Tigers	Pavlova, Ltd.

4   Bring up the *Advanced Filter* dialog.

Click: Data→Sort & Filter→Advanced.

5   Set the *List range* to all cells in column C within the range.

1.   Click in the *List range* text box.

2.   Click into cell C1.

3.   Press: **<Cmd>+<Shift>+<DownArrow>**

The range C1:C70 appears in the *List Range* text box.

List range: | entory!$C$1:$C$70

6   Leave the *Criteria Range* box blank and check the *Unique records only* check box.

☑ Unique records only

7   Click the *Copy to another location* option button.

8   Click in the *Copy to:* box and then click once in cell I1.

The dialog should now look like this:

9   Click the *OK* button.

A list of suppliers appears in column I:

In Stock	Value		Supplier		
13	130.00		Exotic Liquids		
123	2,263.20		New England Seafood Cannery		
19	646.00		Gai pâturage		
42	2,625.00		Pavlova, Ltd.		
39	702.00		Aux joyeux ecclésiastiques		
17	323.00		New Orleans Cajun Delights		

Notice that there are no duplicate entries in the list. The *Unique records only* feature has ensured that each supplier is only listed once.

10   Delete column I.

11   Save your work as *Inventory-5*.

Lesson 1-11: Convert a range into a table and add a total row

This lesson introduces tables (originally added to Excel in the Excel 2007 version). While tables have now been with us for nine years, they remain a mystery to many professional Excel users.

Tables provide a completely new way to work with tabular data and are particularly powerful when dealing with dynamic data. A table is very similar to a range but incorporates several very useful extra features.

You can freely convert a table into a range, or a range into a table. The key difference between ranges and tables is that table references shrink and grow dynamically.

For example, if you create a chart from a table and then add more rows to the table, the chart's source data will automatically adjust to include the new rows. This doesn't happen with a range.

1   Open *Inventory-5* from your sample files folder (if it isn't already open).

2   Convert the range into a table.

   1.   Click anywhere inside the range

   2.   Click: Insert→Tables→Table.

        The *Create Table* dialog is displayed:

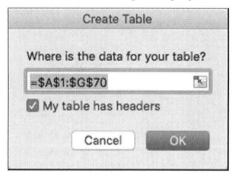

   3.   Click the *OK* button.

        The range is converted into a table. The appearance of the range changes and filter arrows appear in the header row.

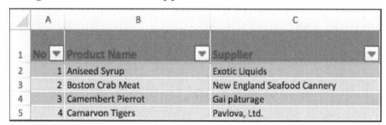

3   Scroll down the table and notice the "sticky" column headers.

   1.   Click inside the table

   2.   Scroll down the worksheet until the headers disappear from the top row.

---

tip

You can also convert a range into a table using the keyboard shortcut:

<Cmd>+<T>

Inventory-5

In a range you would have to freeze panes in order to continue to view the range headers (freeze panes was covered in the Essential Skills book in this series). Tables are much easier to work with. The table headers and filter buttons are always visible, as they replace the column letters when scrolled off the screen:

No	Product Name	Supplier
19	18 Grandma's Boysenberry Spread	Grandma Kelly's Homestead
20	19 Gravad lax	Svensk Sjöföda AB
21	20 Gudbrandsdalost	Norske Meierier

4   Add a total row.

Tables have a built-in ability to add total rows.

1.   Click anywhere inside the table.

The *Table* tab appears on the ribbon.

2.   Click: Table→Table Style Options→Total Row.

A total row appears at the bottom of the table.

Category	Unit Price	In Stock	Value
Grains/Cereals	33.25	22	731.50
Confections	9.50	36	342.00
			69,598.25

3.   Re-size the *Value* column if needed to view the total.

By default, the total row contains the SUM of all values in the right-most column. Excel uses the SUM function indirectly via the SUBTOTAL function (see sidebar).

5   Change the total from SUM to AVERAGE and add a total for the *In Stock* column.

1.   Click cell G71 (the cell containing the total).

A drop-down arrow appears next to the total.

2.   Click the drop-down arrow and choose *Average* from the function list.

3.   Click on cell F71 at the bottom of the *In Stock* column (the cell in the dark blue total row).

A drop-down arrow appears next to the empty cell.

4.   Click the drop-down arrow and then click *Sum* from the function list.

The sum of units in stock is now also displayed.

6   Change the AVERAGE in cell G71 back to a SUM.

	E	F	G
69	33.25	22	731.50
70	9.50	36	342.00
71		3018	69,598.25

7   Save your work as *Inventory-6*.

Lesson 1-12: Format a table using table styles and convert a table into a range

When you have formatted your data as a table, you can customize the appearance of the table using Excel's powerful *table styles* feature.

You can either apply a table style from the *table styles gallery* or you can create your own custom table styles.

All of the pre-defined styles in the *table styles gallery* follow best practice by restricting color choices to theme colors. Themes are covered in great depth in the *Essential Skills* book in this series.

In this lesson you will explore the simpler of the two options by applying some of the standard pre-defined table styles. Later, in *Lesson 1-13: Create a custom table style,* you'll create your own custom-designed table style.

1   Open *Inventory-6* from your sample files folder (if it isn't already open).

2   Apply the *Berlin* theme to the workbook.

Click: Page Layout→Themes→Themes→Berlin.

The *Berlin* theme is applied and the colors used in the table change.

The reason the colors change is that Microsoft used best practice when creating the built-in table styles and restricted their color and font choices to theme colors and theme fonts.

3   Change the theme back to the default *Office* theme.

4   Choose a new table style from the *Table Styles Gallery*.

1.   Click anywhere inside the table.

2.   Click: Table→Table Styles→More.

The *More* button appears when you hover the mouse cursor over the bottom of the Table Styles group:

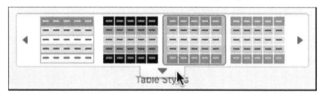

The table styles gallery is displayed.

3.   Click any of the table styles that you find attractive.

The chosen table style is applied.

4.   Restore the table style to the default *Table Style Medium 9*.

5   Change the table's appearance using *Table Style Options*.

1.   Click inside the table.

2.   Click the *Table* tab and focus upon the *Table Style Options* group.

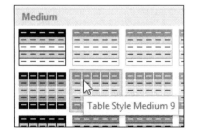

Inventory-6

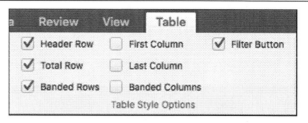

note

Formatting mayhem when converting tables into ranges and back

When you convert a table into a range, all of the formatting applied to the table remains.

Removing this formatting after conversion can be problematic.

The biggest problem occurs if you need to convert the range back into a table again.

Because each cell contains formatting information, Excel politely avoids changing any of the colors. This makes it impossible to change the table style using the table styles gallery.

The table's appearance then becomes very strange when you add rows to the table. Newly added rows will use the table style, while the rows imported from the range will keep their old formatting (because Excel thinks that the formatting has been manually applied).

The simple solution is to always obey the important rule:

Apply the None style before converting a table into a range, except when you are sure that you will never want to convert the range back into a table again.

tip

How to quickly identify tables and ranges

A quick way to tell tables from ranges is to click inside the table/range.

If you see the *Table* tab on the ribbon, you will immediately know that you are looking at a table.

The easiest way to understand the options is to experiment by switching each option on and off. The function of each option will then be obvious.

6 Apply the *None* quick table style to remove all table style formatting.

The *None* style is extremely useful.

In a moment you're going to convert the table back into a range. You'll nearly always want to remove table style formatting prior to conversion (see sidebar for more on this).

1. Click anywhere inside the table.

2. Click: Table→Table Styles→More→None.

The *None* style is the one in the top left corner of the gallery.

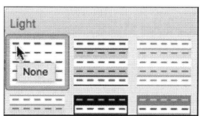

The table now looks more like a range, but it is still a table and still provides all table features.

7 Set the *None* style as the default.

I always like to work with the *None* style as the default. Excel's default table styles are a little too colorful for me. Note that this sets the default style only for this workbook. When you open a different workbook, the default table style will revert to *Table Style Medium 9*.

1. Click inside the table.

2. Click: Table→Table Styles→More.

3. Right-click on the *None* style and click *Set As Default* from the shortcut menu.

Every time you create new tables in the *Inventory-6* workbook, they will now display with the *None* style.

8 Convert the table back into a range.

1. Click anywhere inside the table.

2. Click: Table→Convert to Range.

3. Click the *Yes* button.

The table has now been converted back into a range.

9 Save your work as *Inventory-7*.

note

Why it is a good idea to restrict custom style colors to theme colors

If you restrict your color choices to the 60 *Theme Colors,* your worksheet design will be compatible with documents that use other themes.

If you use non-theme colors, your worksheets will not seamlessly integrate (from a design point of view) with PowerPoint presentations, Word documents, and other Office documents that use a different theme.

Example

John creates a worksheet using the default *Office* theme.

Mary wants to use this in her PowerPoint presentation that uses the *Berlin* theme. John e-mails the worksheet to her and then she simply pastes the required cells into her presentation and changes the theme to *Berlin.*

Joe sees the presentation and wants to use the same worksheet in his Word report that uses the *Circuit* theme. Mary e-mails the presentation to him and then he simply pastes the required slides into his Word document and changes the theme to *Circuit.*

The same worksheet has been used without modification and it blends perfectly into both Joe and Mary's work because John followed best practice and restricted his color choices to theme colors.

Themes are covered in great depth in the *Essential Skills* book in this series.

Inventory-7

Lesson 1-13: Create a custom table style

Perhaps none of the huge selection of styles in the *table styles gallery* is suitable for your requirements. In this case you can create a custom table style from scratch.

Another great feature of a custom table style is that you can set it as the default for this workbook. This saves you from continually reapplying a style every time you create a table.

1   Open *Inventory-7* from your sample files folder (if it isn't already open).

Notice that this range, (created from a table with a total row in: *Lesson 1-12: Format a table using table styles and convert a table into a range*), has totals in row 71.

2   Convert the range into a table.

This was covered in: *Lesson 1-11: Convert a range into a table and add a total row.*

3   Convert the *range total row* into a *table total row.*

If you click the Table tab, you will see that the *Total Row* check box is unchecked.

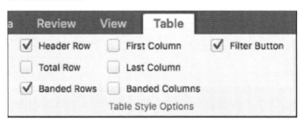

Why then does the table appear to have a total row in row 71?

	D	E	F	G
69	Grains/Cereals	33.25	22	731.50
70	Confections	9.50	36	342.00
71			3018	69,598.25

The reason is that row 71 is the total row defined in the range and has nothing to do with the total row that is available as a table feature.

1.   Check: Table→Table Style Options→Total Row.

A second total row appears beneath the first. This is the *table total row:*

	D	E	F	G
69	Grains/Cereals	33.25	22	731.50
70	Confections	9.50	36	342.00
71			3018	69,598.25
72				69,598.25

2.   Delete row 71 to remove the range total row.

4   Create a custom table style based upon an existing style.

1.   Click anywhere inside the table.

2. Click: Table→Table Styles→More.

The *More* button appears when you hover the mouse cursor over the bottom of the Table Styles group:

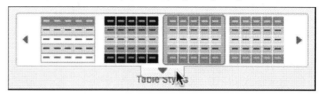

The table styles gallery is displayed.

3. Right-click one of the existing styles and then click *Duplicate* from the shortcut menu.

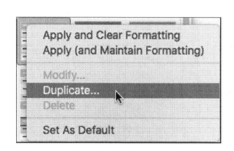

The *Modify Table Style* dialog is displayed:

4. Name the new table style: **TSM**

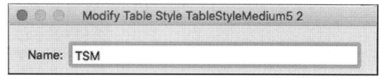

Each of the table's elements are listed on the left of the dialog.

Elements that aren't affected by this style are greyed out.

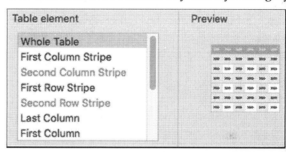

5. Choose a table element and then click the *Format* button to set the *Font, Border* and *Fill* formatting.

To follow best practice, you should restrict your color and font choices to theme colors and theme fonts (see sidebar on facing page).

6. Customize as many other elements as you wish.

7. Click the *OK* button.

5 Apply your new custom style to the table.

1. Click on any cell inside the table.

2. Click: Table→Table Styles→More.

Notice the new *Custom* section at the top of the gallery containing your new style.

3. Hover the mouse cursor over your new style and the style name will appear.

4. Click the style to apply it to the table.

5. Change the style back to *None*.

6 Save your work as *Inventory-8*.

Lesson 1-14: Sort a range or table by rows

1   Open *Inventory-8* from your sample files folder (if it isn't already open).

2   Sort the categories from Z-A.

    1.   Click anywhere in the *Category* column.

    2.   Click: Data→Sort & Filter→Z-A.

       The categories are now sorted in reverse alphabetical order:

	Category	Unit Price	In Stock	Value
13	Seafood	12.00	95	1,140.00
14	Produce	10.00	4	40.00
15	Produce	53.00	20	1,060.00
16	Produce	23.25	35	813.75

3   Sort the categories from A-Z.

    1.   Click anywhere in the *Category* column.

    2.   Click: Data→Sort & Filter→A-Z.

       The categories are now sorted in alphabetical order:

	Category	Unit Price	In Stock	Value
11	Beverages	14.00	111	1,554.00
12	Beverages	18.00	20	360.00
13	Condiments	10.00	13	130.00
14	Condiments	22.00	53	1,166.00

4   Sort by both Category and Supplier.

    There's a small problem with the existing sort. It can be seen that one category often has many suppliers:

	C	D	E
55	Tokyo Traders	Produce	10.00
56	G'day, Mate	Produce	53.00
57	Mayumi's	Produce	23.25
58	Grandma Kelly's Homestead	Produce	30.00

    In the above example it would be nice to also have the suppliers listed in alphabetical order. This can be achieved with a two-column sort.

    1.   Click: Data→Sort & Filter→Sort.

       The *Sort* dialog appears:

Inventory-8

note

You can also sort from the Home tab

The *Home* tab also has a *Sort & Filter* menu button in the *Editing* group.

This is one of the unusual cases where a feature is repeated on two different ribbon tabs.

It doesn't matter which you use as the functionality is identical.

2. Click the ⊞ button to add a second sort that will sort *Suppliers* from A-Z.

3. Click the *OK* button.

The table is now sorted first by *Category* and then by *Supplier*.

	Supplier	Category
55	G'day, Mate	Produce
56	Grandma Kelly's Homestead	Produce
57	Mayumi's	Produce

5 Select all of the data cells in column G.

1. Scroll to the top of the table so that row 1 is visible.

2. Hover the mouse cursor over the top of cell G1 until you see a black down-arrow with a black bar above it. Note that you *must* overlap the bottom of the column header button. If you hover inside the button, you'll see a black arrow with no bar and your selection will include every cell in column G (rather than the value cells within the table).

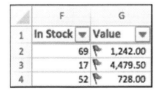 **The arrow must overlap the bottom of this button.**

3. When you see the arrow, click once to select cells G2:G70.

6 Add a *Three Flags* conditional format icon set to column G.

Conditional formatting was covered in depth in the *Essential Skills* book in this series.

1. Click: Home→Styles→Conditional Formatting→Icon Sets→ 3 Flags.

2. If necessary, widen column G to make room for the flags.

Values in column G have red, yellow or green flags added depending upon their value.

tip

Sort with a right-click

The fastest sort method of all is to right-click any cell and select *Sort* from the shortcut menu.

The fly-out menu then provides every sort option available from the ribbon.

Sort Smallest to Largest
Sort Largest to Smallest
Cell Color on Top
Font Color on Top
Icon on Top
Custom Sort...

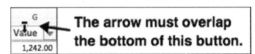

	F	G
1	In Stock ▼	Value ▼
2	69	1,242.00
3	17	4,479.50
4	52	728.00

7 Sort by icon so that the green flagged cells appear first, the yellow flagged second and the red flagged last.

1. Click any value in column G.

2. Click: Data→Sort & Filter→Sort.

3. Click the ⊟ button twice to remove existing sort conditions.

4. Add the following three sort conditions to sort by flag.

5. Click the *OK* button.

8 Save your work as *Inventory-9*.

Lesson 1-15: Sort a range by columns

Students often come to my classes with long "wish lists". Usually by the end of the course they have ticked all of their requirements off and don't have to ask any of the questions they had arrived with.

An item that seems to be on everybody's wish list is a way to sort data by columns. This lesson will teach you a simple technique to achieve this.

Note that this technique will work for ranges but not for tables. If you need to sort a table by columns, you'll have to convert it to a range first. That's exactly what you'll do in this lesson.

1   Open *Inventory-9* from your sample files folder.

2   Convert the table into a range.

This was covered in: *Lesson 1-12: Format a table using table styles and convert a table into a range.*

3   Add a blank row at the top of the range.

4   Add numbers to enable a column sort order of: *No, Category, Supplier, Product Name, Price, Stock, Value.*

The blank row that you have just added is a dummy row that will enable you to set the sort order.

Type numbers into row 1 that numerically describe the desired sorted position for each column:

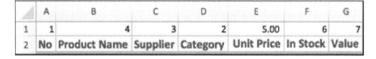

	A	B	C	D	E	F	G
1	1	4	3	2	5.00	6	7
2	No	Product Name	Supplier	Category	Unit Price	In Stock	Value

Note that the value in cell E1 only appears to be different to the others because it has inherited the two decimal place format from the *Price* field in the table.

5   Sort the range by reference to row one.

1.   Click anywhere inside the range.

2.   Press **<Cmd>+<A>** to select every cell in the range (including the dummy header row).

3.   Click: Data→Sort & Filter→Sort.

Notice that row 1 is no longer included in the selected range. This is because the *My list has headers* box is checked.

4.   Uncheck the *My list has headers* check box.

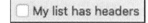

The entire range (including row 1) is now selected.

5.   Remove any existing sort condition(s) by clicking the ⊟ button.

Inventory-9

6. Click the *Options...* button.

    A dialog appears with additional sorting options.

7. Click the *Sort left to right* option button.

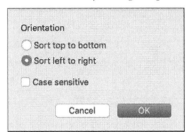

8. Click the *OK* button.

    A new sort appears in the dialog, sorting on *Row 1, Values, Smallest to Largest.*

9. Click the *OK* button.

    The worksheet is now sorted in the same order as the dummy sort row.

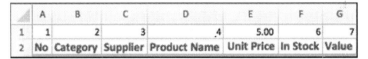

6 Delete row 1.

7 Convert the range back into a table.

This was covered in: *Lesson 1-11: Convert a range into a table and add a total row.*

8 Save your work as *Inventory-10.*

Lesson 1-16: Sort a range or table by custom list

Sometimes you need a sort order that is not alphabetical.

For example, you might run a support desk and be given support incidents marked as *Low, Medium, High, Urgent* and *Critical*. You would want to sort such a list in order of priority, but these priorities do not lend themselves to an alphabetic sort.

If you create a custom sort list with each incident listed in order of importance, you can then use the list to sort a range or table. This lesson will show you how.

1   Open *Help Desk-1* from your sample files folder.

This worksheet lists several support incidents sent to the help desk and prioritized from *Low* to *Critical*.

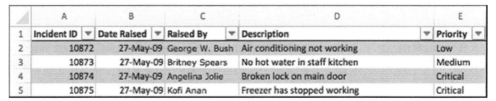

	A	B	C	D	E
1	Incident ID	Date Raised	Raised By	Description	Priority
2	10872	27-May-09	George W. Bush	Air conditioning not working	Low
3	10873	27-May-09	Britney Spears	No hot water in staff kitchen	Medium
4	10874	27-May-09	Angelina Jolie	Broken lock on main door	Critical
5	10875	27-May-09	Kofi Anan	Freezer has stopped working	Critical

2   Create a custom list.

1.   Click: ➔Excel➔Preferences➔Formulas and Lists➔ Custom Lists.

The *Custom Lists* dialog is displayed.

2.   Type each of the support incidents priority levels followed by the **<Enter>** key into the *List entries* box in the following order:

3.   Click the *Add* button to add your new custom list.

4.   Click the Close button to close the dialog. ⊛

3   Sort the table using the custom list.

1.   Click anywhere in column E.

2.   Click: Data➔Sort & Filter➔Sort.

The *Sort* dialog appears.

Help Desk-1

3. Select *Priority* from the *Column* drop down.

4. Select *Custom List...* for the *Order:*

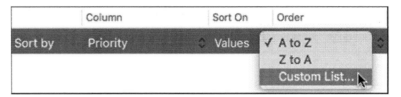

A dialog appears, showing all defined custom lists.

5. Click on your newly added custom list and then click the *OK* button twice to close both dialogs.

The worksheet is now sorted in order of priority from lowest to highest.

4   Reverse the sort order to show the higher priority incidents first.

1. Click anywhere inside the range.

2. Click: Data→Sort & Filter→Sort.

3. Click the drop-down arrow under *Order.* Notice that your custom sort order is shown twice as *Low to Critical* and as *Critical to Low.*

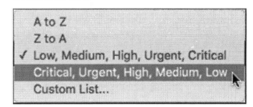

4. Click *Critical to Low.*

5. Click the *OK* button.

The worksheet is now sorted with higher priority incidents listed first.

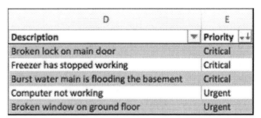

5   Save your work as *Help Desk-2.*

important

Because structured table references were only introduced in Excel 2007, this feature will not work if you have saved a workbook in *Excel 97-2003 Workbook* format to maintain compatibility with earlier versions.

note

If this feature doesn't work for you, somebody may have switched it off

Excel allows structured references to be switched off.

You really wouldn't ever want to do this, as structured references are one of the most useful features of tables.

If you simply want to maintain compatibility with Excel 2003, you can save the workbook in *Excel 97/2003 Workbook* format. The structured references feature will then be automatically disabled.

You can check that this feature is enabled by clicking:

→Excel→Preferences→ Tables & Filters→ Use table names in formulas

When the check box is checked, the feature is switched on (the default).

Lesson 1-17: Name a table and create an automatic structured table reference

One of the key differences between a range and a table is that tables shrink and grow dynamically.

The table's ability to shrink and grow wouldn't be useful without a way to enter a cell reference into a formula that points to all of the rows in a table column (no matter how many rows the table contains).

Consider the following range:

	A	B	C	D	E	F	G
1	Sales						
2							
3	Month	Net	Tax	Total		Total Sales	
4	Jan	15,249.00	2,287.35	17,536.35			
5	Feb	18,320.00	2,748.00	21,068.00			
6	Mar	21,260.00	3,189.00	24,449.00			

To calculate the total sales in cell G3 you could use the formula:

=SUM(D4:D6)

A recurring problem with data ranges is that when you add a new row to the range for April's sales, the SUM formula has to be adjusted (to D4:D7).

In order to exploit the power of dynamic tables, the Excel designers had to figure out a whole new way of referencing cell ranges. They needed a cell reference that would mean:

=SUM(All of the cells in column D that are inside this table)

Because there may be several tables on a single worksheet, the cell reference needs to indicate which table the range is in. This has been solved by adding the ability to name tables. If the table in this example was called *Sales* and the column was called *Total*, the formula would be:

=SUM(Sales[Total])

This type of reference is called a *structured reference.*

In this lesson, you'll use structured references to create some formulas that will always give the correct result, no matter how many rows you add or remove from a table.

1   Open *Sales Summary-1* from your sample files folder.

2   Convert the range into a table.

     1.   Click anywhere inside the range (A3:D6).

     2.   Click: Insert→Tables→Table.

        The *Create Table* dialog is displayed.

     3.   Click *OK* to accept the automatically detected range A3:D6.

3   Set the table name to: **Sales**

     1.   Click anywhere inside the table.

Sales Summary-1

Notice that a *Table* tab has appeared on the ribbon.

2. Click: Table→Properties→Table Name.

3. Type **Sales** into the table name text box.

4. Press the **<Enter>** key.

4 Add a SUM function to cell G3 using a structured reference.

1. Click in cell G3 and type:

    =SUM(

2. Hover the mouse cursor over the top of cell D3 until you see a black down-arrow with a black bar above it.

3. When you see the arrow, click once to select cells D4:D7 (all of the data cells in the column).

4. Note the structured reference that has been automatically entered:

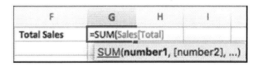

5. Press the **<Enter>** key.

    There's no need to close the bracket; Excel is clever enough to add this for you automatically.

The structured reference means:

The sum of all values in the Total column in the Sales table.

5 Add another row to the Sales table by entering the following values in row 7:

6	Mar	21,260.00	3,189.00	24,449.00
7	Apr	24,400.00	3,660.00	28,060.00

You only have to enter a value in cell B7. Cells C7 and D7 will automatically calculate as Excel automatically adds formulas to new table rows (see sidebar for more on this).

Notice that the total in cell G3 has updated to include April's sales figure. You can now appreciate the power of structured table references.

6 Save your work as *Sales Summary-2*.

Lesson 1-18: Create a manual structured table reference

In the last lesson you created a structured reference automatically by selecting a range inside a table.

In this lesson you'll appreciate the powerful tools that are built into Excel to make the creation of manual structured references very easy and intuitive.

1   Open *Sales Summary-2* from your sample files folder (if it isn't already open).

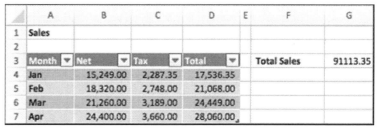

2   Add a formula to cell G4 that will calculate average sales using a manual structured reference.

1. Type the words **Average Sales** into cell F4.

2. Press the **<Tab>** key to move to cell G4.

3. Type:

    =AVERAGE(Sa

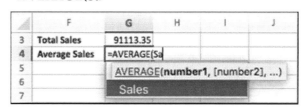

    Notice that a menu has appeared with the name *Sales*. If there was more than one table on any worksheet in this workbook that began with **Sa**, you'd see them all listed here. It doesn't matter whether you type **Sa** or **SA**. Table names are not case sensitive.

4. Press the **<Tab>** key.

    The remaining letters in the table name are entered into the formula.

    The table name references all of the data in a table, excluding the header and totals row.

    In this case, and at this time, it will reference cells A4:D7.

    As rows are added and removed from the table, the cells referenced by the table name will dynamically adjust to continue to reference all of the data in the table.

5. Type **[T** after the word *Sales* (a square bracket followed by the letter T).

Sales Summary-2

Excel lists all of the columns in the table that begin with the letter T:

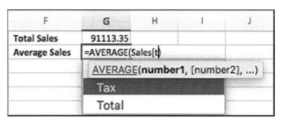

6. Use the **<Down Arrow>** key to move the highlight to the *Total* field.

7. Press the **<Tab>** key.

8. Close the square bracket.

9. Close the round bracket.

The formula should now look like this:

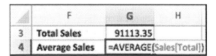

In a similar way to the table name, the column name will reference all of the data in the *Total* column excluding the header and total rows.

In this case, and at this time, it will reference cells D4:D7.

As rows are added and removed from the table, the cells referenced by the table name and column name will dynamically adjust to continue to reference all of the data in the column.

10. Press the **<Enter>** key to view the result of the formula.

Average sales during the period Jan-Apr were 22,778.34.

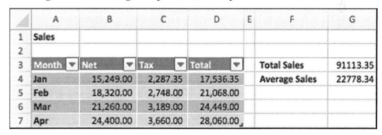

3 Save your work as *Sales Summary-3*.

Lesson 1-19: Use special items in structured table references

1   Open *Sales Summary-3* from your sample files folder (if it isn't already open).

2   Add a total row to the table.

This was covered in: *Lesson 1-11: Convert a range into a table and add a total row.*

3   Change the total at the bottom of column D so that it displays the maximum sales in any one month (using the *Max* option).

1.   Click in cell D8.

2.   Click the drop-down arrow next to the cell and select *Max* from the shortcut menu.

4   Type the words: **Max Sales** into cell F5 and then press the **<Tab>** key to move to cell G5.

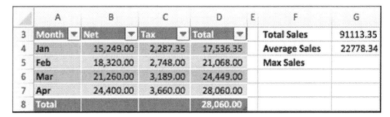

5   Examine the possible special items.

Type: **=Sales[#**

To enter the # symbol on a standard Mac keyboard, press: **<Alt>+<3>**

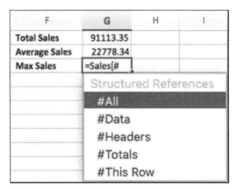

These are called *special items*. They can be used to reference different parts of a table.

The *#Data* special item is rarely used, because it is the default and doesn't have to be explicitly stated. In the last lesson you created the structured reference:

Average Sales	=AVERAGE(Sales[Total])

You could have entered the same formula in a different (and needlessly complex) way by adding the *#Data* special item like this:

=Average(Sales[[#Data],[Total]])

Sales Summary-3

The #Data special item simply means:

All of the data excluding the header and totals row.

6   Add an automatic structured reference to cell G5 that will reference the total at the bottom of the *Sales* table.

This time you're going to reference the value in cell D8 by using the special item: *#Totals*.

1.   Press **<Escape>** twice to discard the formula that you started to enter into cell G5.

2.   Press the equals key (=) to start a new formula.

3.   Click in cell D8.

An automatic structured reference is created that uses the special item *#Totals* to point to the *Total* row.

This means:

Reference the value in the Totals row of the Sales table that is at the bottom of the Total column.

4.   Press the **<Enter>** key to save the formula into the cell.

The *Max Sales* figure is displayed.

7   Apply the comma style to cells G3:G5.

1.   Select cells G3:G5.

2.   Click: Home→Number→Comma Style.

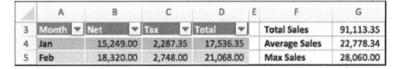

8   Understand all of the special items.

Here's what the other special items mean:

Special item	What it references
#All	Every cell in the table (this includes the header and total rows).
#Data	The entire contents of the table excluding the header and total rows (this is the default).
#Headers	The header row.
#Totals	The total row.
@ - This Row	Covered in the next lesson.

9   Save your work as *Sales Summary-4*.

Lesson 1-20: Understand unqualified structured table references

A qualified structured reference is a reference that includes the table name such as:

=Sum(Sales[Net])

An unqualified structured reference may be used in formulas within the table itself. In this case you do not have to use the table name as well as the field name because it is obvious.

For example, if you wanted to add *Net sales* and *Tax*, you could use the qualified structured reference:

=Sales[Net]+Sales[Tax]

… but it would be easier and more readable to use the unqualified structured reference:

=[Net]+[Tax]

This reference works because the @ (meaning *This Row*) special item is the default when entering structured references into tables.

You could have entered the same formula in a different way by adding the @ (meaning *This Row*) special item like this:

=[@Net]+[@Tax]

The @ special item is useful when you want to place a formula *alongside* a table and then want to AutoFill the formula to reference each row in the table.

1 Open *Sales Summary-4* from your sample files folder (if it isn't already open).

2 Convert the A1 style references within the table to unqualified structured references.

   1. Double-click in cell C4 and note the existing A1 style reference:

      The formula is calculating sales tax as 15% of the net sales value.

   2. Delete this formula and replace it with the unqualified structured reference:

      =[Net]*0.15

   3. Press the **<Enter>** key.

   4. Double-click in cell D4 and note the existing A1 style reference:

      The formula is adding the sales tax to the net value.

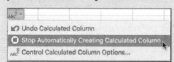
5. Delete this formula and replace it with the unqualified structured reference:

=[Net]+[Tax]

6. Press the **<Enter>** key.

7. Click: Formulas→Formula Auditing→Show Formulas to view the formulas in each cell:

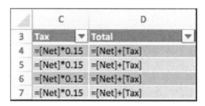

Notice that, even though you didn't AutoFill the formulas in cells C4 and D4, Excel has automatically converted all of the formulas in columns C and D into structured references.

This has happened because Excel now regards column D as being a *Calculated Column*. This provides a major advantage of tables over ranges.

Unfortunately, there's a huge potential pitfall that you can encounter by accidentally switching off the *Calculated Columns* feature (see important sidebar).

8. Click: Formulas→Formula Auditing→Show Formulas once again to display values.

3 **Convert the table back into an unformatted range.**

1. Click anywhere inside the table.

2. Click: Table→Table Styles→More→None.

The formatting is removed from the table. In: *Lesson 1-12: Format a table using table styles and convert a table into a range,* you learned why this step is essential before converting a table into a range.

3. Click: Table→Tools→Convert to Range.

4. Click the *Yes* button.

Notice that the filter buttons have now disappeared.

Notice also that the structured references have now changed to (rather verbose) A1 style references.

4 **Convert the range back into a table.**

1. Click anywhere inside the range.

2. Click: Insert→Tables→Table.

3. Click *OK* to accept the data range A3:D8.

Notice that the filter buttons have now re-appeared. Notice also that the A1 style references remain. They are not converted into structured references when you convert a range into a table.

5 **Save your work as *Sales Summary-5*.**

Session 1: Exercise

1   Open *Land Speed Records* from your sample files folder.

2   Convert the range A1:F13 into a table.

3   Name the table: **SpeedRecord**

4   Use a simple filter to only show speed records achieved at Bonneville Salt Flats.

5   Remove the filter to show all speed records.

6   Use an advanced filter to show speed records:

- At Bonneville Salt Flats that are greater than 575 mph.

- Together with all records held by Tom Green (irrespective of location and top speed).

   Another way of expressing this is:

   Where Location = Bonneville Salt Flats AND MPH > 575
   OR where Driver = Tom Green.

	A	B	C	D	E	F
5	Date	Location	Driver	Vehicle	Power	MPH
7	05-Oct-64	Bonneville Salt Flats	Tom Green	Wingfoot Express	Turbojet	413.199
13	07-Nov-65	Bonneville Salt Flats	Art Arfons	Green Monster	Turbojet	576.553
14	15-Nov-65	Bonneville Salt Flats	Craig Breedlove	Spirit of America - Sonic 1	Turbojet	600.601
15	23-Oct-70	Bonneville Salt Flats	Gary Gabelich	Blue Flame	Rocket	622.407

7   Remove the advanced filter to show all records and remove the rows that you added for the advanced filter criteria.

8   Sort the table A-Z, first by *Location* and then by *Driver*.

9   Add a total row to the table and use the MAX function to display the maximum value in column F.

10   Type **Km/h** into cell G1.

11   Use a formula containing a structured reference to show speeds in kilometers per hour in column G.

12   Save your work as *Land Speed Records-1*.

	A	B	C	D	E	F	G
1	Date	Location	Driver	Vehicle	Power	MPH	Km/h
2	15-Oct-97	Black Rock Desert	Andy Green	ThrustSSC	Turbofan	766.000	1232.758
3	04-Oct-83	Black Rock Desert	Richard Noble	Thrust2	Turbojet	633.000	1018.715
4	07-Oct-64	Bonneville Salt Flats	Art Arfons	Green Monster	Turbojet	434.022	698.4907
5	27-Oct-64	Bonneville Salt Flats	Art Arfons	Green Monster	Turbojet	536.710	863.751
6	07-Nov-65	Bonneville Salt Flats	Art Arfons	Green Monster	Turbojet	576.553	927.8721
7	05-Sep-63	Bonneville Salt Flats	Craig Breedlove	Spirit of America	Turbojet	407.447	655.7224
8	13-Oct-64	Bonneville Salt Flats	Craig Breedlove	Spirit of America	Turbojet	468.719	754.3301
9	15-Oct-64	Bonneville Salt Flats	Craig Breedlove	Spirit of America	Turbojet	526.277	846.9607
10	02-Nov-65	Bonneville Salt Flats	Craig Breedlove	Spirit of America - Sonic 1	Turbojet	555.485	893.9665
11	15-Nov-65	Bonneville Salt Flats	Craig Breedlove	Spirit of America - Sonic 1	Turbojet	600.601	966.5736
12	23-Oct-70	Bonneville Salt Flats	Gary Gabelich	Blue Flame	Rocket	622.407	1001.667
13	05-Oct-64	Bonneville Salt Flats	Tom Green	Wingfoot Express	Turbojet	413.199	664.9793
14	Total					766.000	

Land Speed Records

If you need help slide the page to the left

Session 1: Exercise Answers

These are the four questions that students find the most difficult to answer:

Q 11	Q 8	Q 6	Q 2
1. Click in cell G2. 2. Type: = 3. Click on cell F2. 4. Type: / 5. Click on cell B17. 6. Press the **<Fn>+<F4>** keys to change the reference to cell B17 into an absolute reference. Absolute references were covered in: *Essential Skills Book-Lesson 3 12: Understand absolute and relative cell references,* available for free viewing at http://ExcelCentral.com. The function should now read: **=[@MPH]/$B$17** 7. Press the **<Enter>** key. This was covered in: *Lesson 1-20: Understand unqualified structured table references.*	1. Click anywhere inside the table. 2. Click: Data→ Sort & Filter→Sort. 3. Set *Sort By, Location, A to Z.* 4. Click ⊞. 5. Set *Then by, Driver, Values, A to Z.* 6. Click the *OK* button. This was covered in: *Lesson 1-14: Sort a range or table by rows.*	1. Insert four blank rows at the top of the worksheet. 2. Copy the table headers from row 5 to row 1. 3. In cell F2, type : **>575** 4. In cell B2 type: **Bonneville Salt Flats** 5. In cell C3 type: **Tom Green** 6. Click anywhere inside the table and then click: Data→Sort & Filter→ Advanced. 7. Set the *Criteria Range* to A1:F3. 8. Click the *OK* button. This was covered in: *Lesson 1-8: Apply an advanced filter with complex criteria.*	1. Click anywhere inside the range. 2. Click: Insert→Tables→Table This was covered in: *Lesson 1-11: Convert a range into a table and add a total row.*

If you have difficulty with the other questions, here are the lessons that cover the relevant skills:

3   Refer to: *Lesson 1-17: Name a table and create an automatic structured table reference.*

4   Refer to: *Lesson 1-5: Apply a simple filter to a range.*

5   Refer to: *Lesson 1-5: Apply a simple filter to a range.*

7   Refer to: *Lesson 1-7: Apply an advanced filter with multiple OR criteria.*

9   Refer to: *Lesson 1-11: Convert a range into a table and add a total row.*

Session Two: Data Integrity, Subtotals and Validations

> The longer I live the more I see that I am never wrong about anything, and that all the pains I have so humbly taken to verify my notions have only wasted my time.
>
> *George Bernard Shaw, Irish dramatist & socialist (1856 - 1950)*

In an ideal world, all data entry personnel would be just like George Bernard Shaw and never make any mistakes. Unfortunately, the world is not ideal and we have to give users of our worksheets a little help by validating their input.

In this session you will learn how to validate cells and entire columns in order to restrict the values that users are able to enter. As well as simple validations you'll learn several advanced Excel validation techniques.

Excel's ability to automatically add subtotals never fails to elicit a gasp of amazement during my courses. In this session you'll find out why, when you add sophisticated grouped multi-level subtotals with just a few clicks of the mouse.

Session Objectives

By the end of this session you will be able to:

- Split fixed width data using Text to Columns
- Split delimited data using Text to Columns
- Automatically subtotal a range
- Create nested subtotals
- Consolidate data from multiple data ranges
- Use data consolidation to generate quick subtotals from tables
- Validate numerical data
- Create user-friendly messages for validation errors
- Create data validation input messages
- Add a formula-driven date validation and a text length validation
- Add a table-based dynamic list validation
- Use a formula-driven custom validation to enforce complex business rules
- Remove duplicate values from a table
- Use a custom validation to add a unique constraint to a column

Sales Analysis

Lesson 2-1: Split fixed width data using Text to Columns

Over the years, students have brought some very interesting workbooks to my classes from many diverse areas of business and commerce.

Often the workbook has become extremely complex and unmanageable with convoluted formulas that are difficult to audit.

Many times, all of the problems can be traced to the workbook designer breaking one simple golden rule of data table design:

"Keep data atomic"

This is one of Dr Codd's rules for efficient database design (see sidebar) that is equally relevant to Excel tables and ranges. In the same way that the atom is the smallest basic unit you can divide matter into, a column should contain the smallest possible amount of data.

Here's a simple example to illustrate the concept:

	A	B
1	Name	Age
2	Mr John Smith	42
3	Ms Jane Johnson	28

In the example above it wouldn't be easy to sort or filter column A by first name or last name. If you had observed the *keep data atomic* rule, you would have split the data into multiple columns like this:

	A	B	C	D
1	Title	First Name	Last Name	Age
2	Mr	John	Smith	42
3	Ms	Jane	Johnson	28

The benefits provided by this simple example are obvious. It is not as easy to see the problem when a general ledger code or part number contains many different pieces of data. Here's an example:

	A	B	C	D
1	Part Number	Units	Unit Price	Ext Price
2	GB480Z	2	42.70	85.40
3	EU522S	3	22.50	67.50

The error isn't so easy to see here. In this particular example, the *Part Number: GB480Z* is actually made up of three pieces of data:

1. GB: Where the product is made
   (GB=Great Britain, EU=Rest of Europe, US=USA).

2. 480: Product ID.

3. Z: Sales tax rate (Z=Zero rated, S=Standard rated, E=Exempt).

When you see this type of number in your data, you should immediately break it up into its constituent parts.

Excel 2016 for Mac now provides two different ways to split text:

1. **Using Functions:** You can use the MID, LEFT, RIGHT and FIND functions to split text. (You'll learn about these functions later in: *Lesson 3-20: Extract text from fixed width strings using the LEFT, RIGHT*

and *MID functions*). This is the most complex technique, but is the only method that will automatically update when the source text changes.

2. **Using the *Text to Columns* tool**: This is the method used in this lesson.

1   Open *Sales Analysis* from your sample files folder.

The table contains a list of products sold during March, April and May 2016. But there's a problem with this list: column B contains part numbers that break the atomic data rule.

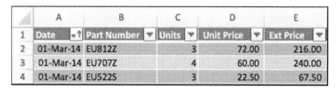

2   Insert two blank columns to the left of column C.

These columns, along with the original column, will receive the new atomic values.

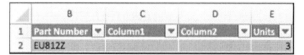

3   Split column B into atomic data elements.

   1.   Select all of the values in column B of the table (B2:B54).

   2.   Click: Data→Data Tools→Text to Columns.

   3.   Click *Fixed width* (you'll learn about delimited data in *Lesson 2-2: Split delimited data using Text to Columns*).

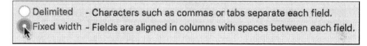

   4.   Click the *Next* button.

   5.   Click in the *Preview of selected data* window to break up each data element within the part number.

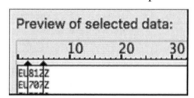

   6.   Click the *Finish* button.

The part number is split into atomic data.

4   Rename the columns B, C and D as **Region, Part Number** and **Tax**.

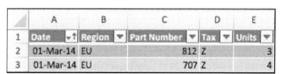

5   Save your work as *Sales Analysis-2*.

note

Splitting delimited data using functions

You can use the FIND and LEN functions to split delimited data.

You'll learn about these functions later in: *Lesson 3-21: Extract text from delimited strings using the FIND and LEN functions.*

This is the most complex technique, but is the only method that will automatically update when the source text changes.

Lesson 2-2: Split delimited data using Text to Columns

Fixed width data

In *Lesson 2-1: Split fixed width data using Text to Columns*, you worked with data that can be split into its constituent parts by reference to the character position of each piece of information.

Several accounting packages export data in a similar fixed width format:

Mr	John	Smith	19-Mar-14	2,220.24	2	4,440.48
Ms	Susan	Phillips	22-Mar-14	125.45	1	125.45
Mrs	Jennifer	Scott	23-Mar-14	1,145.60	2	2,291.20

This type of data is easy to recognize because all of the data elements "line up".

Delimited data

You'll often encounter delimited data. This type of data uses a special character (such as a comma or semicolon) to split each data element. Delimited data will be structured like this:

```
Mr;John;Smith;19-Mar-14;2,220.24;2;4,440.48
Ms;Susan;Phillips;22-Mar-14;125.45;1;125.45
Mrs;Jennifer;Scott;23-Mar-14;1,145.60;2;2,291.20
```

In the above example, the semicolon (;) is used as the delimiter.

1   Open *US Labor Force-1* from your sample files folder.

	A	B
1	US Labor Force - by occupation:	
2		
3	farming, forestry, and fishing: 0.7%	
4	manufacturing, extraction, transportation, and crafts: 20.3%	
5	managerial, professional, and technical: 37.3%	
6	sales and office: 24.2%	
7	other services: 17.6%	
8		
9	note: figures exclude the unemployed (2009)	

This worksheet contains some data that has been cut and pasted from the *CIA World Fact book* web site.

When you cut and paste information from other documents, (such as web pages), the information usually isn't in a format that is "Excel friendly".

In this lesson you'll split this data into a structured table so that you can display the division of labor as a pie chart.

2   Split the data in column A into text and percentages.

1.   Select cells A3:A7.

2.   Click: Data→Data Tools→Text to Columns.

3. Click *Delimited*.

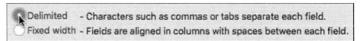

Delimited - Characters such as commas or tabs separate each field.
Fixed width - Fields are aligned in columns with spaces between each field.

4. Click the *Next >* button.

5. Set the delimiter to a colon (see sidebar).

Delimeters

☐ Tab
☐ Semicolon
☐ Comma
☐ Space
☑ Other: `:`

You can see that there is a colon before each percentage value in column A. By setting this as a delimiter you can extract the percentages.

6. Click the *Next >* button.

7. Click the *Finish* button.

The percentages are moved to their own column.

	A	B
1	US Labor Force - by occupation:	
2		
3	farming, forestry, and fishing	0.70%
4	manufacturing, extraction, transportation, and crafts	20.30%
5	managerial, professional, and technical	37.30%
6	sales and office	24.20%
7	other services	17.60%
8		
9	note: figures exclude the unemployed (2009)	

3 Create a pie chart to display the data visually.

1. Select cells A3:B7.

2. Click:

Insert→Charts→Recommended Charts→Pie

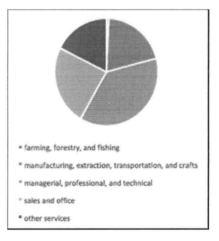

- farming, forestry, and fishing
- manufacturing, extraction, transportation, and crafts
- managerial, professional, and technical
- sales and office
- other services

Charting is covered in depth in the *Essential Skills* book in this series.

4 Save your work as *US Labor Force-2*.

Lesson 2-3: Automatically subtotal a range

1   Open *Inventory-10* from your sample files folder.

2   Remove conditional formatting from the table.

      1.   Click anywhere inside the table.

      2.   Click: Home→Styles→Conditional Formatting→Clear Rules→ Clear Rules from This Table.

3   Sort the table by *Category* in ascending order (A-Z).

      This was covered in: *Lesson 1-14: Sort a range or table by rows.*

	A	B	C
11	42	Beverages	Pavlova, Ltd.
12	49	Beverages	Plutzer Lebensmittelgroßmärkte AG
13	57	Condiments	Forêts d'érables
14	18	Condiments	Grandma Kelly's Homestead

4   Convert the table into a range.

      This was covered in: *Lesson 1-12: Format a table using table styles and convert a table into a range.*

      You must convert the table into a range because you cannot add subtotals to tables.

5   Delete the total row (row 71).

6   Add subtotals to the *In Stock* and *Value* columns for each category.

      1.   Click anywhere inside the range.

      2.   Click: Data→Outline→Subtotal.

      The *Subtotal* dialog appears:

Inventory-10

note

Other subtotal options

Note the three subtotal options:

☑ Replace current subtotals
☐ Page break between groups
☑ Summary below data

You can use the first option to add different types of subtotal to different columns.

For example, if you wanted to view both the average and the sum at the same time, you could add a second subtotal by unchecking this box.

The new subtotal is then shown above the old one:

Beverages Average
Beverages Total

note

Copying subtotals to another location

A very common request in my courses is:

"How can I copy the subtotals only (ie the level two outline) to another worksheet. When I copy the subtotals and paste I get the detail rows as well – but I just want the subtotals".

The secret here is to only select the visible cells on the worksheet before copying.

Here's how it is done:

1. Display level two subtotals by clicking the ② button.

2. Click: ⌘→Edit→Find→Go To

3. Click: *Special.*

4. Click *Visible Cells Only,* and then click *OK.*

5. Copy.

6. Paste to the destination cells.

---

3. Tell Excel which column of repeating data you wish to add subtotals to by choosing *Category* in the *At each change in:* drop down.

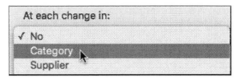

4. Make sure that the *Sum* function is selected.

5. Click the check boxes to add subtotals to the *In Stock* and *Value* columns:

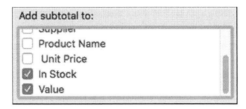

6. Click the *OK* button.

The worksheet is now subtotaled and Excel has added an outline bar to the left hand side:

1 2 3		A	B	C	D	E	F	G
	55	64	Grains/Cereals	PB Knäckebröd AB	Tunnbröd	9.00	61	549.00
	56	68	Grains/Cereals	Plutzer Lebensmittelg	Wimmers gute Semm	33.25	22	731.50
	57		Grains/Cereals Total				282	5,230.50
	58	43	Meat/Poultry	Ma Maison	Pâté chinois	24.00	115	2,760.00
	59	63	Meat/Poultry	Ma Maison	Tourtière	7.45	21	156.45
	60		Meat/Poultry Total				136	2,916.45

7 Collapse and expand the entire outline.

Notice the small ⬚123 buttons in the top left corner of the worksheet.

- When you click button 1 only the grand total is shown.

- When you click button 2 each category subtotal is shown.

- When you click button 3 all items are shown.

8 Collapse and expand categories within the outline.

Note the ⊞ and ⊟ buttons in the left-hand sidebar.

Experiment by clicking them and notice how you can selectively expand and collapse any group within the outline.

9 Remove the subtotals from the range.

1. Click anywhere within the range.

2. Click: Data→Outline→Subtotal→Remove All.

10 Save your work as *Inventory-11*.

Lesson 2-4: Create nested subtotals

Sometimes you'll find a need for more than one level of subtotal.

Consider this data:

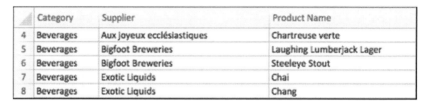

	Category	Supplier	Product Name
4	Beverages	Aux joyeux ecclésiastiques	Chartreuse verte
5	Beverages	Bigfoot Breweries	Laughing Lumberjack Lager
6	Beverages	Bigfoot Breweries	Steeleye Stout
7	Beverages	Exotic Liquids	Chai
8	Beverages	Exotic Liquids	Chang

In the example above, both *Bigfoot Breweries* and *Exotic Liquids* supply more than one product in the *Beverages* category.

As well as wishing to know subtotals for each *category* you may also wish to know subtotals for each *supplier* within each *category*. In other words:

What is the value of Bigfoot Breweries' inventory in each category?

By nesting subtotals, you can quickly cater for this requirement.

1 Open *Inventory-11* from your sample files folder (if it isn't already open).

2 Apply a two-level A-Z sort, first by *Category* and then by *Supplier*.

This was covered in: *Lesson 1-14: Sort a range or table by rows*.

	Column	Sort On	Order
Sort by	Category	◇ Values ◇	A to Z ◇
Then by	Supplier	◇ Values ◇	A to Z ◇

3 At each change in *Category*, use the *Sum* function to add subtotals to the *In Stock* and *Value* columns.

You learned how to do this in:
Lesson 2-3: Automatically subtotal a range.

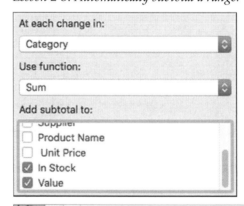

At each change in:

Category

Use function:

Sum

Add subtotal to:

☐ Supplier
☐ Product Name
☐ Unit Price
☑ In Stock
☑ Value

	60		Meat/Poultry Total	
	61	34	Produce	G'day, Mate	Manjimup Dried Apples
	62	65	Produce	Grandma Kelly's Homestead	Uncle Bob's Organic Dried Pears
	63	62	Produce	Mayumi's	Tofu
	64	31	Produce	Tokyo Traders	Longlife Tofu

Inventory-11

4 Add a nested subtotal to show totals by *Supplier* within each category.

1. Click anywhere within the range.

2. Click: Data→Outline→Subtotal.

3. Uncheck the *Replace current subtotals* check box.

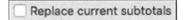

This is the secret when creating nested subtotals. If you didn't uncheck this box, the new subtotal would simply replace the old one. By keeping the current subtotal, you'll add a nested subtotal.

4. At each change in *Supplier,* add a *Sum* function to subtotal the *In Stock* and *Value* columns:

5. Click the *OK* button.

Nested subtotals are now shown by category/by supplier:

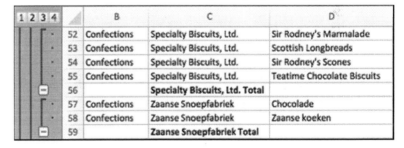

Notice that there's an extra level button too:

The fourth level is the nested subtotal, allowing you to collapse and expand the *Supplier* subtotals.

5 Save your work as *Inventory-12.*

Lesson 2-5: Consolidate data from multiple data ranges

Totaling data from multiple worksheets onto a summary sheet is a very common business requirement. Excel can automatically consolidate data if each worksheet has an identical structure.

If you use this technique, it is a good idea to use templates for each of the worksheets that will be consolidated in order to ensure that they are identical. (Templates are covered in depth in the *Essential Skills* book in this series).

1 Open *Sales and Profit by Employee-1* from your sample files folder.

This worksheet shows each employee's sales, cost and profit data for the first three months in the quarter.

The *January, February, March* and *Summary* worksheets have an identical structure. This makes the consolidation feature very easy to use.

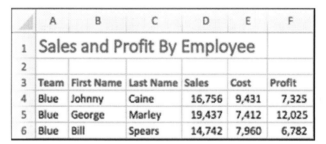

2 Consolidate data for the first three months into the summary sheet.

1. Click into the destination cell for the consolidated data. This is cell D4 on the *Summary* sheet.

2. Click: Data→Data Tools→Consolidate.

   The *Data Consolidation* dialog appears.

3. Make sure that the *Function* drop-down displays the *Sum* function, because you want to add together the values in the *January, February* and *March* worksheets:

4. Click in the *Reference* box.

5. Click the *January* worksheet tab and select cells D4:F17:

6. Click the ⊞ button to add the reference to the list of references to be consolidated:

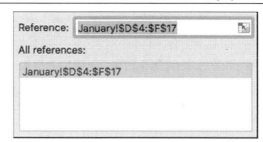

7. Click the *February* worksheet tab. This time the same range (on the *February* worksheet) is automatically displayed in the dialog.

8. Click the ⊞ button to add the *February* range to the list of references to be consolidated.

9. Repeat the same operation for the *March* range.

   The dialog should now look like this:

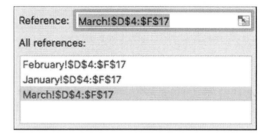

10. Click the *OK* button to display the consolidated totals on the summary sheet:

	A	B	C	D	E	F
1	Sales and Profit By Employee					
2						
3	Team	First Name	Last Name	Sales	Cost	Profit
4	Blue	Johnny	Caine	52,713	22,243	30,470
5	Blue	George	Marley	46,320	20,824	25,496
6	Blue	Bill	Spears	40,847	20,085	20,762

3   Create a data consolidation that is linked to the source data.

In the previous operation, the consolidated values were not linked to the source worksheets. If a value on a source worksheet changes, the summary worksheet will not update.

1. Delete the range D4:F17 on the *Summary* worksheet.

2. Click in cell D4 on the *Summary* worksheet.

3. Click: Data→Data Tools→Consolidate.

4. Check the *Create links to source data* check box:

5. Click the *OK* button.

This time the data consolidation links to the source data and also displays a grouped outline similar to an automatic subtotal, enabling you to view each of the source data values for the consolidation.

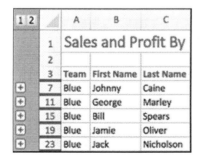

4   Save your work as *Sales and Profit by Employee-2*.

Lesson 2-6: Use data consolidation to generate quick subtotals from tables

In: *Lesson 2-3: Automatically subtotal a range* you used Excel's fantastic *Automatic Subtotal* feature to quickly add subtotals to a range. Unfortunately, automatic subtotals do not work with tables.

Another problem with automatic subtotals is that you have little control over the formatting of the subtotal data.

Data consolidation can overcome both of these problems by allowing full control of formatting, along with the ability to work with both ranges and tables.

1   Open *Inventory-12* from your sample files folder.

2   Remove subtotals from the range.

    1. Click anywhere inside the range.

    2. Click: Data→Outline→Subtotal→Remove All.

3   Convert the range into a table.

    This was covered in: *Lesson 1-11: Convert a range into a table and add a total row.*

4   Add quick subtotals by category using data consolidation.

    1. Click in cell I1.

    2. Click: Data→Data Tools→Consolidate.

        The *Consolidate* dialog is displayed.

    3. Make sure that *Sum* is shown in the *Function* box. This should be the case, as *Sum* is the default.

    4. Click in the *Reference* box and select the range B1:G70.

        A quick way to do this is to click in cell B1,
        press **<Cmd>+<Shift>+<DownArrow>**,
        and then press **<Cmd>+<Shift>+<RightArrow>**.

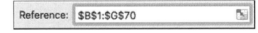

    5. Click the ⊞ button to add B1:G70 to the list of references to be consolidated.

    6. Check the two check boxes: *Use labels in Top row, Left column.*

    7. Click the *OK* button.

Subtotals appear beginning in cell I1 for every column.

Inventory-12

	Supplier	Product Na	Unit Price	In Stock	Value
Beverages			451.25	539	12,390.25
Condiments			255.40	507	12,023.55
Confections			327.08	386	10,392.20
Dairy Products			287.30	393	11,271.20

note

Consolidated subtotals cannot be linked to source data on the same worksheet

In: *Lesson 2-5: Consolidate data from multiple data ranges,* you learned how to create consolidated totals that are linked to source data.

You did this by checking the *Create links to source data* checkbox.

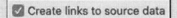

This is really useful, as linked consolidated totals will update whenever an existing row in the source data is changed or deleted.

The consolidated totals will not, however, update when new rows are added to the source data.

Unfortunately, the option to link only works when the consolidated data is on a different worksheet to the source data.

If you try to link consolidated totals on the same worksheet as the source data, you will see this dialog:

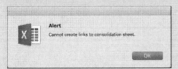

If you need to display linked consolidated totals on the same worksheet, there's a simple work-around.

1. Create linked consolidated totals on a different worksheet

2. Create cross-worksheet formulas that reference the values on the worksheet containing the linked consolidated totals.

5 Delete columns J:L.

Subtotals are impossible on the text columns: *Supplier* and *Product Name.* They are also of no interest for the *Unit Price* column.

6 Re-size columns I, J and K.

Useful subtotals are now displayed:

	I	J	K
1		In Stock	Value
2	Beverages	539	12,390.25
3	Condiments	507	12,023.55
4	Confections	386	10,392.20
5	Dairy Products	393	11,271.20
6	Grains/Cereals	282	5,230.50
7	Meat/Poultry	136	2,916.45
8	Produce	74	2,363.75
9	Seafood	701	13,010.35

7 Add averages alongside the totals using the same technique.

1. Click in cell L1.

2. Do exactly the same thing you did for the *Sum,* but choose the *Average* function in the consolidate dialog:

3. Click the *OK* button.

4. Delete columns L:O.

5. Change the label in cell L1 to: **Average In Stock**

6. Change the label in cell M1 to **Average Value**

7. Change the number of decimal places shown for the values in column L to zero.

8. Re-size columns L and M.

	I	J	K	L	M
1		In Stock	Value	Average In Stock	Average Value
2	Beverages	539	12,390.25	49	1,126.39
3	Condiments	507	12,023.55	46	1,093.05

8 Save your work as *Inventory-13.*

	I	J
2	The Rules	
3		
4	Age	
5	Minimum age	17
6	Maximum age	100
7		
8	Date	
9	today or later	
10		
11	Names	
12	Min length	2
13	Max length	20
14		
15	Price	
16	Minimum	10.00
17	Maximum	100.00
18		
19	Discounts	
20	Minimum price for discount	20.00
21		

Health Club Bookings-1

Lesson 2-7: Validate numerical data

In the next lessons you'll explore the power of Excel's data validation features. You can prevent a huge number of data entry errors by catching them when they are entered and then politely informing your users that they have made a mistake.

1   Open *Health Club Bookings-1* from your sample files folder.

This worksheet manages all of the treatments sold in a health club.

There are several rules that must not be broken when entering data (see sidebar). These types of rules are often referred to as *business rules* when designing data systems.

At the moment the worksheet doesn't police these rules itself but relies upon all personnel understanding and applying them.

	A	B	C	D	E	F	G
1	Health Club Bookings						
2							
3	Period	From:					
4		To:					
5							
6	Date	Name	Age	Group	Price	Discount	Total
7	05-Apr-14	Depp, Julia	22	Aerobics	22.00	12%	19.36
8	01-Apr-14	Nicholson, Johnny	23	Weight Training	9.00		9.00
9	12-Apr-14	Dickens, Bob	18	Aromatherapy	23.00	10%	20.70
10	15-Apr-14	Oliver, Jamie	38	Weight Training	23.00	15%	19.55

2   Apply the Age rule (see sidebar) to column C.

1. Select all of column C by clicking the column header.

You need to select the entire column when you want to add data validation to every cell in the column.

2. Click: Data→Data Tools→Data Validation.

The *Data Validation* dialog appears.

3. Click the *Settings* tab.

At the moment, Excel is allowing *Any value*. This is the default, meaning that the user is free to type anything at all into any cell in column C.

4. Choose *Whole number* from the *Allow* drop-down list.

Whole number will not allow the user to enter decimal values such as 22.8. As ages cannot have decimal places, this is a good validation rule for a column containing age data.

Criteria now appear that are relevant to whole numbers.

5. Click in the *Data* box and select *between*:

6. Click in the *Minimum* box and then click on cell J5.

note

Absolute and relative cell references

Absolute and relative cell references are covered in depth in:

Lesson 3-11: Understand absolute and relative cell references.

... in the *Essential Skills* book in this series.

If you are unsure about how to use absolute and relative cell references, you can watch a video lesson (recorded using Excel 2013) free of charge on our website.

http://ExcelCentral.com.

note

How to quickly find invalid values

The Data Validation button on the ribbon is a split button. If you click the right side of the:

Data→Data Tools→ Data Validation

... button, you'll see some more options:

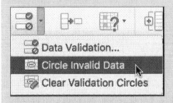

Click: *Circle Invalid Data* to show red circles around all invalid values on this worksheet:

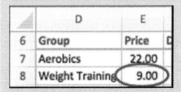

When you have reviewed the invalid data, you can use the *Clear Validation Circles* command to remove the circles.

7. Make J5 into an absolute reference (see sidebar).

8. Click in the *Maximum* box and then click on cell J6.

9. Make J6 into an absolute reference.

    The dialog should now look like this:

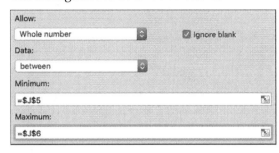

10. Click the *OK* button.

3 Test the data validation.

Data validation will now ensure that any new values entered into column C are valid. It will not change any existing invalid values in the column. (See sidebar for a quick way to find existing invalid values).

Enter an invalid value (such as an age of 101 or 15) into any cell in column C.

A rather unfriendly error message appears, advising that an error has occurred:

In the next lesson you'll discover how to make this message a little friendlier.

4 Add another data validation.

Use the same technique to apply the business rule: *Prices must be between 10.00 and 100.00* (stated in cells I16:J17) to column E.

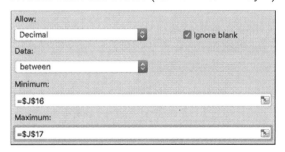

Notice that cell E8 now violates the validation criteria. When you apply a new validation rule to a cell, any values that already exist will remain without any error warnings. It will, however, be impossible to change the value to another that violates the validation criteria.

5 Save your work as *Health Club Bookings-2*.

Lesson 2-8: Create user-friendly messages for validation errors

A very useful design goal when developing computer software is to create a user interface that requires no user training. The interface should be so simple, and the features so obvious, that users can train themselves by experimentation and discovery.

For this reason, a user needs to be provided with an informative error message whenever they do something that is not allowed.

1 Open *Health Club Bookings-2* from your sample files folder (if it isn't already open).

2 Add an error message to column C.

   1. Select all of column C.

   2. Click: Data→Data Tools→Data Validation.

   3. Click the *Error Alert* tab.

   4. Type: **Invalid Age** into the *Title* box.

   5. Click in the *Error message* box and type:

      Age must be at least 17 and no more than 100.

      Your dialog should now look like this:

   6. Click the *OK* button.

3 Test the error message.

When you enter an invalid age into any cell in column C, you will see the error message:

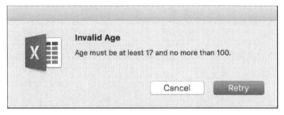

4 Change the validation from mandatory to advisory.

This validation is called *mandatory* because there is absolutely no possibility of the user entering an invalid value.

Sometimes this restriction is too strict. You may want to tell the user that an age of over 100 is unusual, but if the user is really sure that the client is over 100 they can still continue.

1. Select all of column C.

2. Click: Data→Data Tools→Data Validation.

3. Change the error message to read: **Age is usually between 17 and 100. Are you sure this is correct?**

4. Change the *Style* of the error message from *Stop* to *Warning*.

5. The dialog should now look like this:

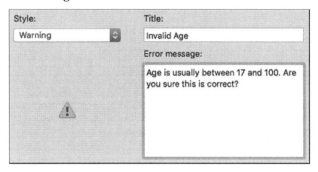

6. Click the *OK* button.

5 Test the error message.

When you enter an invalid age into any cell in column C, you will now see a different style of error message:

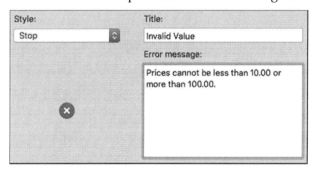

You then have the opportunity to click the *Yes* button and override the validation.

6 Add an informative error message to column E.

Use the same technique to add an error message to column E.

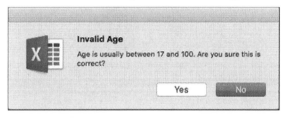

7 Save your work as *Health Club Bookings-3*.

Lesson 2-9: Create data validation input messages

In the last lesson: *Lesson 2-8: Create user-friendly messages for validation errors,* you discovered how to provide an informative error message whenever the user breaks a business rule.

Users can become frustrated if they can only discover business rules by first making mistakes and then being informed of the error. To make applications more efficient and user-friendly, it is sometimes better to inform the user of the business rules before they attempt to enter a value.

In this lesson you'll use data entry input messages to provide a better user experience.

1   Open *Health Club Bookings-3* from your sample files folder (if it isn't already open).

2   Add a data validation input message to column C.

In *Lesson 2-7: Validate numerical data,* you added a validation to column C to ensure that ages are entered as whole numbers between 17 and 100.

You will now use the *Input Message* feature to inform the user of this business rule before an attempt is made to enter an age.

1. Select all of column C by clicking the column header.

   You must select the entire column when you want to add an input message to every cell in the column.

2. Click: Data→Data Tools→Data Validation.

   The *Data Validation* dialog appears.

3. Click the *Input Message* tab.

4. In the *Title* box type: **Age**

5. In the *Input message* box type: **Ages must be whole numbers in the range 17-100.**

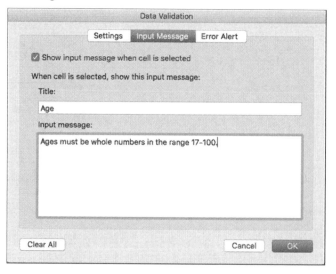

note

Data validation input messages can be annoying on columns of data

The sample workbook used in this lesson isn't a good candidate for data validation input messages.

The little yellow box may have been welcome the first time the user saw it. Once the business rule is known to the user, however, it becomes very irritating.

I've found that the best use for this feature is on one-time forms.

In this scenario each message is added to only one cell and provides useful information to aid completion of the form.

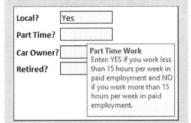

6. Click the *OK* button.

3   Test the data validation input message.

Click any cell in column C. The input message is displayed:

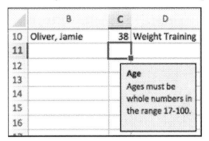

4   Use the same technique to add a data validation input message to column E.

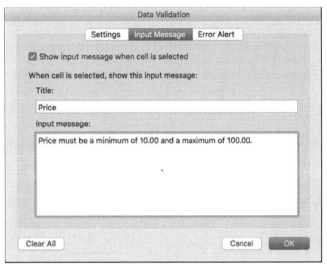

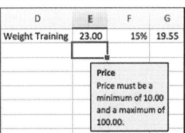

5   Save your work as *Health Club Bookings-4*.

Lesson 2-10: Add a formula-driven date validation and a text length validation

Validation parameters do not have to be simple values. They can also be set to the value returned by a formula.

In this lesson, you'll use Excel's TODAY function to add a validation that will not allow a date to be entered that is in the past.

1 Open *Health Club Bookings-4* from your sample files folder (if it isn't already open).

2 Add a validation to column A that will not allow dates that are in the past to be entered.

    1. Select all of column A.

    2. Click: Data→Data Tools→Data Validation.

    3. Click the *Settings* tab.

    4. Set the *Allow:* box to *Date.*

    5. Set the *Data:* box to *greater than or equal to.*

    6. Add a TODAY function to the *Start date* text box by typing:

       =TODAY()

       The TODAY function returns today's date. The TODAY function will be covered in depth later in: *Lesson 3-8: Understand common date functions.*

       Your dialog should now look like this:

3 Add an appropriate error alert message.

    1. Click the *Error Alert* tab.

    2. Type: **Date Error** into the *Title* box.

    3. Type: **Dates cannot be in the past** into the *Error message* box.

    4. Click the *OK* button.

Health Club Bookings-4

4   Test the validation.

Attempt to enter a date that is in the past.

An error message is displayed:

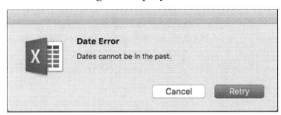

5   Apply a text length validation to column B to enforce the rule: "Minimum name length = 2 characters, Maximum name length = 20 characters".

The validation dialog will look like this:

Note that it is important to use the absolute references $J$12 and $J$13 rather than the relative references J12 and J13.

See sidebar for more on absolute and relative references.

6   Add an appropriate *Error Alert* for this validation.

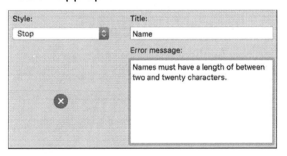

7   Test the validation.

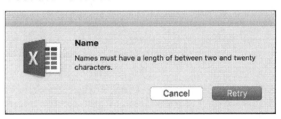

8   Save your work as *Health Club Bookings-5*.

Lesson 2-11: Add a table-based dynamic list validation

List validations prevent the user from entering any value into a cell that is not contained within a pre-defined list.

1 Open *Health Club Bookings-5* from your sample files folder (if it isn't already open).

2 Create a table (with a header) in cells I24:I30 containing a list of the valid groups: *Yoga, Aerobics, Weight Training, Aromatherapy, Massage* and *Aquarobics.*

   1. Type **Group** into cell I24.

   2. Type the valid group names (shown below) into cells I25:I30.

   3. Convert cells I24:I30 into a table.

     This was covered in: *Lesson 1-11: Convert a range into a table and add a total row.*

   4. Name your new table: **ValidGroups**

     This was covered in: *Lesson 1-17: Name a table and create an automatic structured table reference.*

3 Add a validation to column D that will only allow groups defined in the *ValidGroups* table (cells I24:I30) to be entered.

   1. Select all of column D.

   2. Click: Data→Data Tools→Data Validation.

   3. Click the *Settings* tab.

   4. In the *Allow* drop down, click *List.*

   5. Click in the *Source* box and then select cells I25:I30 with the mouse.

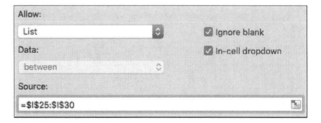

At this point you may wonder why you don't simply type: **=ValidGroups** into the *Source* box. While this makes perfect sense, Excel won't allow this (see the important sidebar for more on this).

Health Club Bookings-5

There are five ways to define validation source data

1. Type values directly into the Source box.

When you do this you need to type a comma in between each value:

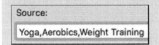

2. Define values as a range.

Simply select a regular range to define the values:

3. Define values as a table.

Convert the source values from a range to a table before setting the source data.

This seems to be the same as method 2. It differs because Excel treats source cells that are in a table differently from source cells that are in a range (but only when the table is on the same worksheet as the cells to be validated).

When the source cells originate in a table on the same worksheet, Excel will automatically grow and shrink the range as items are added and removed from the table.

4. Define values as a named range.

You'll learn all about named ranges in: *Session Four: Using Names and the Formula Auditing Tools.*

5. Define values as a named range that references a table.

This is the best method of all, as the validation table can reside on any worksheet. You'll use this technique, in: *Lesson 4-7: Create table-based dynamic range names.*

---

6. Add an appropriate *Error Alert.*

   You learned how to do this in: *Lesson 2-8: Create user-friendly messages for validation errors.*

   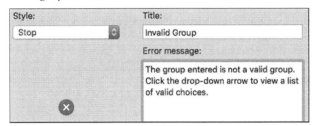

7. Click the *OK* button.

4 **Test the validation.**

1. Click anywhere in column D.

   Notice that a drop down arrow appears on the right-hand side of the cell.

2. Click the drop-down arrow.

   A list of all valid groups is displayed:

3. Click any of the valid groups.

   The selected value is displayed in the cell.

5 **Add *Circuit Training* as a valid group.**

1. Click in cell I31.

2. Type: **Circuit Training**

3. Press the **<Enter>** key.

   The new item is added to the table.

6 **Test the validation again.**

Click on the drop-down arrow to the right of any cell in column D.

Note that *Circuit Training* is now a valid item in the list.

This only happened because you converted the source cells I24:I30 into a table. If you hadn't done this, *Circuit Training* would not have been valid (see the important sidebar for more on this).

7 **Save your work as *Health Club Bookings-6*.**

Lesson 2-12: Use a formula-driven custom validation to enforce complex business rules

The simple dialog-driven validations have served all of your requirements up to now.

Sometimes you will have to implement a validation that is too complex for any of the dialog-driven validations to handle. In this case you will have to write a formula-driven custom validation.

There is a requirement (listed in the business rules) that states:

Discounts	
Minimum price for discount	20.00

This means that the value in column F will depend upon the value in column E.

	E	F	G
6	Price	Discount	Total
7	22.00	12%	19.36
8	9.00		9.00
9	23.00	10%	20.70
10	23.00	15%	19.55

In cell F8 above, it is prohibited to enter a discount because the price is less than 20.00. Right now there's nothing to stop a user doing this. You need to enforce this business rule with a formula-driven custom validation.

1   Open *Health Club Bookings-6* from your sample files folder (if it isn't already open).

2   Add a validation to column F that will enforce the business rule: *Minimum price for discount = 20.00*.

   1. Select all of column F.

   2. Click: Data→Data Tools→Data Validation→Data Validation.

   3. Click the *Settings* tab.

   4. Select *Custom* from the *Allow* drop-down list.

Custom validations require a formula. The validation will only allow a value to be entered if the formula returns a value of TRUE.

It is necessary to get a little ahead of yourself at this point, because this validation requires the use of an IF function. The IF function will be thoroughly covered later in: *Lesson 3-5: Use the IF logic function.*

Health Club Bookings-6

5. Click in the *Formula* text box and type the following text:

=IF(E1<$J$20, FALSE, TRUE)

Don't worry if the function doesn't make too much sense just yet. It will return FALSE if the value in E1 is less than the value in cell J20, and TRUE if the value in E1 is greater than or equal to the value in cell J20.

Note that E1 is a relative cell reference (ie it does not have the dollar prefixes $E$1). This is because you want it to adjust to the current row.

For example, when the user enters a percentage into cell F11, you want to check the value in cell E11.

6. Add an appropriate *Error Alert*:

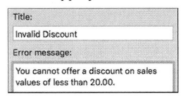

7. Click the *OK* button.

3 Test the validation.

1. Enter a discount into cell F8. Because the value in cell E8 is only 9.00, an error alert is displayed:

2. Click the *Cancel* button.

3. Change the value in cell E8 to **21.00**.

4. Enter a discount of **10%** in cell F8.

5. This time the value is accepted.

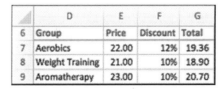

	D	E	F	G
6	Group	Price	Discount	Total
7	Aerobics	22.00	12%	19.36
8	Weight Training	21.00	10%	18.90
9	Aromatherapy	23.00	10%	20.70

4 Save your work as *Health Club Bookings-7*.

trivia

Spot the famous hybrid names

The names in the Employees file were generated by using Excel's RANDBETWEEN function.

I used this function to randomly mix the first and last names of some of the world's most famous people.

See how many famous half-names you can spot.

Some of them would make really good names for the film stars of the future, while others are definite non-starters!

Lesson 2-13: Remove duplicate values from a table

Duplicate entries are a common problem in data systems of all types.

When tables contain duplicate entries they are said to be corrupt.

Unfortunately, just about every corporate database I've ever worked with has contained corrupt data. You'll almost certainly have to clean up data sets containing duplicate values at some point in your Excel career.

This lesson will show you how to quickly weed out duplicate entries from tables.

Note that the technique taught in this lesson will only work with tables. If you have a range that needs to have duplicate values removed, you will need to first convert it into a table using the skills learned in: *Lesson 1-11: Convert a range into a table and add a total row.*

1   Open *Employees-1* from your sample files folder.

The table contains a list of employees along with their *EmployeeID* (a unique identification number). Every employee should only be listed once, but you suspect that the list contains duplicate entries.

	A	B	C
1	EmployeeID ▼	First Name ▼	Last Name ▼
2	362281	Brad	Cruise
3	324794	Ian	Dean
4	998783	Paris	Smith

2   Sort *EmployeeID* from smallest to largest.

If the list was very short, you could manually identify duplicate *EmployeeID* rows by simply sorting column A. This skill was covered in: *Lesson 1-14: Sort a range or table by rows.*

When the numeric EmployeeID values are sorted, part of the problem is instantly revealed:

	A	B	C
1	EmployeeID ▼↑	First Name ▼	Last Name ▼
2	117362	Johnny	Caine
3	117362	Johnny	Caine
4	118657	George	Marley
5	118657	George	Marley
6	128947	Bill	Spears

Johnny Caine and George Marley clearly have duplicate entries in the table.

Employees-1

note

A formula-driven approach to identifying duplicate values

Imagine that the problem posed in this lesson occurred in a real-life business scenario involving a large amount of data.

The primitive "sort and look" or "remove duplicates without review" features discussed in this lesson wouldn't provide a reasonable solution.

Here's one way that you could solve the problem.

1. Open the *Employees-1* sample file (this still contains duplicate Employee ID numbers).

2. Sort *EmployeeID* (column A) from *Smallest to Largest*.

3. Insert a new column to the left of column B.

4. Type: **Duplicate** into cell A1 (the new column's column header).

5. Enter this formula into cell A2:

=IF(B2=B1, TRUE, FALSE)

This is an IF function. You will learn more about these later, in: *Lesson 3-5: Use the IF logic function.*

The function only returns TRUE if the value in column B is the same as the value above (ie a duplicate entry).

6. Filter column A so that only TRUE values are shown.

The duplicate entries are now revealed:

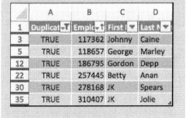

3   Automatically remove employees with duplicate *EmployeeID* values.

1.   Click any cell inside the table.

2.   Click: Table→Tools→Remove Duplicates.

The *Remove Duplicates* dialog is displayed:

Notice that, by default, Excel has selected every field in the table.

3.   Click the *Remove Duplicates* button.

All of the duplicate entries are deleted.

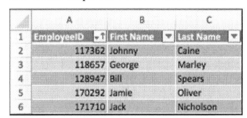

This is a very fast method, but not very sophisticated as there's no opportunity to review the values that have been deleted.

In: *Lesson 2-14: Use a custom validation to add a unique constraint to a column,* you'll discover how to catch duplicate entries at the point of entry.

4   Save your work as *Employees-2*.

Lesson 2-14: Use a custom validation to add a unique constraint to a column

You'll often find yourself working with a table or range that contains a column that must have unique values.

For example, consider this list of employees:

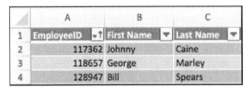

The *EmployeeID* column should never contain the same number listed twice. If it does, an error has occurred because no two employees can have the same *EmployeeID*.

In cases such as this, it would be very useful to refuse to let the user add duplicate values to column A. This type of restriction is called a *unique constraint* and is a fundamental feature of database products such as Microsoft Access, SQL Server and Oracle.

Excel doesn't provide an easy way to apply unique constraints directly (hopefully it will in a later version). Fortunately, there's an easy way to leverage upon the custom validation feature to add this functionality to Excel 2016 tables.

1   Open *Employees-2* from your sample files folder (if it isn't already open).

In this table, each employee should have a unique *EmployeeID*. At the moment the table does not enforce this rule.

2   Add a duplicate EmployeeID.

1. Press the **<Cmd>+<End>** keys to move to the end of the table (cell C120).

2. Press the **<Tab>** key.

If you press the **<Tab>** key in the last cell of a table, a new row is added to the table.

	A	B	C
119	997371	Michal	Marley
120	998783	Paris	Smith
121			

3. Add a duplicate entry for *Paris Smith*.

	A	B	C
119	997371	Michal	Marley
120	998783	Paris	Smith
121	998783	Paris	Smith

Notice that Excel allows the duplicate entry. In a moment you'll add a unique constraint to make this impossible.

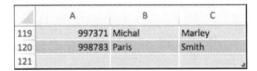
Employees-2

3   Delete the duplicate EmployeeID (row 121).

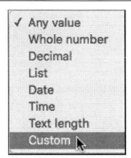

note

The COUNTIF function

The COUNTIF function will be covered in depth later, in: *Lesson 3-6: Use the SUMIF and COUNTIF functions to create conditional totals.*

If you are curious about how it works in this lesson, here's a quick explanation.

COUNTIF(range, criteria)

The COUNTIF function returns the number of cells in a *range* that meet a stated condition (the *criteria* argument).

In this lesson, **A:A** is used for the *range* argument. This means all of the cells in column A.

The relative reference **A2** is used for the *criteria* argument.

The COUNTIF function compares the value in the current row within column A to every other value in column A. It should always result in finding only one value (the value you are currently entering).

If your entry is unique, the COUNTIF function will return 1. If it is not unique, the function will return a number greater than 1.

As 1=1 is TRUE, the function returns TRUE (passing the validation) when the value is unique and FALSE (failing the validation) when the value is not unique.

4 Add a unique constraint to column A.

1. Select all of the table cells in column A except the header row.

   A quick way to do this is to click in cell A2 and then press **<Cmd>+<Shift>+<DownArrow>**.

2. Click: Data→Data Tools→Data Validation.

3. Click the *Settings* tab.

4. In the *Allow* drop-down, select *Custom.*

5. Type the following function into the *Formula* box:

   =COUNTIF(A:A,A2)=1

   See sidebar for a discussion of the COUNTIF function.

6. Add an appropriate error alert.

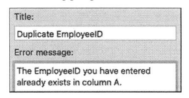

7. Click the *OK* button.

5 Test the unique constraint.

1. Attempt to change the *EmployeeID* in row 3 so that it is the same as the *EmployeeID* in row 2.

   Note that you must type the values in. If you copy and paste, the entry is not validated.

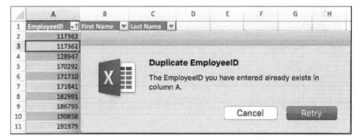

2. Attempt to add a new row at the end of the table with a duplicate ID:

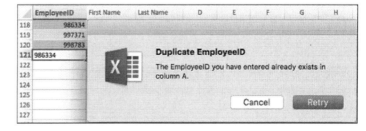

6 Save your work as *Employees-3.*

Session 2: Exercise

1 Open *Sales Performance Analysis-1* from your sample files folder.

	A	B	C	D
3	Salesman	Country	Salary	Sales
4	Alan Shearer	England	60,000	489,817
5	Bobby Charlton	England	34,000	844,935

2 Using *Text to Columns*, break the data in the *Salesman* column into two columns: *First Name* and *Last Name*.

Make sure that you also type the column labels **First Name** and **Last Name** into cells A3 and B3.

	A	B	C	D	E
3	First Name	Last Name	Country	Salary	Sales
4	Alan	Shearer	England	60,000	489,817
5	Bobby	Charlton	England	34,000	844,935

3 Automatically subtotal by *Country*, showing subtotals for *Salary* and *Sales*.

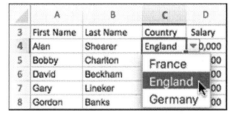

1 2 3		C	D	E
	3	Country	Salary	Sales
	11	England Total	364,000	3,657,627
	26	France Total	767,000	7,339,298

4 Remove the subtotals.

5 Add a validation to column C so that the country may only be entered as *England, France* or *Germany*.

	A	B	C	D
3	First Name	Last Name	Country	Salary
4	Alan	Shearer	England	0,000
5	Bobby	Charlton	France	00
6	David	Beckham	England	00
7	Gary	Lineker	Germany	00
8	Gordon	Banks		00

6 Add a user-friendly Error Alert to column C.

Country Error
Invalid Country. Click the drop-down arrow next to the country to see a list of valid entries.

Cancel   Retry

7 Add an input message to column C to inform users which countries are valid.

	A	B	C	D	E
3	First Name	Last Name	Country	Salary	Sales
4	Alan	Shearer	England	0,000	489,817
5	Bobby	Charlton	Engla		44,935
6	David	Beckham	Engla		66,277
7	Gary	Lineker	Engla		30,707
8	Gordon	Banks	Engla		00,950
9	Kevin	Keegan	Engla		34,433

Country
Country must be France, England or Germany.

8 Save your work as *Sales Performance Analysis-2*.

Sales Performance Analysis-1

If you need help slide the page to the left

Session 2: Exercise Answers

These are the four questions that students find the most difficult to answer:

Q 6	Q 5	Q 3	Q 2
1. Select all of column C. 2. Click: Data→ Data Tools→ Data Validation. 3. Click the *Error Alert* tab. 4. In the *Title* box, enter the text: **Country Error** 5. In the *Error message* box, enter the text: **Invalid Country. Click the drop-down arrow next to the country to see a list of valid entries.** 6. Click the *OK* button. This was covered in: *Lesson 2-8: Create user-friendly messages for validation errors.*	1. In cell G3, type the text: **Valid Countries** 2. Type the text: **France, England** and **Germany** into cells G4, G5 and G6. 		G
---	---
3	Valid Countries
4	France
5	England
6	Germany | 3. Select all of column C. 4. Click: Data→ Data Tools→ Data Validation. 5. Click the *Settings* tab. 6. Set up the dialog as follows: Allow: List Data: between Source: =$G$4:$G$6 7. Click the *OK* button. This was covered in: *Lesson 2-11: Add a table-based dynamic list validation.*	1. Click on any of the countries in column C. 2. Click: Data→Sort & Filter→ A-Z …to sort column C in ascending order. 3. Click: Data→Outline→Subtotal 4. Set up the dialog as follows: At each change in: Country Use function: Sum Add subtotal to: ☐ First Name ☐ Last Name ☐ Country ☑ Salary ☑ Sales 5. Click the *OK* button. This was covered in: *Lesson 2-3: Automatically subtotal a range.*	1. Insert a column to the left of column B. 2. Select cells A4:A34. 3. Click: Data→ Data Tools→ Text to Columns. 4. Leave the data type as *Delimited* and click the *Next* button. 5. Select *Space* in the *Delimiters* option group. ☑ Space 6. Click *Finish*. 7. Type: **First Name** and **Last Name** into cells A3 and B3. This was covered in: *Lesson 2-2: Split delimited data using Text to Columns.*

If you have difficulty with the other questions, here are the lessons that cover the relevant skills:

4   Refer to: *Lesson 2-3: Automatically subtotal a range.*

7   Refer to: *Lesson 2-9: Create data validation input messages.*

Session Three: Advanced Functions

> All animals are equal, but some animals are more equal than others.
>
> *George Orwell, "Animal Farm"*
> *English essayist, novelist, & satirist (1903 - 1950)*

There are 348 functions in the Excel function library. This would be a very large book if I tried to cover all of them.

In this session, I'll cover the most important Excel functions and put them into context by demonstrating real-world examples of how they can be used.

With the insights that you'll gain from using these functions, you'll be able to confidently explore the vast array of other functions in Excel's huge library should you ever need them.

Session Objectives

- Understand precedence rules
- Use common functions with Formula AutoComplete
- Use the Formula Builder task pane and the PMT function
- Use the PV and FV functions to value investments
- Use the IF logic function
- Use the SUMIF and COUNTIF functions to create conditional totals
- Understand date serial numbers
- Understand common date functions
- Use the DATEDIF function
- Use date offsets to manage projects using the scheduling equation
- Use the DATE function to offset days, months and years
- Enter time values and perform basic time calculations
- Perform time calculations that span midnight

- Understand common time functions and convert date serial numbers to decimal values
- Use the TIME function to offset hours, minutes and seconds
- Use the AND and OR functions to construct complex Boolean criteria
- Understand calculation options (manual and automatic)
- Concatenate strings using the concatenation operator (&)
- Use the TEXT function to format numerical values as strings
- Extract text from fixed width strings using the LEFT, RIGHT and MID functions
- Extract text from delimited strings using the FIND and LEN functions
- Use a VLOOKUP function for an exact lookup
- Use an IFERROR function to suppress error messages
- Use a VLOOKUP function for an inexact lookup

Lesson 3-1: Understand precedence rules

In my classroom courses, I put up a slide and ask the class the answer to the following sums:

6+(2*3) = ?

(6+2)*3 = ?

6+2*3 = ?

The class always agrees that **6+(2*3) = 12**. They are also very happy that **(6+2)*3 = 24**.

Nearly always I manage to divide opinion about the answer to **6+2*3**. Half the class usually goes for 24 and the other half for 12. Mostly, they are guessing!

Bearing in mind that most of my classes are taught to office workers who work with numbers every day of their lives, I am confident in my assertion that the rules of precedence are a mystery to at least half of the adults who work with Excel for a living!

Because of the rules of precedence:

6+2*3 = 12

That's because multiplication has precedence over addition (in other words, Excel does all of the multiplication before it does the addition).

Here are Excel's precedence rules:

Operator	Description
Parentheses (brackets)	Any expression in brackets is always evaluated first. **(6+2)*3=24**
Exponent	Exponents are always evaluated next. Exponents tend to be used in engineering/scientific scenarios and are rarely seen in accounting scenarios. **(1+1)*6^2=72**
Multiply and Divide	Multiplication and Division operators have the same precedence and are evaluated from left to right.
Add and Subtract	Addition and Subtraction operators have the same precedence and are evaluated from left to right.

If you only ever work with accounting scenarios, all you really need to remember is:

- Brackets are evaluated first.

- Multiplication and Division are evaluated next.

- Addition and Subtraction are evaluated last.

Payroll-1

1   Open *Payroll-1* from your sample files folder.

This worksheet contains some simple formulas required to compute *Net Pay* from *Hours Worked* (see *Payroll Rules* grab on facing page).

Most tax regimes have more complicated rules than those defined in this simple example. Employees are paid the same hourly rate for all hours worked. A different percentage of gross pay is then deducted for Tax, Social Security and Pension contributions.

2   Examine the formula in cell B23.

A formula that uses a rather long winded way of calculating *Net Pay* has been inserted into cell B23:

Because of the rules of precedence, the formula works correctly. It could also have been written with parentheses like this:

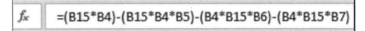

The parentheses are not needed, because the precedence rules state that multiplication happens before subtraction. I still prefer the formula with redundant parentheses (see sidebar).

---

tip

Use parentheses to make formulas more readable

I often use parentheses even when they are not needed.

There are two reasons for this:

1. The formula is easier to read.

2. Errors caused by precedence–related mistakes are eliminated.

---

note

If AutoComplete doesn't work

As with so many other features, Microsoft allows you to turn this very useful feature off.

You'd never want to do this, but you may work on a machine that has had *Formula AutoComplete* switched off and need to turn it on again. To do this click:

→Excel→Preferences→ AutoComplete

...and make sure that *Use AutoComplete* is checked.

The World's Tallest Buildings-1

Lesson 3-2: Use common functions with Formula AutoComplete

The functions most often seen in workbooks are: SUM, AVERAGE, COUNT, MAX and MIN. In this lesson, you'll use Excel's *Formula AutoComplete* feature to add these formulas to a workbook.

1   Open *The World's Tallest Buildings-1* from your sample files folder.

This worksheet contains information about the world's 20 tallest buildings. You'll use the SUM, MAX, MIN, AVERAGE and COUNT functions to populate cells B25:B29.

2   Click into cell B25 and type **=S** into the cell.

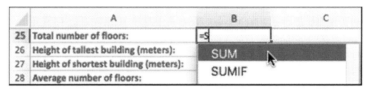

A list appears, showing every function in the Excel function library beginning with S. This feature (introduced in Excel 2007) is called *Formula AutoComplete*. (If this didn't work for you, see the sidebar).

3   Continue typing: **=SU**

Notice that the list now only shows functions beginning with SU. You can see the SUM function, three down in the list.

4   Select the SUM function.

There are two methods for selecting the SUM function:

Press the **<Down Arrow>** key until SUM is highlighted and then press the **<Tab>** key.

OR

Click on the function name with the mouse.

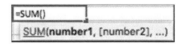

Notice that a little box has appeared beneath the function call. This is the *Syntax box* (see sidebar for more information).

5   Display detailed help for the SUM function.

Click the blue underlined *SUM* link in the *Syntax box*.

The Excel help system opens, showing detailed help for the SUM function.

This will not work if you are not connected to the Internet as the help system in Excel 2016 is only available online.

Read the help text if you are interested and then close the help window.

note

The Syntax box

The Syntax box tells you which arguments (sometimes called parameters) the function needs.

Arguments in square brackets are optional.

In the case of the SUM function, the first argument does not have square brackets, meaning that you can't leave it out.

For such a simple function as SUM, the syntax box is hardly needed, but later you'll discover functions that require several arguments and then the syntax box will be invaluable.

trivia

How the foot got shorter in 1959

This workbook uses the foot-to-meter conversion factor of 0.3048. Before 1959, a foot was slightly longer at 0.3048006096012 meters!

In 1893, the US Office of Weights and Measures (now the National Bureau of Standards) fixed the value of the US foot at 0.3048006096012 meters. Unfortunately, the rest of the world used a slightly different factor.

Because this caused problems, an international agreement was reached in 1959 to re-define the standard conversion factor at exactly 0.3048 meters – making a post-1959 foot slightly shorter than a pre-1959 foot!

Because the new standard upset existing survey data, it was further agreed that, for geodetic purposes only, the old conversion factor would remain valid. To avoid confusion, survey data is now defined in a new unit called the *US Survey Foot.*

6   Select the cells that you need to sum (cells F4:F23) with the mouse or keyboard.

You can select the cells with the keyboard using the following technique:

1. Erase the current contents of cell B25 (to start again).

2. Type: **=SUM(**

3. Press the **<Up Arrow>** and **<Right Arrow>** keys until you reach cell F4.

4. Press **<Cmd>+<Shift>+<Down Arrow>** to select cells F4:F23.

7   Press the **<Enter>** key to finish the formula.

There's no need to type the closing bracket, as Excel is clever enough to enter it for you. The total number of floors in all 20 buildings is now displayed in cell B25.

	A	B
25	Total number of floors:	2099

8   Use the same technique to add a MAX function to cell B26.

1. Click in cell B26.

2. Type **=MA**

3. Press the **<Down Arrow>** key to move the cursor over the MAX function.

4. Press the **<Tab>** key to automatically enter the MAX function into cell B26.

5. Select the range D4:D23 using either the mouse or the keyboard.

    The formula should now be: **=MAX(D4:D23**

6. Press the **<Enter>** key.

    There's no need to type the closing bracket as, once again, Excel helps you out by entering it automatically.

9   Use the same technique to add MIN, AVERAGE and COUNT functions to cells B27:B29.

	A	B
25	Total number of floors:	=SUM(F4:F23)
26	Height of tallest building (meters):	=MAX(D4:D23)
27	Height of shortest building (meters):	=MIN(D4:D23)
28	Average number of floors:	=AVERAGE(F4:F23)
29	Number of buildings in the list:	=COUNT(D4:D23)

10 Save your work as *The World's Tallest Buildings-2.*

Lesson 3-3: Use the Formula Builder task pane and the PMT function

note

Differences in the Windows version of Excel 2016

The Windows version of Excel 2016 uses an *Insert Function* dialog instead of the *Formula Builder* task pane.

The *Insert Function* dialog looks a lot different to the task pane that's used in the Mac version, but has all of the same features.

The advantage of the *Formula Builder* is that it can remain open while you edit your workbook. This means that you can very easily edit the arguments of existing formulas without needing to re-open the task pane.

This is an area where the Mac version of Excel 2016 could be said to be more advanced than the Windows version.

For more on the differences between the Mac and Windows versions of Excel 2016, see: *Appendix A: Differences between the Windows and Mac versions of Excel 2016.*

Calculates the payment for a loan based on constant payments and a constant interest rate.

In this lesson, you'll use a complex function with five parameters that will calculate the monthly repayments on a mortgage loan.

1 Open *Mortgage Repayments-1* from your sample files folder.

This worksheet contains details of mortgages for loans from 50,000 to 300,000 with a 25-year term and an interest rate of 6.7%. You will use the PMT function to calculate the monthly repayments.

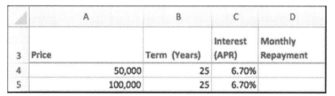

	A	B	C	D
3	Price	Term (Years)	Interest (APR)	Monthly Repayment
4	50,000	25	6.70%	
5	100,000	25	6.70%	

2 Calculate the monthly repayments using the PMT function and the *Formula Builder* task pane.

1. Click in cell D4.

2. Click the *Insert Function* button at the left of the formula bar:

D4	▲▼	✕	✓	*fx*	
		A			Insert Function

The *Formula Builder* task pane appears.

3. Type **PMT** into the *Search* box in the *Formula Builder* pane.

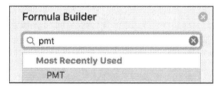

The PMT function is found and shown beneath the *Search* box.

Look at the help text below the list of functions. You can see what the PMT function is used for.

Below the help text, you can see an explanation of all of the PMT function's arguments.

Note also that there is a hyperlink pointing to the help page for this function.

More help on this function

The help page provides detailed information about each argument.

4. Click the *Insert Function* button.

A list of the function's arguments appear in the *Formula Builder* task pane.

note

What are the Fv and Type arguments used for?

Fv

Fv is the Future Value. It is an amount that will still be owed, or a cash bonus that will be paid to the borrower at the end of the loan. This is sometimes called a balloon payment.

If a positive amount is entered into the Fv box, this amount will be paid to the borrower at the end of the loan.

If a negative amount is entered, it will represent an amount still owed at the end of the loan.

This type of loan is common in vehicle loan agreements and can also be used to model *interest only* mortgages.

Example:

A car is sold for 10,000 across three years. At the end of the three years, the borrower is able to buy the car for 3,000 or to hand it back to the dealer.

To model this loan, the Pv would be 10,000 and the Fv would be -3000.

Type

Most loans require the repayment to be made at the end of the period (in this example, at the end of each month). Some insurance-backed loans require the repayment to be made at the beginning of the period.

Payments for this type of loan can be calculated by setting the *Type* argument to 1.

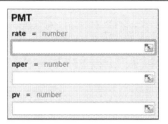

The last two arguments are optional (Fv and Type). You won't be using the Fv and Type arguments in this lesson, but if you are interested in their purpose see the sidebar for more information.

5.   Click in the first box (*rate*). Notice that the help text is still visible at the bottom of the dialog:

> • **rate**: is the interest rate per period for the loan. For example, use 6%/4 for quarterly payments at 6% APR.

6.   Click in cell C4 and then type **/12**. You need to divide the annual interest rate by twelve to calculate the monthly interest rate.

7.   Complete the next two arguments by studying the help text for each. Your task pane should now look like this:

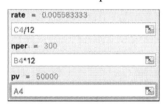

8.   Click the *Done* button below the function arguments.

The monthly repayment is now shown in cell D4, but the amount shown is negative. The number is shown as negative because it represents money going out of your account (a negative cash flow).

The PMT function automatically formats the repayment with a currency prefix matching the currency locale of your computer. Because my computer had a currency locale of pounds sterling, my value was prefixed by a GBP (£) symbol.

9.   Click in cell D4 and add a minus operator to the front of the formula:

> fx =-PMT(C4/12,B4*12,A4)

10.   Press the **<Enter>** key.

The value is now displayed as a positive number, which is more visually pleasing:

	A	B	C	D
			Interest	Monthly
3	Price	Term (Years)	(APR)	Repayment
4	50,000	25	6.70%	£343.88

11.   AutoFill the formula to the end of the list to show monthly repayments for all six loan amounts.

3   Save your work as *Mortgage Repayments-2*.

	C	D
	Interest	Monthly
3	(APR)	Repayment
4	6.70%	£343.88
5	6.70%	£687.76
6	6.70%	£1,031.64
7	6.70%	£1,375.51
8	6.70%	£1,719.39
9	6.70%	£2,063.27

Lesson 3-4: Use the PV and FV functions to value investments

> Compound interest is the eighth wonder of the world. He who understands it, earns it … he who doesn't … pays it
>
> *Albert Einstein, theoretical physicist (1879-1955)*

Present Value

Present Value is the total amount that a series of future payments is worth now.

Present Value can be used to value an existing loan. This would be useful if you wanted to sell the loan to another party.

In this lesson, you will explore the following scenario:

I have loaned my friend John $20,000 to buy a car. John has agreed to repay $1,000 per month for two years (making me $4,000 in interest on the deal). I want to sell the loan on to my other friend Bill. Bill says he is happy to buy it from me, but he needs a return of 12% on his investment. I can use the PV function to work out what the loan is worth today based upon Bill's requirement for a 12% return.

Future Value

Future value is used to work out how much capital will accumulate if a fixed amount is saved each month at a specified compound interest rate.

In this lesson, you will also explore the following scenario:

I save $100 each month towards my retirement fund. If I save for 30 years and the interest rate during this time will be 10%, how much money will I have in my fund upon retirement?

1   Open *Investments-1* from your sample files folder.

This worksheet contains details of the retirement fund and car loan scenarios described above.

2   Use the FV function to calculate the retirement fund value.

In the last lesson, you discovered how to use the *Insert Function* button fx to access functions in Excel's vast function library.

You can also access the library by using the *Function Library* buttons on the ribbon.

1.   Click in cell B7.

2.   Click: Formulas→Function Library→Financial→FV.

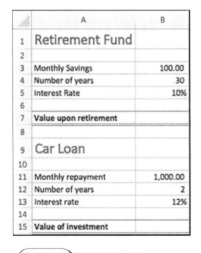

	A	B
1	Retirement Fund	
2		
3	Monthly Savings	100.00
4	Number of years	30
5	Interest Rate	10%
6		
7	Value upon retirement	
8		
9	Car Loan	
10		
11	Monthly repayment	1,000.00
12	Number of years	2
13	Interest rate	12%
14		
15	Value of investment	

Investments-1

3. Add the correct values in the *Formula Builder* task pane:

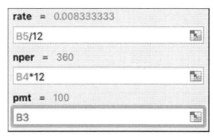

4. Click the *Done* button.

The retirement fund is shown as a negative because it represents money leaving your account.

5. Add a minus sign in front of *FV* in the formula bar to convert it into a more visually pleasing positive value:

f_x | =-FV(B5/12,B4*12,B3)

Although only 36,000 was paid into the retirement fund, compound interest has boosted the amount saved to 226,048.79.

You can now appreciate why Einstein described compound interest as the eighth wonder of the world!

3 **Use the PV function to calculate the value of the car loan.**

1. Click in cell B15.

2. Click: Formulas→Function Library→Financial→PV.

3. Add the correct values in the *Formula Builder* task pane:

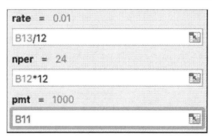

4. Click the *Done* button.

5. Add a minus sign in front of *PV* in the formula bar to convert it to a positive value:

f_x | =-PV(B13/12,B12*12,B11)

The result is 21,243.39 so you turned a profit on the deal!

(The *Fv* and *Type* arguments are discussed in: *Lesson 3-3: Use the Formula Builder task pane and the PMT function*).

4 **Save your work as *Investments-2*.**

Earnings Summary-1

Lesson 3-5: Use the IF logic function

The IF function is one of Excel's most widely used and useful functions. It is also a function that often confuses my students, so I'll begin this lesson by explaining the concept of the logical test. Later, you'll construct a worksheet containing three examples of the IF function at work.

The IF function requires a *logical test* and then performs one action if the test returns TRUE and a different action if the test returns FALSE.

Here are some examples of logical tests:

Expression	Returns	Why?
6=2	FALSE	Because six does not equal two.
100<90	FALSE	Because 100 is not less than 90.
6+2 = 4+4	TRUE	Because eight does equal eight.

In this lesson, you'll use three different logical tests in order to calculate several employees' earnings during a week.

1 Open *Earnings Summary-1* from your sample files folder.

Notice the *Payroll Rules* section:

	A	B	C	D	E	F
3	**Payroll Rules:**					
4	*All hours up to 35 hours per week paid at hourly rate*					
5	*All hours over 35 hours per week paid at time and a half (150% of hourly rate)*					
6	*Bonus of 5% paid on all sales above target*					

Logical tests will be constructed to calculate *Standard Pay, Overtime Pay* and *Bonus*:

	A	B	C	D	E	F	G	H	I
8	Name	Sales	Target	Hourly Rate	Hours Worked	Standard Pay	Overtime Pay	Bonus	Total
9	Brad Cruise	22,000	10,000	15.00	40				

2 Use an IF function to calculate standard pay.

In the case of *Standard Pay*, the logical test will be:

"Did this employee work more than 35 hours this week?"

The formula for the logical test is: **E9<=35** (Cell E9 is less than or equal to 35).

If this returns *TRUE*, then standard pay will be:

*Hours Worked * Hourly Rate* (E9*D9)

...because the employee worked for 35 hours or less.

If this returns **FALSE**, then standard pay will be:

*35*Hourly Rate* (35*D9)

... because the employee worked more than 35 hours (and the first 35 hours of this time will be paid at standard rate).

tip

Avoid nesting IF functions

My students often bring their own workbooks to my courses in order to find a solution to their real-world problems.

Some hideously complex and completely unfathomable workbooks turn up at my courses!

A common theme to many of these difficult-to-understand workbooks is the use of nested IF functions.

Here's an example of a two-level nested IF function:

=IF(A31="Apples",10%,IF(A31="Lemons",20%,0))

This would return 10% if the value in A31 was *Apples*, 20% if the value was *Lemons* and zero if the value was anything else. Note that the words *Apples* and *Lemons* are enclosed in quotation marks. You must refer to text in this way within Excel formulas.

Whenever I see nested IF functions, I know that there's almost certainly a better, less complex, and more understandable solution. In the above example, a VLOOKUP function would provide a better solution (VLOOKUP functions will be covered in: *Lesson 3-22: Use a VLOOKUP function for an exact lookup*).

Excel 2016 allows you to nest IF functions up to 64 levels deep (which is 63 too many).

1. Click in cell F9.

2. Click: Formulas→Function Library→Logical→IF.

   The *Formula Builder* task pane appears.

3. Complete the task pane as follows:

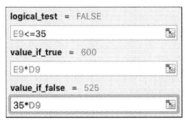

   If you do not completely understand why the above formulas are used, read the introduction to this lesson again.

4. Click the *Done* button.

   Standard Pay is correctly displayed in cell F9 (525.00).

3   Use an IF function to calculate overtime pay.

   It should now be clear to you why the correct arguments for the IF function, this time, are:

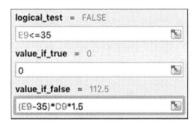

4   Use the IF function to calculate bonus.

   Once again, it should be clear to you why the correct arguments for the IF function this time are:

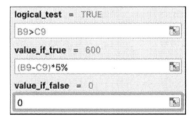

5   Add a formula to cell I9 to calculate total pay.

   The correct formula could be either of the following:

   =F9+G9+H9
   =SUM(F9:H9)

6   AutoFill the formulas in cells F9:I9 to cells F10:I17.

   The payroll worksheet is now complete.

	A	B	C	D	E	F	G	H	I
8	Name	Sales	Target	Hourly Rate	Hours Worked	Standard Pay	Overtime Pay	Bonus	Total
9	Brad Cruise	22,000	10,000	15.00	40	525.00	112.50	600.00	1,237.50
10	Ian Dean	9,000	8,000	13.00	35	455.00	-	50.00	505.00
11	Paris Smith	10,000	12,000	15.00	42	525.00	157.50	-	682.50

7   Save your work as *Earnings Summary-2*.

note

The SUMIFS and COUNTIFS functions

The SUMIFS and COUNTIFS functions work in exactly the same way as the SUMIF and COUNTIF functions used in this lesson but they accept multiple criteria.

For example, if you needed to know the combined total salary for Male employees in the *Sales* department, you'd set the SUMIFS arguments as follows:

Lesson 3-6: Use the SUMIF and COUNTIF functions to create conditional totals

In the previous lesson, you used the IF logical function to return different values based upon a logical test that returned TRUE or FALSE.

SUMIF and COUNTIF are similar functions but are used to sum or count values within a range based upon a similar logical test.

This session's sample workbook lists all of an organization's employees along with their gender and department:

	A	B	C	D
3	Name	Sex	Salary	Department
4	Johnny Caine	M	37,864	Sales
5	George Marley	M	26,148	Purchasing
6	Betty Anan	F	26,345	Logistics
7	Paris Winfrey	F	23,562	Sales

You'll use the SUMIF and COUNTIF functions to list the total salary and headcount for each department, along with the total salary and headcount for each gender.

1　Open *Headcount & Salaries-1* from your sample files folder.

2　Use the SUMIF function to calculate the total salary for each department.

　　1.　Click in cell B21.

　　2.　Click: Formulas→Math & Trig→SUMIF.

　　　　The *Formula Builder* task pane appears.

　　　　There are three arguments for the SUMIF function:

　　　　The *range* argument defines the range in which to look for the department name. In this case, it is the range D4:D17 (the cells containing the *Departments*.

　　　　The *criteria* argument is the thing to look for within the stated range. In this case, it is the word "Sales" contained in cell A21.

　　　　The *sum_range* argument is the range containing numerical data that needs to be added up when the criteria is true. In this case, it is the range C4:C17 (the cells containing *Salary* values).

　　3.　Complete the task pane with the following arguments:

　　　　Note the use of absolute references for each range. This will allow you to AutoFill the function for the *Purchasing* and *Logistics* totals. See sidebar for more on absolute references.

tip

Absolute references and the Formula Builder task pane

You might remember that you can quickly change a cell reference into an absolute reference by pressing the <Fn>+<F4> keys.

If you try this in the *Formula Builder*, however, you'll find that it doesn't work.

The solution is to click the cell references in the *Formula Bar* before pressing <Fn>+<F4>. You'll then be able to quickly convert them into absolute references.

Headcount & Salaries-1

note

Using wildcards in logical criteria

Sometimes you will only have a partial idea of what you need to find.

In this case, you can use the wildcard characters – the asterisk (*) and the question mark (?). It is easiest to explain how wildcards work with a few examples:

C*g   Finds **Containing**
        Finds **Citing**
        Finds **Changing**

S?d   Finds **Sid**
        Finds **Sad**
        Finds **Syd**
        Finds **Sud**

In the above examples, you can see that the first search finds all words that begin with C and end with g. The second example only finds three letter words that begin with S and end with d.

Later in this session, in: *Lesson 3-18: Concatenate strings using the concatenation operator (&)*, you'll learn about concatenating strings. After this lesson, you will understand the following examples:

Imagine you have a range containing the values:

22 Cherry Walk
144 Cherry Road
Cherry Tree House
Cherry Tree Lodge

... and you want to construct a COUNTIF or SUMIF function based upon the partial string contained in cell A1 (for this example, let's imagine that the word *Cherry* is in cell A1).

The criteria would be:

"*" & A1 & "*"

This would find all four values.

To find values that begin with the word *Cherry*, you would use the criteria:

A1 & "*"

This would find two values.

4. Click the *Done* button.

5. AutoFill cell B21 to cells B22:B23 to display the total salaries for the *Purchasing* and *Logistics* departments.

3   **Use the COUNTIF function to calculate the headcount for each department.**

COUNTIF works in exactly the same way as SUMIF, but returns a count of all cells that match the criteria.

1. Click in cell C21.

2. Click: Formulas→More Functions→Statistical→COUNTIF.

3. Complete the task pane with the following arguments:

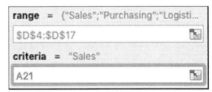

4. Click the *Done* button.

5. AutoFill cell C21 to cells C22:C23 to display the headcount for the *Purchasing* and *Logistics* departments.

4   **Use SUMIF and COUNTIF functions to calculate the salary and headcount for male and female employees in cells B27:C28.**

Use exactly the same technique as you did for *Salary* and *Headcount by Department*. The correct arguments for cells B27 and C27 are:

And:

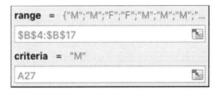

	A	B	C
20	Department	Salary	Headcount
21	Sales	179,898	6
22	Purchasing	137,557	5
23	Logistics	73,601	3
24	Total:	391,056	14
25			
26	Gender	Salary	Headcount
27	M	253,587	9
28	F	137,469	5
29	Total:	391,056	14

5   **Save your work as *Headcount & Salaries-2*.**

trivia

The Julian and Gregorian calendars

When you work with very old dates, you can run into a problem with the Julian and Gregorian calendars.

In 1582 it was noticed that the seasons had drifted by 10 days because the Julian system (named after Julius Caesar who adopted it in 45 BC) had incorrectly miscalculated a year as being 365 ¼ days. A year is actually slightly shorter than this.

Pope Gregory XIII decreed that, in order to put things right, the world had to lose 10 days to make up for all of those extra leap years.

The reformed Gregorian calendar also adopted a new leap year rule to keep things on track in future years.

It took nearly 200 years for everybody to get on board with the Gregorian calendar. The Catholic countries of Spain, Italy and Portugal adopted it at once, but England and parts of America didn't convert until September 14th 1752.

This means that in Spain the dates October 5th 1582 to October 14th 1582 never actually existed. In England it was the dates Sept 3rd 1752 to September 14th 1752.

The strangest case of all was Sweden who decided to "phase it in gradually" between 1700 and 1740, meaning that their calendar was out of step with the rest of the world for 40 years.

If you work with historical data from this era you have to be very careful indeed.

Lesson 3-7: Understand date serial numbers

This lesson was included in the *Essential Skills* book in this series and has been also included in this book as a recap. A full understanding of the date serial number concept is essential in order to understand the date and time functions that will be introduced in later lessons.

Excel stores dates in a very clever way. Understanding Excel's date storage system empowers you to use date arithmetic. You can use date arithmetic to compute the difference between two dates (in days) or to shift date ranges by a given time interval.

How Excel stores dates

Dates are stored as simple numbers called *date serial numbers*. The serial number contains the number of days that have elapsed since 1st January 1900 (where 1st January 1900 is 1).

The world began in 1900

An interesting shortcoming of Excel is its inability to easily work with dates before 1900. Excel simply doesn't acknowledge that there were any dates before this time. If you work with older dates, you will have to work-around this limitation.

In Excel, every time is a date, and every date is a time

You've already realized that 5th January 1900 is stored as the number 5. What would the number 5.5 mean? It would mean midday on 5th January 1900.

It is possible to format a date to show only the date, only the time, or both a time and a date.

When you enter a time into a cell without a date, the time is stored as a number less than one. Excel regards this as having the non-existent date of 00 January 1900!

When you enter a date into a cell without a time, the time is stored as midnight at the beginning of that day.

1   Create a new blank workbook and put the numbers 1 to 5 in cells A1:A5.

2   Type the formula **=A1** into cell B1 followed by the **<Enter>** key, and then AutoFill the formula to the end of the list.

	A	B
1	1	1
2	2	2
3	3	3
4	4	4
5	5	5

trivia

The peculiar case of the Excel date bug and Lotus 1-2-3

Here's the Gregorian leap year rule as defined by 1582 Pope Gregory XIII:

Every year that is exactly divisible by four is a leap year, except for years that are exactly divisible by 100; the centurial years that are exactly divisible by 400 are still leap years.

This means that the year 1900 wasn't a leap year, but 2000 was (causing many millennium software bugs).

The designers of Lotus 1-2-3 weren't paying enough attention to Pope Gregory's rules. Their DATE() function thought that 1900 was a leap year and thus recognised the mythical date February 29th 1900.

Because Excel needed to be compatible with Lotus 1-2-3, Microsoft had to replicate the Lotus bug when they designed Excel.

Try entering 29th Feb 1900 into a worksheet and Excel will gladly accept it.

This bug has the effect of introducing a one-day error into any date arithmetic you may do that spans 29th February 1900.

3. Apply a date format to column A that will show a four-digit year.

	A	B
1	Sunday, 1 January 1900	1
2	Monday, 2 January 1900	2

This reveals that the numbers 1 to 5 represent the dates 1-Jan-1900 to 05-Jan-1900.

4. Set a custom format of **dd mmm yyyy hh:mm** for the dates in column A (to show both dates and times).

Notice that when you enter a date without a time, the time is set to midnight at the beginning of that day.

	A	B
1	01 Jan 1900 00:00	1
2	02 Jan 1900 00:00	2

5. Change the time in cell A2 to 12:00.

Notice that the number in cell B2 has changed to 2.5 showing that times are stored by Excel as the decimal part of a number.

	A	B
1	01 Jan 1900 00:00	1
2	02 Jan 1900 12:00	2.5

6. Compute the number of days that occurred between 01 Jan 1900 and 01 Jan 2000.

Now that you have a good grasp of Excel's serial numbers, this task is easy.

1. Enter the two dates in cells A7 and A8, one beneath the other.
2. Subtract one date from the other by entering the formula: **=A8-A7** into cell A9.
3. Format cell A9 to display numeric (rather than date) values.

	A
7	Sunday, 1 January 1900
8	Saturday, 1 January 2000
9	36,525.00

You now know that 36,525 days occurred during the last millennium (actually 36,524 due to the Lotus 1-2-3 bug – see sidebar).

7. Close the workbook without saving.

Lesson 3-8: Understand common date functions

Excel's primary date functions are TODAY, DAY, MONTH and YEAR. In the previous lesson, you gained an understanding of how Excel stores dates as serial numbers. You can now use this knowledge in conjunction with the above date functions to create some very useful date related formulas.

1   Open *Resources-1* from your sample files folder.

This worksheet contains a list of Employees along with their dates of birth.

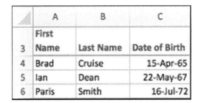

2   Use the YEAR function to calculate the year in which each employee was born.

    1.   Click in cell D4.

    2.   Click: Formulas→Date & Time→Year.

        The *Formula Builder* task pane is displayed.

    3.   Click in cell C4.

        Because you know that all dates are represented by a serial number, and because cell C4 contains a date, this reference will cause the YEAR function to return 1965 (the year Brad Cruise was born).

        Notice that the dialog previews the result as *Result: 1965* and also lets you know that the date serial number for 15th April 1965 is *23,847*.

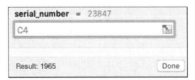

    4.   Click the *Done* button.

        The year in which Brad Cruise was born is now displayed in cell D4.

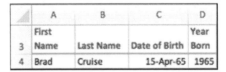

3   Use the DAY function to place the day when Brad Cruise was born into cell E4.

4   Use the MONTH function to place the month when Brad Cruise was born into cell F4.

Resources-1

	E	F
3	Day Born	Month Born
4	=DAY(C4)	=MONTH(C4)

	A	B	C	D	E	F
3	First Name	Last Name	Date of Birth	Year Born	Day Born	Month Born
4	Brad	Cruise	15-Apr-65	1965	15	4

5 Use the TODAY function to place a volatile current date into cell G4.

	G			G
3	Today		3	Today
4	=TODAY()		4	11-Feb-16

The TODAY function returns the current date. The date is volatile. This means that if you were to open this worksheet again tomorrow, you would see tomorrow's date in cell G4.

6 Use the YEAR function to place the current year into cell H4.

By using the value in cell G4 as the argument for the YEAR function, it is possible to insert the current year into cell H4.

Because the value in cell G4 is volatile, the value in H4 is also volatile. This means that if this worksheet was opened again in the year 2017, you would see the value 2017 in cell H4.

	H			H
3	Current Year		3	Current Year
4	=YEAR(G4)		4	2016

7 Add a formula to cell I4 to calculate the employee's maximum age this year.

Calculating the employee's current age from their date of birth using the YEAR, MONTH and DAY functions is quite a feat (although it can be done). You'll discover an easy way to do this in the next lesson using a different technique.

In this lesson, you'll simply calculate what the employee's maximum age will be this year with a simple subtraction of the year born from the current year.

	D	E	F	G	H	I
3	Year Born	Day Born	Month Born	Today	Current Year	Max Age This Year
4	1965	15	4	11-Feb-16	2016	=H4-D4

8 Autofill cells D4:I4 down to row 12.

9 Save your work as *Resources-2*.

note

Why calculating age from date of birth is so difficult

I've seen some weird and wonderful attempts to calculate age from date of birth in my student's worksheets.

At first, it doesn't seem such a big deal. The first solution that occurs is to simply convert each date to days and then divide by 365. Like this:

(TODAY() – BirthDate)/365

If it wasn't for leap years, this would work. To overcome the leap year issue, I've seen solutions based upon the assumption that a year is, on average, 365.25 days long. So why won't this work?

(TODAY() – BirthDate)/365.25

There are two reasons why.

The first reason is that the date may belong to a child who has not yet lived through a leap year.

The second reason is caused by the Gregorian leap year rule that skips a leap year in centurial years (see: *Lesson 3-7: Understand date serial numbers* sidebar).

Lesson 3-9: Use the DATEDIF function

Three may keep a secret, if two of them are dead.

Benjamin Franklin (1706 - 1790)

One of the most useful date-related functions available in Excel is the DATEDIF function. For some reason this is a secret, and you'll find nothing about this wonderful function anywhere in the Excel 2016 documentation. Some have speculated that this may be for legal reasons as the function was originally included for compatibility with Lotus 1-2-3.

Microsoft documented the function in Excel 2000 so, in their spirit of backward compatibility, they continue to support it in Excel 2016 and can be expected to also support it in all future Excel versions.

DATEDIF is able to calculate the difference between two dates for several intervals. In this lesson, you'll use it to calculate an age from a date of birth. This is hugely complex using the YEAR, MONTH and DAY functions (see sidebar).

Because you probably don't have a copy of Excel 2000, here is the syntax for the function:

=DATEDIF(StartDate, EndDate, Interval)

StartDate: The first date.

EndDate: The second date.

Interval: The interval to return, such as the number of months or years between the two dates.

The interval arguments are:

"m"	Months between two dates.
"d"	Days between two dates.
"y"	Years between two dates.
"ym"	Months between two dates, ignoring the year (ie as if both dates were the same year).
"yd"	Days between two dates, ignoring the year.
"md"	Days between two dates, ignoring the months and years.

1 Open *Resources-2* from your sample files folder (if it isn't already open).

2 Change the text in cell I3 to: **Age (Years)**

Resources-2

note

Calculating age from date of birth using the YEARFRAC and INT functions

Excel is also able to calculate an age from a date of birth using the INT and YEARFRAC functions.

YEARFRAC returns the number of years between two dates expressed as a fraction.

The syntax is:

YEARFRAC(start_date, end_date, [basis])

In this lesson's sample file, you would use the function (in cell I4) like this:

=YEARFRAC(C4, G4, 1)

The last argument (basis) tells Excel to take leap years into account when calculating the fractional part of the year.

In this lesson's sample file YEARFRAC produced these results (when this lesson was written on 11th January 2016):

	A	B	I
3	First Name	Last Name	Age (Years)
4	Brad	Cruise	50.8255
5	Ian	Dean	48.7242

This means that Brad Cruise was 50.8255 years old.

In: *Lesson 1-9: Apply an advanced filter with function-driven criteria,* you learned about the INT function. This returns the whole number portion of a number. For example, **=INT(25.99)** would return the whole number **25**.

In the example above, the formula:

=INT(I4)

… would return **50** (Brad Cruise's age).

You could also combine the two functions like this:

=INT(YEARFRAC(C4, G4, 1))

---

3 Delete cells I4:I12.

	C	D	E	F	G	H	I
3	Date of Birth	Year Born	Day Born	Month Born	Today	Current Year	Age (Years)
4	15-Apr-65	1965	15	4	11-Feb-16	2016	
5	22-May-67	1967	22	5	11-Feb-16	2016	
6	16-Jul-72	1972	16	7	11-Feb-16	2016	

4 Add the following formula to cell I4:

=DATEDIF(C4,TODAY(),"y")

Notice that *Formula AutoComplete* doesn't even want to admit that this function exists.

The function works by comparing the date of birth (in cell C4) with today's date (returned by the TODAY function) and returns the interval between the date of birth, and today's date, in years.

5 Calculate each resource's precise age in years, months and days.

This requirement illustrates the use of the "ym" and "md" arguments.

1. Type the text: **Age (Months)** into cell J3.

2. Type the text: **Age (Days)** into cell K3.

3. Match the formatting of cells J3 and K3 to that in cell I3.

   (Formatting is an elementary skill covered in the *Essential Skills* book in this series).

	H	I	J	K
3	Current Year	Age (Years)	Age (Months)	Age (Days)
4	2016	50		

(You will probably see a different age depending upon whatever today's date is at the time you read this book).

4. Add the following formula to cell J4:

   =DATEDIF(C4,TODAY(),"ym")

5. Add the following formula to cell K4:

   =DATEDIF(C4,TODAY(),"md")

6. Autofill cells I4:K4 to the end of the range.

	A	B	C	D	I	J	K
3	First Name	Last Name	Date of Birth	Year Born	Age (Years)	Age (Months)	Age (Days)
4	Brad	Cruise	15-Apr-65	1965	50	9	27
5	Ian	Dean	22-May-67	1967	48	8	20

The above was calculated on 11th January 2016. They'll all be a little older by the time you complete this exercise.

6 Save your work as Resources-3.

---

note

Project Management and Excel

Excel is often misused to manage projects.

Project Management involves scheduling tasks and assigning resources to complete each task. For example, to build a house you would have tasks such as *lay bricks* and *fit windows*.

Each task has a *start* and *end* date, along with one or more *dependencies* (for example you cannot fit the windows until you have laid the bricks).

Each task also has one or more *resources* assigned to it (for example you may assign Bill and Bob to lay the bricks and Colin to fit the windows).

The best way to illustrate a project plan is the Gantt chart, named after Henry Gantt (1861–1919). It is quite easy to produce a primitive Gantt chart using Excel (but not a true Gantt chart showing inter-task dependencies).

Now that you understand Excel's date functions, you might think that Excel is a great tool for managing projects – but there's a far, far better way.

Microsoft Project is a tool designed specifically to manage projects and produce excellent Gantt charts.

If you have complex workbooks that seek to manage the type of scenario described above, you really should check out Microsoft Project – it is a superb tool.

Many students that attend my Project Management courses have first tried hard and failed using Excel.

Project-1

Lesson 3-10: Use date offsets to manage projects using the scheduling equation

In this lesson, you'll use date offsets in conjunction with the scheduling equation to create a worksheet that will manage a small project.

In order to understand project management, you need to first understand the scheduling equation:

Time = Work/Units

Let's pose the age-old primary school math problem:

"If it takes one man ten days to dig a hole, how long will it take two men to dig the same hole"?

The answer is, of course, five days (in mathematics, if not in reality).

To use the scheduling equation, each unit can be described (in this example) as being a man and the work can be defined in days.

In the first example:

10 days = 10 days/1 Man

In the second example:

5 days = 10 days/2 Men

If you increase your estimate of 10 days' work, then the time will increase. If you add more men to the task, then the time will decrease, as the equation will always balance.

In this lesson, you'll learn how to create formulas that will enable task lengths to dynamically re-scale as you either add more resources to each task, or revise your estimate for the amount of work needed to complete each task.

1 Open *Project-1* from your sample files folder.

The worksheet contains a simple project plan consisting of four linked tasks:

	A	B	C	D
3	Task Name	Start date	Work (Man-Days)	Units
4	Dig Foundations	15-Jun-16	3	3
5	Pour Footings		2	1
6	Lay Bricks to DPC		8	4
7	Pour floor slab		2	1

Each task has a *start to finish dependency*. This means that each task must be completed before the following task can begin.

2 Calculate the *End Date* for the first task.

Enter the formula: **=B4+C4/D4-1** into cell E4.

Note that, because of the rules of precedence, this is the equivalent of **=B4+(C4/D4)-1**

(Precedence was covered in: *Lesson 3-1: Understand precedence rules*).

One day is subtracted because a job of one day's duration will begin and end on the same day. The formula calculates the *End Date* using the scheduling equation discussed at the beginning of this lesson.

	A	B	C	D	E
			Work		
3	Task Name	Start date	(Man-Days)	Units	End Date
4	Dig Foundations	15-Jun-16	3	3	15-Jun-16
5	Pour Footings		2	1	
6	Lay Bricks to DPC		8	4	
7	Pour floor slab		2	1	

The *End Date* is 15-Jun-16 because three men have been assigned to a task that has three man-day's work. The task thus takes one day to complete and so begins and ends on the same day.

3   Test the scheduling equation.

If you were to take two men off the job, the single remaining man would take three days to complete the task.

1.   Change the value in cell D4 to 1.

Notice that the task now takes three days to complete.

	A	B	C	D	E
			Work		
3	Task Name	Start date	(Man-Days)	Units	End Date
4	Dig Foundations	15-Jun-16	3	1	17-Jun-16

2.   Revise your estimate of the work to 8 Man-Days and assign two men to the task.

This time, the task takes four days to complete.

	A	B	C	D	E
			Work		
3	Task Name	Start date	(Man-Days)	Units	End Date
4	Dig Foundations	15-Jun-16	8	2	18-Jun-16

4   Add a formula to show the start date for the *Pour Footings* task.

The start date of the *Pour Footings* task will be the day after the End Date of the *Dig Foundations* task.

Enter the formula: **=E4+1** into cell B5.

5   AutoFill cells B5 and E4 to the end of the range.

You now have a dynamic project plan that will adjust the end date of the project based upon your work estimates and the number of resources that you assign to each task.

	A	B	C	D	E
			Work		
3	Task Name	Start date	(Man-Days)	Units	End Date
4	Dig Foundations	15-Jun-16	8	2	18-Jun-16
5	Pour Footings	19-Jun-16	2	1	20-Jun-16
6	Lay Bricks to DPC	21-Jun-16	8	4	22-Jun-16
7	Pour floor slab	23-Jun-16	2	1	24-Jun-16

6   Save your work as *Project-2*.

Lesson 3-11: Use the DATE function to offset days, months and years

Now that you understand the TODAY, DAY, MONTH and YEAR functions, you will be able to use the DATE function to dynamically manage more sophisticated date offsets.

1 Open *Service Schedule-1* from your sample files folder.

In this example, the service schedule requires that vehicles are inspected 20 days after first supply, 3 months after the 20-day inspection, and then every year thereafter.

	A	B	C	D	E	F
1	Service Schedule					
2						
3	Vehicle Supplied On	20 Day Inspection	3 month Inspection	12 Month Services Thereafter...		
4	16-Jan-15					
5	18-Feb-16					
6	16-Mar-16					

2 Put a formula in cell B4 that will calculate the date for the 20-day inspection based upon the date in cell A4.

1. Type **=D** into cell B4.

   Press the **<Down Arrow>** key to select the *DATE* function:

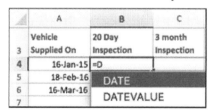

2. Press the **<Tab>** key to enter the formula into the cell.

3. Click the *Insert Function* button on the left of the formula bar:

The *Formula Builder* task pane is displayed.

The DATE function demands three numerical arguments: *Year, Month* and *Day.* For example:

=DATE(2016,9,20)

… would return 20th September 2016.

Because the DATE function requires numerical arguments, you need to use the YEAR, MONTH and DAY functions to convert each part of the date into numbers.

tip

You can also use the keyboard shortcut:

<Ctrl>+<A>

…to bring up the *Formula Builder* task pane when you are entering a function.

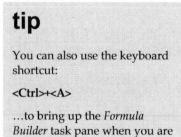

Service Schedule-1

4.   Complete the task pane as follows:

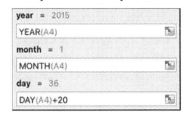

You can see from the arguments in the above grab that you are requesting the date: *36ᵗʰ January 2015*. This is not, of course, a valid date.

Notice that in the *Day* argument, the number 20 has been added to 16, creating 36 for the day argument.

Fortunately, Excel is intelligent enough to understand that you really require the date: *5ᵗʰ February 2015.*

5.   Click the *Done* button.

A date is shown that is 20 days after 16ᵗʰ January 2015:

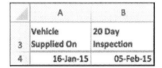

3   Put a DATE formula in cell C4 that will calculate a date that is three months later than the 20-day inspection date.

This time your task pane should look like this:

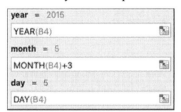

4   Put a DATE formula in cell D4 that will calculate a date that is twelve months later than the 3-month inspection date.

This time your task pane should look like this:

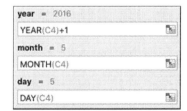

5   AutoFill the formula in cell D4 to cells E4:G4.

6   AutoFill the formulas in cells B4:G4 to the end of the range.

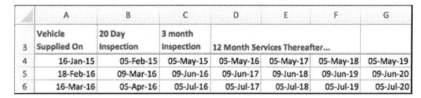

	A	B	C	D	E	F	G
3	Vehicle Supplied On	20 Day Inspection	3 month Inspection	12 Month Services Thereafter...			
4	16-Jan-15	05-Feb-15	05-May-15	05-May-16	05-May-17	05-May-18	05-May-19
5	18-Feb-16	09-Mar-16	09-Jun-16	09-Jun-17	09-Jun-18	09-Jun-19	09-Jun-20
6	16-Mar-16	05-Apr-16	05-Jul-16	05-Jul-17	05-Jul-18	05-Jul-19	05-Jul-20

7   Save your work as *Service Schedule-2.*

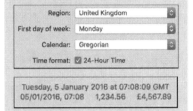
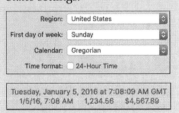
Lesson 3-12: Enter time values and perform basic time calculations

Serial number recap

In: *Lesson 3-7: Understand date serial numbers,* you learned how Excel combines time and date information in a single date serial number.

Excel represents dates by counting from 1st January 1900 to the present day. For example, the date serial number 2.0 represents midnight (00:00) on 2nd January 1900.

Excel represents time using the decimal part of the serial number. For example, the date serial number 3.5 represents midday on 3rd January 1900.

Excel also allows you to work with pure time values (times that do not have an associated date). In this case, the non-existent date of 0 Jan 1900 is used. For example, the date serial number 0.3333 represents the time 08:00 but does not represent any date.

In this lesson, you'll focus on entering time values into a worksheet without any associated date and learn how to avoid the mistakes commonly made when working with time values.

1 Open *Time Sheet-1* from your sample files folder.

This worksheet contains details of the hours worked by an employee during a single week.

2 Add a start time of 08:00 and finish time 17:00 for Monday.

24-hour notation is the best way to enter times, as it is the least error prone and easiest to read.

Type **08:00** into cell B8 and **17:00** into cell C8.

	A	B	C
7	Day	Start	Finish
8	Monday	08:00	17:00

3 Add a start time of 10:00 AM and finish time 6:00 PM for Tuesday.

AM/PM notation is preferred by some users, but is more error prone than the recommended 24-hour notation.

Type **10:00 AM** into cell B9 and **6:00 PM** into cell C9. Make sure that you leave a space between the time and the AM/PM indicator, otherwise Excel will interpret the value as text rather than time.

	A	B	C
7	Day	Start	Finish
8	Monday	08:00	17:00
9	Tuesday	10:00 am	6:00 pm

Time Sheet-1

tip

You can also return to *General* format using the shortcut key:

<Ctrl>+<Shift>+<~>

(Control + Shift + Tilde).

The ~ key can be found in the bottom-left corner of a standard Mac keyboard.

tip

Converting time serial numbers to decimal values

In this lesson, you subtracted 08:00 from 17:00, giving a result of 0.375, representing 9 hours as 37.5% of one 24-hour day.

Sometimes, it is convenient to express times as simple decimal numbers (in this case as 9.0). In order to convert a time serial number to a numeric value representing hours, you simply multiply the serial number by 24:

24*37.5% = 9.0 hours

tip

You can also open the *Format Cells* dialog using the shortcut key:

<Cmd>+<1>

	A	B	C
7	Day	Start	Finish
8	Monday	08:00	17:00
9	Tuesday	10:00	18:00
10	Wednesday	21:00	03:00
11	Thursday	22:00	04:00
12	Friday	08:00	17:00

4 Complete the rest of the time sheet as follows:

	A	B	C
7	Day	Start	Finish
8	Monday	08:00	17:00
9	Tuesday	10:00 am	6:00 pm
10	Wednesday	21:00	03:00
11	Thursday	10:00 pm	4:00 am
12	Friday	08:00	17:00

Depending upon which country you are in, your dates and times may display differently to those shown above. See the sidebar on the facing page for more information about how your regional settings affect the default format of dates and times.

5 Examine the date serial numbers in cells B8:C12.

1. Select cells B8:C12.

2. Right-click the selected cells and click *Format Cells…* from the shortcut menu.

3. Click the *Number* tab and click *General* in the *Category* list.

4. Click the *OK* button.

   Notice that all of the time values begin with zero. This is because no date is associated with them. Understanding this is very important when creating time formulas.

   Notice that the time in cell B8 is 0.333333. This is because at 08:00, approximately 33.333333% of the day has elapsed, as eight hours is approximately 33.333333% of 24.

6 Add a formula to cell D8 that will calculate the number of hours worked.

Add the formula **=C8-B8** to cell D8.

	A	B	C	D
7	Day	Start	Finish	Hours Worked
8	Monday	0.333333	0.708333	0.375

The result shows that Frank worked for 37.5% of the day on Monday.

7 Format cells B8:D12 to show times in the 24-hour format.

1. Select cells B8:D12.

2. Right-click the selected cells and click *Format Cells…* from the shortcut menu.

3. From the *Custom* category, set the format to: **hh:mm**

4. Click the *OK* button.

   The number of hours and minutes worked is now shown in cell D8.

	A	B	C	D
7	Day	Start	Finish	Hours Worked
8	Monday	08:00	17:00	09:00
9	Tuesday	10:00	18:00	

8 Save your work as *Time Sheet-2*.

Type:

hh:mm

Lesson 3-13: Perform time calculations that span midnight

1   Open *Time Sheet-2* from your sample files folder (if it isn't already open).

2   AutoFill the formula in cell D8 to cells D9:D12.

	A	B	C	D
7	Day	Start	Finish	Hours Worked
8	Monday	08:00	17:00	09:00
9	Tuesday	10:00	18:00	08:00
10	Wednesday	21:00	03:00	##############
11	Thursday	22:00	04:00	##############
12	Friday	08:00	17:00	09:00
13	Total:			

A problem is now revealed. On Wednesday and Thursday, Frank's working times spanned midnight. A row of hashes is shown to signify an error, as Excel cannot display a time value that is negative (Frank's Wednesday hours would result in minus 18 hours worked).

3   Correct the formulas in cells D8:D12 so that time is correctly calculated, even when the times span midnight.

Fortunately, it is very easy to correct the formula using the IF logic function covered in: *Lesson 3-5: Use the IF logic function.*

1. Change the formula in cell D8 to the following:

   =IF(C8>B8, C8-B8, C8+1-B8)

   The formula works by adding the number one (representing one day) to the finish time when the finish time is earlier than the start time.

2. AutoFill the formula from cell D8 to cells D9:D12.

   The times are now correctly calculated:

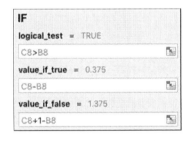

	A	B	C	D
7	Day	Start	Finish	Hours Worked
8	Monday	08:00	17:00	09:00
9	Tuesday	10:00	18:00	08:00
10	Wednesday	21:00	03:00	06:00
11	Thursday	22:00	04:00	06:00
12	Friday	08:00	17:00	09:00

4   Add a formula to show the total hours worked this week in cell D13.

Add a SUM function to cell D13 to sum the values in cells D8:D12.

	D
13	=SUM(D8:D12)

The formula doesn't return an error, but it seems to produce the wrong answer:

Time Sheet-2

	A	B	C	D
7	Day	Start	Finish	Hours Worked
8	Monday	08:00	17:00	09:00
9	Tuesday	10:00	18:00	08:00
10	Wednesday	21:00	03:00	06:00
11	Thursday	22:00	04:00	06:00
12	Friday	08:00	17:00	09:00
13	Total:			14:00

The value in cell D13 is actually correct. The problem lies in the way in which cell D13 is formatted.

Remember that the date serial numbers in cells D8:D12 contain the percentage of each 24-hour day that was worked. When they are added together, they will add up to more than one. Because cell D13 is formatted to show times, it will ignore the whole number part of the date/time serial number, believing that this represents a date.

The actual value in cell D13 is 1.583333 and that represents 14:00 on 1st January 1900.

5 Display the value in cell D13 correctly by adjusting the format.

There are two ways to solve this problem. In this lesson, a custom format is used. The other potential method is discussed in the sidebar.

Because adding time values is a common requirement, Excel provides a special custom format to display times that exceed 24 hours.

1. Right click on cell D13 and click *Format Cells* from the shortcut menu.

2. Click the *Custom* category.

    Notice that the current format is: **hh:mm**

3. Manually type in the new custom format: **[h]:mm**

    The square brackets around the [h] means that where there is a whole number in the date serial number it should be regarded as time data.

    For example, the date serial number 2.0 will be interpreted as meaning 48 hours and not midnight on 2nd January 1900. The serial number 1.5 will be interpreted as 36 hours and not midday on 1st January 1900.

4. Click the *OK* button.

    The worksheet now displays correctly:

	A	B	C	D
11	Thursday	22:00	04:00	06:00
12	Friday	08:00	17:00	09:00
13	Total:			38:00

6 Save your work as *Time Sheet-3*.

---

tip

Another way to sum time serial numbers that exceed 24 hours

In this lesson, you use the **[h]:mm** custom format to display the time data correctly.

The value of **1.5833** then correctly displays as **38:00**.

The value 1.5833 actually means 158.33% of a 24-hour day, so another method of correcting the result would be to multiply it by 24:

=SUM(D8:D12)*24

...and then to format cell D13 as a number.

The advantage of this method is that it is often easier to work with numerical values than with date serial numbers if you need to perform further mathematical calculations.

You'll see this technique in action in: *Lesson 3-14: Understand common time functions and convert date serial numbers to decimal values.*

---

tip

You can also open the Format Cells dialog using the shortcut key:

<Cmd>+<1>

Lesson 3-14: Understand common time functions and convert date serial numbers to decimal values

Excel's primary time functions are NOW, HOUR, MINUTE and SECOND. In this lesson, you'll learn how to use all of them along with some important techniques that are useful when performing calculations with time values.

1   Open *Time Sheet-3* from your sample files folder (if it isn't already open).

2   Add formulas to cells E8:E12 to calculate earnings.

This isn't as straightforward as it first seems.

The actual values in cells D8:D12 represent the percentage of each day that was worked. For example, cell D9 actually contains the value 0.333333, as eight hours are approximately 33.3333% of one 24-hour day.

In order to calculate the correct earnings figure, it is necessary to multiply the date serial number in column D by 24 to convert the date serial number into a decimal value.

1.   Type the formula: **=D8*24*$B$5** into cell E8.

Note the absolute reference for cell B5. This will enable the formula to be AutoFilled to the cells below without adjusting the reference to cell B5.

2.   AutoFill the formula to cells E9:E12.

3.   Select cells E8:E13.

4.   Click: Home→Number→Comma Style ⌐⟩ to show two decimal places.

The correct earnings figure is now shown in every case.

5.   Use a SUM function to show total earnings for the week in cell E13.

	A	B	C	D	E
5	Hourly Rate:	15.00			
6					
7	Day	Start	Finish	Hours Worked	Earnings
8	Monday	08:00	17:00	09:00	135.00
9	Tuesday	10:00	18:00	08:00	120.00
10	Wednesday	21:00	03:00	06:00	90.00
11	Thursday	22:00	04:00	06:00	90.00
12	Friday	08:00	17:00	09:00	135.00
13	Total:			38:00	570.00

3   Add a NOW function to cell B15 to display the current date and time.

1.   Type **Current Date and Time** into cell A15.

2.   Click on cell B15.

Time Sheet-3

3. Type **=NOW**

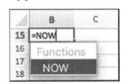

The NOW function returns the current date and time. This is a little like the TODAY function encountered in *Lesson 3-8: Understand common date functions*, except that it returns the current date *and* time rather than midnight on the current date.

The current date and time is the time that the worksheet was last recalculated (you'll learn how to recalculate the worksheet later in this lesson).

4. Press the **<Tab>** key twice.

5. If necessary, widen columns A and B so that they are wide enough to see all of their contents.

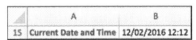

4   Add a TIME function to cell B16 to display the current time.

The TIME function works in a similar way to the DATE function encountered in: *Lesson 3-10: Use date offsets to manage projects using the scheduling equation.*

1. Type **Current Time** into cell A16.

2. Click in cell B16.

3. Click: Formulas→Function Library→Date & Time→TIME.

    The *Formula Builder* task pane is displayed.

4. Enter the following values for each argument:

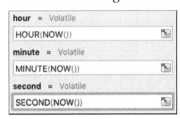

5. Click the *Done* button.

    The current time appears in cell B16.

	A	B
15	Current Date and Time	12/02/2016 12:15
16	Current Time	12:15 pm

5   Re-calculate the worksheet to update the current time.

Click: Formulas→Calculation→Calculate Sheet.

Provided that at least a minute has passed since you created the NOW and TIME functions, you will see the time update to the current time.

6   Save your work as *Time Sheet-4*.

Lesson 3-15: Use the TIME function to offset hours, minutes and seconds

In this lesson, you will use the TIME function in conjunction with the HOUR, MINUTE and SECOND functions to offset time data.

You'll construct a train timetable that will run a service every 10 minutes before 09:00 and every hour thereafter.

1 Open *Train Timetable-1* from your sample files folder.

The formulas in this worksheet will be constructed so that the entire timetable can be automatically updated by simply changing the *First Train* times in column B.

This will work because all of the subsequent journeys will be defined as offsets from the first train's arrival time using the TIME function.

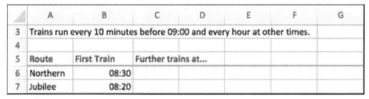

	A	B	C	D	E	F	G
3	Trains run every 10 minutes before 09:00 and every hour at other times.						
4							
5	Route	First Train	Further trains at...				
6	Northern	08:30					
7	Jubilee	08:20					

2 Put formulas in cells C6:K6 that will calculate the arrival times of subsequent trains on the Northern line.

You know that trains arrive every 10 minutes before 09:00, so you would expect trains at 08:40, 08:50 and 09:00. After that, you would expect trains each hour at 10:00, 11:00, 12:00…

1. Click in cell C6.

2. Click: Formulas→Function Library→Date & Time→TIME.

The *Formula Builder* task pane appears.

3. Enter the following values for each argument:

hour	= 8
HOUR(B6)	
minute	= 40
MINUTE(B6)+10	
second	= 0
SECOND(B6)	

4. Click the *Done* button.

The correct time of the next train appears in cell C6.

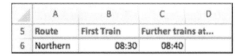

	A	B	C	D
5	Route	First Train	Further trains at...	
6	Northern	08:30	08:40	

5. AutoFill the formula in cell C6 to cells D6:K6.

Unsurprisingly, the formula applies an offset of 10 minutes to each cell:

Train Timetable-1

	A	B	C	D	E	F
5	Route	First Train	Further trains at...			
6	Northern	08:30	08:40	08:50	09:00	09:10

Unfortunately, that isn't what is needed. After the 09:00 train there shouldn't be another until 10:00.

To fix the formula, you need to add an IF function that will check the time of the previous train. If the time is later than or equal to 09:00, the increment should be one hour and not 10 minutes. (The IF function was covered in: *Lesson 3-5: Use the IF logic function*).

6. Copy the function from cell C6 *excluding the = sign* by clicking in cell C6, selecting the function in the formula bar (but not the = sign) and then copying (by pressing **<Cmd>+<C>** or by right-clicking and then selecting *Copy* from the shortcut menu).

fx =TIME(HOUR(B6),MINUTE(B6)+10,SECOND(B6))

7. Press the **<Escape>** key to exit cell edit mode.

8. Click cell C6 again and then press the **<Delete>** key to remove the existing formula from the cell.

9. Click: Formulas→Function Library→Logical→IF.

The *Formula Builder* task pane is displayed.

10. Paste the function (previously copied) into the **value_if_true** and **value_if_false** text boxes.

The dialog should now look like this:

11. Set the *logical_test* argument to:

    HOUR(B6)>=9

12. Edit the *value_if_true* argument so that it offsets the previous train time by one hour rather than ten minutes:

    TIME(HOUR(B6)+1,MINUTE(B6),SECOND(B6))

13. Click the *Done* button.

14. AutoFill cell C6 to cells D6:K6.

3   AutoFill cells C6:K6 down to cells C7:K10 to complete the timetable.

The timetable is now complete and correct:

	A	B	C	D	E	F	G
5	Route	First Train	Further trains at...				
6	Northern	08:30	08:40	08:50	09:00	10:00	11:00
7	Jubilee	08:20	08:30	08:40	08:50	09:00	10:00
8	Circle	08:27	08:37	08:47	08:57	09:07	10:07

4   Save your work as *Train Timetable-2*.

note

The NOT logical function

This session introduces the two Excel logical functions:

AND
OR

There's another logical function that can sometimes make your formulas easier to read (though it is never actually necessary).

This is the NOT function which will invert a logical result.

In other words, it will change TRUE to FALSE and FALSE to TRUE.

The rule:

If Sales > Target AND Years Service > 2

OR

Years Service > 5

Could also be written as:

If Sales > Target AND NOT Years Service < 2

OR

Years Service NOT < 5

Lesson 3-16: Use the AND and OR functions to construct complex Boolean criteria

When using logical functions such as IF, COUNTIF and SUMIF, you need to construct a logical test (sometimes also called Boolean criteria) that will return TRUE or FALSE.

You've already used simple Boolean criteria such as:

E9<=35

This Boolean expression returns TRUE if the value in cell E9 is less than or equal to 35. Otherwise, it returns FALSE.

In this lesson, you'll use the logical functions AND and OR to create more complex Boolean criteria.

The sample file for this lesson computes bonuses for employees, based upon the following rules:

Bonus rules				
A bonus of 2% of sales will be paid to employees who meet the following criteria:				
1/ Sales are above target.				
2/ Have worked for the company for more than two years.				
Note: *Employees with more than five years service will receive the bonus even if sales are below target.*				

Here are the bonus figures for the first three employees:

	A	B	C	D	E
9	Name	Years service	Sales	Target	Bonus
10	Johnny Caine	2	11,000	9,000	
11	George Marley	7	7,000	9,000	
12	Betty Anan	3	13,000	5,000	

- You can see that Johnny Caine exceeded his target, but received no bonus because he only has two years' service.

- George Marley has over five years' service and thus receives a bonus, even though he didn't reach his sales target.

- Betty Annan has three years' service and she has also exceeded her sales target, so she receives a bonus.

Another way of expressing the logical test that governs when bonus will be paid is:

If Sales > Target AND Years Service > 2
OR
Years Service > 5

A logical expression can be created to implement the rules using Excel's AND and OR functions.

Here's how you can use the AND function to test that Johnny Caine's sales are above his target AND that he has more than two years' service:

Bonus Calculator-1

=AND(C10>D10, B10>2)

The AND function will return TRUE only if both expressions evaluate true. In Johnny's case, it will return FALSE because Johnny only has two years' service.

You also need to check whether the employee has over five years' service. Here's how you can use the OR function to do this:

=OR(B10>5, AND(C10>D10, B10>2)**)**

The OR function will return true if either of the arguments return true. In Johnny's case, this will still return FALSE as he also has less than five years' service, but in George's case, it would return TRUE since George has seven years' service.

Now that you understand how to construct the logical test for the bonus calculation, you can create the IF function for the sample file.

1   Open *Bonus Calculator-1* from your sample files folder.

    1. Click in cell E10.

    2. Click: Formulas→Function Library→Logical→IF.

    3. Enter the following values into the *Formula Builder* task pane (see text above for explanation):

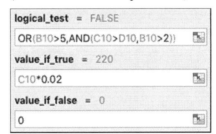

    4. Click the *Done* button.

    5. AutoFill the formula from cell E10 to the end of the range.

	A	B Years service	C Sales	D Target	E Bonus
9	Name	service	Sales	Target	Bonus
10	Johnny Caine	2	11,000	9,000	-
11	George Marley	7	7,000	9,000	140
12	Betty Anan	3	13,000	5,000	260
13	Paris Winfrey	1	11,000	10,000	-
14	Ozzy Dickens	5	9,000	9,000	-
15	Johnny Roberts	2	6,000	7,000	-
16	Charles Monroe	8	10,000	5,000	200

2   Save your work as Bonus Calculator-2.

note

Gross profit and mark up

Newcomers to the retail business often confuse mark up with gross profit.

In general business, gross profit is the more widely accepted metric when discussing profits.

Here's an example of mark up:

Bob buys a watch for $500 and marks it up by 50%. This means that he adds 50% to the cost price and sells it for $750. In this case, the formula is:

Selling Price = Cost Price * (1+MarkUp)

$750 = $500 * 1.5

Here's an example of gross profit:

Bill buys a hard disk for $100. His company needs to make 50% gross profit on all goods sold. This means that they need to sell the hard drive for $200, making 50% of the selling price ($100) in profit. In this case, the formula is:

Selling Price = Cost Price/ (1-Gross Profit%)

$200 = $100/(1-0.5)

You can see from the above example that a gross profit of 50% is the same as a mark up of 100%.

Terminology

I use the term *Gross Profit* when discussing both cash amounts and percentages.

There's a lot of controversy about correct terminology. Some purists would argue that the correct terms are *Gross Margin* (or simply *Margin*) for % *Gross Profit*, and *Gross Profit* for a Gross Profit cash value.

Lesson 3-17: Understand calculation options (manual and automatic)

It is possible to change the calculation mode used by Excel. The three modes available are:

1. *Automatic:* Whenever you change the value in a cell, all values that reference that cell are automatically recalculated. This is the default.

2. *Automatic except for data tables:* This is similar to *Automatic*, but tables will only be recalculated when one of the values within a table is changed (you learned about tables in: *Session One: Tables, and Ranges*).

3. *Manual:* Calculation will only take place when the **<Fn>+<F9>** keys are pressed.

Most users are unaware that the calculation options exist and leave Excel set to the default *Automatic* at all times.

So why would you ever need the other two options? The answer is that Excel worksheets can be very large indeed (over a million rows and over 16,500 columns). A workbook could contain many millions (or even many billions) of formulas. Such a workbook is very unusual, but could take a substantial amount of time to recalculate. You wouldn't want to have to pause for recalculation every time you edited any cell in such a workbook, so you would switch to one of the other two calculation modes under those circumstances.

1   Open *Classic Watches-1* from your sample files folder.

This worksheet calculates the selling prices for a classic watch dealer.

	A	B	C	D	E
5			Gross Profit	33%	
7	Description	Date	Cost price	Selling Price	Profit
8	Breitling Duograph 18K	1948	11,500.00	17,164.18	5,664.18
9	Cartier Tank 18K	1974	3,200.00	4,776.12	1,576.12
10	Rolex Tudor Oyster	1966	300.00	447.76	147.76

The dealer makes 33% Gross Profit (sometimes also called *Margin, Gross Margin* or *Gross Profit Margin*) on all watch sales (see sidebar for a discussion of the difference between gross profit and mark up).

The formula in column D:

=C8/(1-$D$5)

... calculates the selling price based upon the gross profit stated in cell D5.

2   Change the gross profit to 25%.

When the value in cell D5 is changed to 25%, the worksheet recalculates to show the new selling prices.

important

Calculation mode is set at application level

It would be quite reasonable to assume that the calculation mode could be set for a specific worksheet or workbook. Unfortunately, Excel doesn't work in this way, causing great confusion amongst users who begin to believe that Excel is randomly changing the calculation mode.

You can't set the calculation mode for a single worksheet or workbook. When you change the calculation mode, it also changes for all other worksheets and all other open workbooks.

Consider the following scenario:

1/ You create a workbook and set the calculation mode to *Manual*.

2/ You then open another workbook without closing the first one. The second workbook is also in manual calculation mode because only one calculation mode can exist for all open workbooks.

Things become even more confusing, because the calculation mode is saved with the workbook.

Suppose that you had two workbooks called *Manual* and *Automatic*. The first was saved in manual calculation mode and the second saved in automatic calculation mode.

If you open the *Manual* workbook followed by the *Automatic* workbook, then both workbooks will be set to *Manual* calculation mode, as this was the mode of the first workbook opened.

If you open the *Automatic* workbook followed by the *Manual* workbook, then both workbooks will be set to *Automatic* calculation mode.

	A	B	C	D	E
5			Gross Profit	25%	
7	Description	Date	Cost price	Selling Price	Profit
8	Breitling Duograph 18K	1948	11,500.00	15,333.33	3,833.33
9	Cartier Tank 18K	1974	3,200.00	4,266.67	1,066.67
10	Rolex Tudor Oyster	1966	300.00	400.00	100.00

This is exactly what you would expect, because this workbook is using the default *automatic* calculation mode.

3   Change the calculation mode to manual.

Click: Formulas→Calculation→Calculation Options→Manual.

4   Change the gross profit to 30%.

This time nothing happens, because the worksheet will only recalculate when you explicitly request a recalculation.

	A	B	C	D	E
5			Gross Profit	30%	
7	Description	Date	Cost price	Selling Price	Profit
8	Breitling Duograph 18K	1948	11,500.00	15,333.33	3,833.33
9	Cartier Tank 18K	1974	3,200.00	4,266.67	1,066.67
10	Rolex Tudor Oyster	1966	300.00	400.00	100.00

5   Manually recalculate the workbook.

EITHER

Press the <Fn>+<F9> keys.

OR

Click: Formulas→Calculation→Calculate Now.

The workbook recalculates to show the new selling prices at 30% gross profit.

	A	B	C	D	E
5			Gross Profit	30%	
7	Description	Date	Cost price	Selling Price	Profit
8	Breitling Duograph 18K	1948	11,500.00	16,428.57	4,928.57
9	Cartier Tank 18K	1974	3,200.00	4,571.43	1,371.43
10	Rolex Tudor Oyster	1966	300.00	428.57	128.57

Note that you can also click:

Formulas→Calculation→Calculate Sheet

You would use this option to save calculation time when other worksheets in the workbook contained large numbers of formulas. In the case of this simple workbook (that contains only one worksheet), there is no calculation time difference between using *Calculate Now* and *Calculate Sheet*.

6   Change the calculation mode back to automatic.

Click: Formulas→Calculation→Calculation Options→Automatic.

7   Save your work as *Classic Watches-2*.

note

ASCII

ASCII (pronounced Askey) is an acronym for: *American Standard Code for Information Interchange.*

In 1968, the US President (Lyndon B. Johnson) ordered that all computers purchased by the United States Federal Government must support ASCII.

ASCII defines a number (between 0 and 127) for the numbers **0-9**, lowercase letters **a** to **z**, uppercase letters **A** to **Z**, basic punctuation symbols, the space character, and 33 non-printable control characters (many of which are now obsolete).

For example, the ASCII code for an upper-case **A** character is 65.

Excel has two ASCII related functions:

CHAR(number)

This function returns an ASCII character from the corresponding ASCII code. For example:

=CHAR(65)

… would result in an upper-case **A** character appearing in the cell.

CODE(text)

This function returns an ASCII code number from a character. For example:

=CODE("A")

… would return the number 65 (the ASCII code number for an upper-case A).

Lesson 3-18: Concatenate strings using the concatenation operator (&)

About strings

In the world of computers, letters, numbers, spaces, punctuation marks and other symbols are referred to as *characters*.

When several characters are grouped together (perhaps to spell out words), they are referred to as a *string*.

Here are some examples of strings:

Abc123

John Smith

Strings may be of any length, from a single character to thousands of words.

The concatenation operator (&)

When numbers are added together, the addition operator (+) is used to return the sum of the numbers. For example:

4+2=6

The concatenation operator joins two strings together. For example:

4 & 2 = 42

Concatenation is rarely used with numbers. It is more likely that you may wish to concatenate *Title*, *First Name* and *Last Name* cells to produce a full name. For example:

= "Mr" & "John" & "Smith" = "MrJohnSmith".

Note the use of double quotation marks to indicate that each value is a string.

In this example, it would be nice to have spaces between each of the words. To do this, you would concatenate a string containing only a space between each word. Here's how it's done:

= "Mr" & " " & "John" & " " & "Smith" = "Mr John Smith"

Classic Watches-2

note

Concatenating CHAR(10) or CHAR(13) control codes for line breaks

In the (previous page) sidebar, it was stated that there are 33 non-printable control characters defined by ASCII, many of which are now obsolete.

Two of these control codes can sometimes be very useful when you need to create a formula that outputs multiple-line text. These are:

Line Feed (ASCII 10)
and
Carriage Return (ASCII 13)

Excel 2016 for Mac recognizes a *Carriage Return* control code for a new line. Strangely, this doesn't work in *Excel 2016 for Windows*, which recognizes a *Line Feed* control code instead.

Here's an example of concatenating an ASCII 10 control code (in a cell with word-wrap enabled) in order to force line breaks:

	A
1	="One, Two"

Results in:

	A
1	One, Two

... While

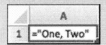

Results in:

	A
1	One, Two

Note that if you wanted your workbook to be compatible with both Windows and Mac Excel versions you would need to use the formula:

1 Open *Classic Watches-2* from your sample files folder (if it isn't already open).

2 Type **Classified Ad** into cell F7 and apply the *Heading 3* style.

To apply the *Heading 3* style, select cell F7 and then click:

Home→Styles→Style Gallery→Titles and Headings→Heading 3

Cell styles were covered in depth in Session 4 of the *Essential Skills* book in this series.

Cells F8:F17 will contain text to be included in a classified ad listing in the local newspaper. You want to show the description of the watch, the year of manufacture and the selling price.

	A	B	C	D	E
7	Description	Date	Cost price	Selling Price	Profit
8	Breitling Duograph 18K	1948	11,500.00	16,428.57	4,928.57

3 Round the values in cells D8:D17 to the nearest five dollars.

The Breitling Duograph is priced at $16,428.57. It would be cleaner to round all of the prices up (or down) to the nearest five dollars. This can easily be achieved using the MROUND (multiple round) function.

1. Change the formula in cell D8 from:

    =C8/(1-$D$5)

    To:

    =MROUND(C8/(1-$D$5),5)

2. AutoFill the formula to the end of the range.

4 Use the concatenation operator to place the classified ad into cell F8 in the format:
Breitling Duograph 18K (1948) -$16,430

As described in the introduction to this lesson, this can easily be achieved using the concatenation operator. The correct formula is:

fx =A8 & " (" & B8 & ") -$" & D8

This very nearly provides the required result:

	E	F	G	H	I
7	Profit	Classified Ad			
8	4,930.00	Breitling Duograph 18K (1948) -$16430			

The only thing that isn't correct is the comma in the cash price of the watch ($16430 should be $16,430). In the next lesson, you'll discover how to solve this problem using the TEXT function.

5 AutoFill the formula in cell F8 to cells F9:F17.

	E	F	G	H	I
7	Profit	Classified Ad			
8	4,930.00	Breitling Duograph 18K (1948) -$16430			
9	1,370.00	Cartier Tank 18K (1974) -$4570			
10	130.00	Rolex Tudor Oyster (1966) -$430			

6 Save your work as Classic Watches-3.

Lesson 3-19: Use the TEXT function to format numerical values as strings

Custom format strings recap

The TEXT function allows numbers to be explicitly formatted as strings. The *Essential Skills* book in this series extensively covers the (rather cryptic) formatting codes available in Excel.

Zeroes are used in formatting codes to define the number of decimal places that are required, along with leading and trailing zeroes. Here are some examples (reproduced from the *Essential Skills* book).

Custom Format String	Value	Display
0	1234.56	1235
0.0	1234.56 1234.5 .5	1234.6 1234.5 0.5
0.00	1234.56 1234.5 .5	1234.56 1234.50 0.50
00.000	4.56	04.560
0.000	1234.56	1234.560

The hash symbol (#) is mainly used to add comma separators to thousands and millions. Here are some examples (once again, reproduced from the *Essential Skills* book).

Custom Format String	Value	Display
#	123.4500	123
#.##	123.45 123.50	123.45 123.5
#,#	1234.56	1,235
#,#.##	1234.56 1234.50 12341234.56	1,234.56 1,234.5 12,341,234.56

Because the hash symbol can be used in conjunction with zeroes, it is also possible to indicate that you want both thousand separators *and* a specific number of leading or trailing zeroes.

Custom Format String	Value	Display
#,#0.00	12341234.5	12,341,234.50

Classic Watches-3

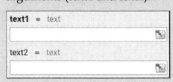
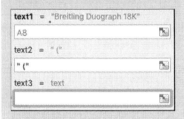
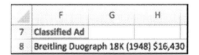

1 Open *Classic Watches-3* from your sample files folder (if it isn't already open).

2 Delete the contents of cells F8:F17.

3 Use the CONCATENATE function to place the classified ad into cell F8 in the format:
Breitling Duograph 18K (1948) - $16,430

The concatenation operator (&) used in the last lesson provides a quick and easy way to concatenate text:

> *fx* =A8 & " (" & B8 & ") -$" & D8

It would be possible to use the TEXT function in conjunction with the concatenation operator (&) to construct the formula but this approach would result in the formula:

> *fx* =A8 & " (" & B8 & ") " & TEXT(D8, "$#,#0")

... which is difficult to read and prone to error. Instead, you'll use the CONCATENATE function.

1. Click in cell F8.

2. Click: Formulas→Function Library→Text→CONCATENATE.

3. Populate the task pane as follows (click the ⊞ button to add more arguments after entering the first two):

Note that each string is enclosed in double quotation marks to denote text.

Note also the use of the TEXT function with a reference to cell D8 followed by the custom format string:

"$#,#0"

This format string means "show a leading dollar sign, show a comma after thousands and show only whole numbers (no decimal places)".

4. Click the *Done* button.

The text is displayed as specified.

4 Autofill cell F8 to the end of the range (cells F9:F17).

	F	G	H
7	Classified Ad		
8	Breitling Duograph 18K (1948) $16,430		
9	Cartier Tank 18K (1974) $4,570		

5 Save your work as *Classic Watches-4*.

Lesson 3-20: Extract text from fixed width strings using the LEFT, RIGHT and MID functions

In *Lesson 2-1: Split fixed width data using Text to Columns*, you learned how to extract fixed width data using Excel's *Text to Columns* feature.

While these methods work well, you'll often need to extract data dynamically using a formula. In this lesson, you'll use the LEFT, RIGHT and MID functions to do just that.

1 Open *Best Selling Books-1* from your sample files folder.

This worksheet lists some of the bestselling fiction books of all time:

	A	B	C	D	E
3	Title	Author	Year	Copies (millions)	ISBN-13
4	A Tale of Two Cities	Charles Dickens	1859	200	978-0141439600
5	The Lord of the Rings	J.R.R. Tolkein	1954	150	978-0618640157
6	The Hobbit	J.R.R. Tolkein	1937	141	978-0345235121

For this lesson, the interesting data is in column E: the *International Standard Book Number* (ISBN-13).

ISBN numbers are a good example of fixed-width strings. At first they simply seem to be a jumble of numbers but they actually contain four discrete pieces of data:

	A	B	C	D
17	Anatomy of an ISBN Number			
18	Digits 1-3	EAN (European Article Number)		
19	Digit 4	Group Identifier (country or language code)		
20	Digits 5-12	publisher prefix and title identifier		
21	Digit 13	Check digit (proves accuracy)		

2 Use a LEFT function to extract the EAN from the ISBN code.

You know that the leftmost three digits represent the EAN. The LEFT function extracts a given number of digits from the left part of a string.

1. Click in cell F4.

2. Click: Formulas→Function Library→Text→LEFT.

3. Complete the task pane as follows:

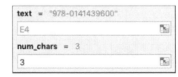

4. Click the *Done* button.

The EAN is extracted into cell F4.

Best Selling Books-1

3 Use a RIGHT function to extract the Check Digit from the ISBN code.

You know that the rightmost single digit represents the *Check Digit*. The RIGHT function extracts a given number of digits from the right part of a string.

1. Click in cell I4.

2. Click: Formulas→Function Library→Text→RIGHT.

3. Complete the task pane as follows:

4. Click the *Done* button.

The *Check Digit* is extracted into cell I4.

4 Use a MID function to extract the Group from the ISBN code.

The MID function extracts text from within a string. You know that digit 4 is the *Group Identifier* that indicates the language that the book is written in. Because the ISBN has a dash between the third and fourth digits, you'll have to extract a single character from position five in the string.

1. Click in cell G4.

2. Click: Formulas→Function Library→Text→MID.

3. Complete the task pane as follows:

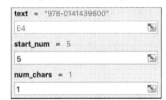

4. Click the *Done* button.

The *Group* is extracted into cell G4.

5 Use a MID function to extract the *Publisher and Title* code from the ISBN code.

This time, the correct arguments for the task pane will be:

6 Autofill the formulas in cells F4:I4 to cells F5:I15.

You can now see from the Group (country or language code) that *Le Petit Prince* was published in French.

7 Save your work as *Best Selling Books-2*.

Lesson 3-21: Extract text from delimited strings using the FIND and LEN functions

Here are two examples of international telephone numbers.

+44 (0)113-4960227 (a UK telephone number)
+356 (0)2138-3393 (a Maltese telephone number)

The *country code* (or international dialing code) is shown as a + symbol followed by one or more numbers. The *NDD* (National Direct Dialing prefix) is shown in brackets. This is the access code used to make a call within the relevant country, but it is omitted when calling from outside the country. The *Area Code* consists of the numbers after the closing bracket but before the hyphen.

In this lesson, you'll use the FIND and LEN functions, in combination with the LEFT and MID functions, to extract the country code, area code and phone number from an international telephone number.

1   Open *Phone Book-1* from your sample files folder.

2   Insert a FIND function into cell C4 to find the first occurrence of an opening bracket within the telephone number.

   1.   Click in cell C4.

   2.   Click Formulas→Text→FIND.

        The FIND function has three arguments. The first is the character to find (in this case the opening bracket), the second is the text to search within (in this case the telephone number in cell B4). There's also an optional argument that allows you to begin the search at a specified position within the string.

   3.   Complete the task pane as follows:

        Note that you don't have to manually type the quotation marks around the text in the *find_text* argument. Excel will helpfully add them for you automatically.

   4.   Click the *Done* button.

        The number 5 is shown in cell C4. This is because the opening bracket is positioned five characters from the left of the string **+44 (**. Note that the space before the opening bracket is counted as a character.

3   Insert a FIND function into cell D4 to find the first occurrence of a closing bracket within the telephone number.

    Repeat *Step 2,* but use a closing bracket for the *find_text* argument.

Phone Book-1

note

Avoid leading and trailing spaces with the TRIM function

In *Step 6* you extracted the country code using the LEFT function. This could result in strings with a trailing space such as:

"+44 "
"+356 "

Because you can't see the trailing space, this doesn't seem to matter.

Trailing spaces cause many problems when comparing data because strings that appear to be the same visually are, in fact, different:

="+44 " = "+44"
(returns FALSE)

="+44" = "+44"
(returns TRUE)

For this reason, it is good practice to always remove leading and trailing spaces using the TRIM function.

You could have used the TRIM function in *Step 6* like this:

=TRIM(LEFT(B4,C4-1))

If this seems a little too complex, you could also have placed the trimmed country code in a different column and then used the untrimmed result as an argument like this:

=TRIM(G4)

4   Insert a FIND function into cell E4 to find the first occurrence of a hyphen within the telephone number.

Repeat *Step 2,* but use a hyphen ("-") for the *find_text* argument.

5   Insert a LEN function into cell F4 to find the total number of characters in the telephone number.

1.   Click in cell F4.

2.   Click: Formulas→Text→LEN.

3.   Click cell B4 for the single argument for this function.

4.   Click the *Done* button.

   The length of the telephone number string (18 characters) is displayed in cell F4.

6   Insert a LEFT function into cell G4 to extract the country code.

The correct arguments are:

Note that C4-1 is used for the number of characters to avoid returning the opening bracket. This could result in a trailing space (see sidebar for a way to remove trailing spaces).

7   Insert a MID function into cell H4 to extract the area code.

The MID function was covered in: *Lesson 3-20: Extract text from fixed width strings using the LEFT, RIGHT and MID functions.*

The correct arguments are:

8   Insert a MID function into cell I4 to extract the phone number.

See sidebar for the correct arguments.

9   AutoFill cells C4:I4 into cells C5:I18.

	A	B	C	D	E	F	G	H	I
3	Company	Telephone	Position of opening bracket (	Position of closing bracket)	Position of Hyphen	Length of entire string	Country Code	Area Code	Phone Number
4	Books A Million	+44 (0)113-4960227	5	7	11	18	+44	113	4960227
5	Maltese Books	+356 (0)2138-3393	6	8	13	17	+356	2138	3393

10   Hide columns C:F.

Select columns C:F, right click the selected cells and then click *Hide* from the shortcut menu.

11   Save your work as *Phone Book-2*.

note

The MATCH function can be used to make a VLOOKUP more resilient

The syntax for the MATCH function is:

MATCH(lookup_value, lookup_array, [match_type])

The MATCH function is very similar to the VLOOKUP function, but returns a number relating to the position of a matched cell in a range.

You can use a MATCH function to feed the correct column number to a VLOOKUP. The following function will return a value of 2 (the correct column number for the *Description* in the *Stock* table).

MATCH("Description", Stock[#Headers], FALSE)

Note the use of a structured reference in the above function (you learned about this type of structured reference in: *Lesson 1-19: Use special items in structured table references*).

The above function could be used in place of the number 2 (used for the third argument of the VLOOKUP in this lesson's example).

The VLOOKUP would then continue to work correctly even if one or more new columns were added to the left of column B in the *Stock* table.

Invoice-1

Lesson 3-22: Use a VLOOKUP function for an exact lookup

Consider the following worksheet:

	A	B	C	D	E
5	Code	Description	Date	Cost price	Selling Price
6	BR48	Breitling Duograph 18K	1948	11,500.00	16,430.00
7	CA74	Cartier Tank 18K	1974	3,200.00	4,570.00
8	RO66	Rolex Tudor Oyster	1966	300.00	430.00

The retailer has created a stock code to save time when creating invoices. The code is made up of the first two letters of the watch description, along with the last two numbers of the date of manufacture.

When provided with a stock code, the VLOOKUP function can scan all of the codes in column A until a match is found and then return a value from the same row for any of the other columns.

1   Open *Invoice-1* from your sample files folder.

	A	B	C
5	Code	Description	Price
6	CA74		
7			
8			
9			Total:

In this lesson, you will create a VLOOKUP formula that will automatically return the *Description* of any watch into column B when the user enters a stock code into column A.

2   Convert the range A5:G15 on the *Stock* worksheet into a table named *Stock*.

This was covered in: *Lesson 1-11: Convert a range into a table and add a total row* and *Lesson 1-17: Name a table and create an automatic structured table reference.*

When working with the VLOOKUP function in Excel 2016 it is best practice to use a table for the *table_array* argument (see sidebar on facing page).

Using a table will make the data dynamic. In other words, the VLOOKUP function will still work correctly if you add and remove rows from the *Stock* table.

3   Insert a VLOOKUP function into cell B6 on the *Invoice* worksheet to find the description that matches the *Code* in cell A6.

    1. Click in cell B6 on the *Invoice* worksheet.

    2. Click: Formulas→Function Library→ Lookup & Reference→VLOOKUP.

The *Formula Builder* task pane appears. It can be seen that the VLOOKUP function has four arguments (see sidebar).

4   Add the *lookup_value* argument.

This is the cell on the *Invoice* worksheet that provides the value to be searched for in column A of the *Stock* worksheet. You want to

look up the description for the watch that has the code *CA74*. This is contained in cell **A6**.

5   Add the *table_array* argument.

The table array is the *range, table* or *name* (see sidebar) you will search for a match to the value in cell A6. VLOOKUP always searches the left-most column of the *range, table* or *name*.

Type **Stock** into the *table_array* text box.

It is best practice to use a table for the *table_array* argument (see sidebar).

6   Add the *col_index_num* argument.

Counting from left to right, the *col_index_num* argument is the column that contains the value you want to return. In this case, it is the *Description* column, so you want to return column **2**.

7   Add the *range_lookup* argument.

Beginners often overlook this vital argument because it is optional.

If it is left blank, VLOOKUP will return an inexact match. Later, in *Lesson 3-24: Use a VLOOKUP function for an inexact lookup*, you'll learn why that might be useful, but in this case you want an error to be returned if the stock code is not found, so it is vital to set this argument to **FALSE**.

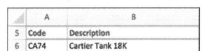

8   Click the *Done* button.

The description of the *Cartier Tank 18K* is returned to cell B6.

	A	B
5	Code	Description
6	CA74	Cartier Tank 18K

9   Save your work as *Invoice-2*.

Lesson 3-23: Use an IFERROR function to suppress error messages

1   Open *Invoice-2* from your sample files folder (if it isn't already open).

2   Add a VLOOKUP formula to cell C6 to return the price that corresponds to the *Code* in cell A6.

You learned how to add a VLOOKUP function in *Lesson 3-22: Use a VLOOKUP function for an exact lookup*. This time, the correct arguments are:

3   AutoFill cells B6:C6 to cells B7:C8.

	A	B	C
5	Code	Description	Price
6	CA74	Cartier Tank 18K	4,570.00
7		#N/A	#N/A
8		#N/A	#N/A
9		Total:	#N/A

This is nearly what is needed. The invoice will work just fine when all three lines are populated:

	A	B	C
5	Code	Description	Price
6	CA74	Cartier Tank 18K	4,570.00
7	RO66	Rolex Tudor Oyster	430.00
8	BR43	Breitling Chronomat 18K	3,070.00
9		Total:	8,070.00

…but you need to cater for customers that only wish to purchase one watch. To make this work, you need to suppress the error messages when some invoice lines have no stock code.

Fortunately, the IFERROR function is designed for precisely this purpose.

4   Wrap each VLOOKUP function with an IFERROR function to return a blank space when an error is encountered.

The IFERROR function can return the value of your choice whenever a formula returns an error.

1. Click in cell B6.

2. Look at the formula in the formula bar:

Invoice-2

f_x | =VLOOKUP(A6,Stock,2,FALSE)

This is the VLOOKUP function that returns the description. You're going to use this formula as the *value* argument for the IFERROR function. When one function is used inside another function in this way, the outside function is sometimes referred to as a *wrapper*.

3. Click just to the right of the equals sign in the formula bar.

f_x | =│VLOOKUP(A6,Stock,2,FALSE)

4. Type **IFERROR(**

f_x | =IFERROR(│VLOOKUP(A6,Stock,2,FALSE)

IFERROR(**value**, value_if_error)

Notice the tip that has appeared. The entire VLOOKUP function is now being used as the *value* argument for the IFERROR function.

5. Click to the extreme right of the formula in the formula bar and add a comma:

f_x | =IFERROR(VLOOKUP(A6,Stock,2,FALSE),│

You are now ready to add the second argument for the IFERROR function. This argument defines what will be displayed if the VLOOKUP function returns an error.

6. Add an empty string to the IFERROR function.

Type **""**. This is an empty string and tells Excel to keep the cell blank when an error is returned.

f_x | =IFERROR(VLOOKUP(A6,Stock,2,FALSE),""

7. Close the bracket to complete the formula.

f_x | =IFERROR(VLOOKUP(A6,Stock,2,FALSE),"")

8. Press the **<Enter>** key.

9. Do the same thing for the *Price* formula in cell C6.

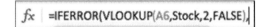

f_x | =IFERROR(VLOOKUP(A6,Stock,5,FALSE),"")

5 AutoFill the formulas in cells B6:C6 to cells B7:C8.

The invoice now works correctly, even when some stock codes are left blank.

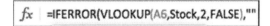

	A	B	C
5	Code	Description	Price
6	CA74	Cartier Tank 18K	4,570.00
7			
8	PA83	Patek Phillipe Jumbo Nautilus	20,355.00
9		Total:	24,925.00

6 Save your work as *Invoice-3*.

---

tip

AutoFill a range of cells in one operation

I've noticed in my classes that many students will respond to the instruction:

"AutoFill the formulas in cells B6:C6 to cells B7:C8"

... by performing two AutoFill operations:

1. Select cell B6.

2. AutoFill cell B6 down to row 8.

3. Select cell C6.

4. AutoFill cell C6 down to row 8.

A quicker way to do this is to AutoFill both cells at the same time:

1. Select cells B6:C6.

2. AutoFill both cells down to row 8.

---

note

The HLOOKUP function works in the same way as the VLOOKUP function

In the VLOOKUP function, V is an abbreviation of *Vertical*. This means that you search for a matching value in a (vertical) column and return a value from any column in that row.

In the HLOOKUP function, H is an abbreviation of Horizontal. This means that you can search for a matching value in a (horizontal) row and return a value from any row in that column.

You'll see the VLOOKUP function used far more often than HLOOKUP, but you may find a scenario where it is useful.

Lesson 3-24: Use a VLOOKUP function for an inexact lookup

In: *Lesson 3-22: Use a VLOOKUP function for an exact lookup*, you set the fourth argument of the VLOOKUP to FALSE in order to perform an *exact* lookup. Most of the time, that's exactly what you want to do.

Sometimes you don't want to search for an exact match, but are interested in the nearest match. This is called an *inexact* lookup. Consider the following exam grades:

	E	F
3	Percentage	Grade
4	0%	Fail
5	60%	C
6	70%	B
7	80%	A
8	90%	A*

An *exact* VLOOKUP for a student with a mark of 80% would correctly return a grade of A.

An *exact* VLOOKUP for a student with a mark of 77% would result in an error, because there is no exact value of 77% in column E.

If you ask VLOOKUP to perform an *inexact* lookup, it will return an exact match if one is found. If an exact match is not found, it will return the largest value *that is less than* the lookup value.

For VLOOKUP to work with inexact matches, it is vital that the lookup column is sorted in ascending order (from the lowest to the highest value).

In the above example, a search for 68% would find row 5 (a C grade) because 60% is the largest value that is less than 68%.

1   Open *Grades-1* from your sample files folder.

	A	B	C	D	E	F
1	Exam Results					
2						
3	Name	Percentage	Grade		Percentage	Grade
4	Johnny Caine	70%			0%	Fail
5	George Marley	68%			60%	C
6	Betty Anan	86%			70%	B
7	Paris Winfrey	80%			80%	A
8	Ozzy Dickens	95%			90%	A*
9	Johnny Roberts	84%				

2   Convert cells E3:F8 into a table named *Grade*.

This was covered in: *Lesson 1-11: Convert a range into a table and add a total row* and *Lesson 1-17: Name a table and create an automatic structured table reference.*

When working with the VLOOKUP function in Excel 2016, it is best practice to use a table for the *table_array* argument.

This will make the data dynamic. In other words, the VLOOKUP function will still work correctly if you add and remove grades from the *Grade* table.

Grades-1

3   Add an inexact VLOOKUP to cell C4 to return the grade that corresponds to the percentage mark in cell B4.

You learned how to add an exact VLOOKUP in *Lesson 3-22: Use a VLOOKUP function for an exact lookup*. An inexact lookup is done in exactly the same way, except that the *range_lookup* argument is set to TRUE (or omitted, as the default is TRUE).

This time, the correct arguments are therefore:

4   AutoFill cell C4 to cells C5:C17.

The correct grades are now shown for each student.

	A	B	C
3	Name	Percentage	Grade
4	Johnny Caine	70%	B
5	George Marley	68%	C
6	Betty Anan	86%	A
7	Paris Winfrey	80%	A
8	Ozzy Dickens	95%	A*
9	Johnny Roberts	84%	A
10	Charles Monroe	55%	Fail
11	Ronnie Bush	58%	Fail
12	Michal Jolie	69%	C
13	JK Spears	77%	B
14	Ozzy Rowling	84%	A
15	Oprah Hilton	60%	C
16	Bill Biggs	58%	Fail
17	Angelina Osbourne	30%	Fail

5   Save your work as *Grades-2*.

Session 3: Exercise

1 Open *Employee Summary-1* from your sample files folder.

	A	B	C	D	E	F	G
					Date	Year	
3	Full Name	Last Name	First Name	Department	Started	Started	Bonus
4	Johnny Caine				16-Jan-04		
5	George Marley				18-Feb-08		

2 Using the RIGHT, LEFT, LEN and FIND functions, split the *Full Name* in column A into *Last Name* and *First Name* in columns B and C.

	A	B	C
3	Full Name	Last Name	First Name
4	Johnny Caine	Caine	Johnny

3 Use an exact VLOOKUP to return the *Department* for each employee (departments are listed on the *Departments* worksheet).

	A	B	C	D
3	Full Name	Last Name	First Name	Department
4	Johnny Caine	Caine	Johnny	Sales

4 Use a COUNTIF function to return the headcount for each department in cells B20:B22.

	A	B
19	Department	Headcount
20	Sales	6
21	Purchasing	5
22	Logistics	3

5 Use the YEAR function to populate column F with the year each employee started.

	A	B	C	D	E	F
3	Full Name	Last Name	First Name	Department	Started	Started
4	Johnny Caine	Caine	Johnny	Sales	16-Jan-04	2004
5	George Marley	Marley	George	Purchasing	18-Feb-08	2008

6 Each employee in the *Sales* department receives a 10% bonus, while all other employees receive a 5% bonus. Use an IF function to populate column G with the correct bonus percentage.

	A	B	C	D	E	F	G
3	Full Name	Last Name	First Name	Department	Started	Started	Bonus
4	Johnny Caine	Caine	Johnny	Sales	16-Jan-04	2004	10%
5	George Marley	Marley	George	Purchasing	18-Feb-08	2008	5%

7 Save your work as *Employee Summary-2*.

Employee Summary-1

If you need help slide the page to the left

Session 3: Exercise Answers

These are the four questions that students find the most difficult to answer:

Q 6	Q 4	Q 3	Q 2
1. Click in cell G4. 2. Click: Formulas→ Function Library→ Logical→IF. 3. Add the following arguments: **logical_test** = D4="Sales" **value_if_true** 10% **value_if_false** 5% 4. Click the *Done* button. 5. AutoFill the formula in cell G4 to cells G5:G17. This was covered in: *Lesson 3-5: Use the IF logic function.*	1. Click in cell B20. 2. Click: Formulas→ Function Library→ More Functions→ Statistical→ COUNTIF. 3. Add the following arguments: **range** = {"Sales"; $D$4:$D$17 **criteria** = "Sales" A20 4. Click the *Done* button. 5. AutoFill the formula in cell B20 to cells B21:B22. This was covered in: *Lesson 3-6: Use the SUMIF and COUNTIF functions to create conditional totals.*	1. Select the *Departments* worksheet. 2. Convert the range A3:B17 into a table named: *Department.* 3. Select the *Employees* worksheet. 4. Click in cell D4. 5. Click: Formulas→ Function Library→ Lookup & Reference→ VLOOKUP. 6. Add the following arguments: **lookup_value** = A4 **table_array** = Department **col_index_num** 2 **range_lookup** FALSE 7. Click the *Done* button. 8. AutoFill the formula in cell D4 to cells D5:D17. This was covered in: *Lesson 3-22: Use a VLOOKUP function for an exact lookup.*	The easiest way to do this is to use the LEFT and RIGHT functions to return a specified number of characters from the left and right hand side of the *Full Name* string. The formula for the *First Name* (in cell C4) is quite easy. You can simply use the FIND function to find the first space and return that number of characters from the left hand side of the string: **=LEFT(A4, FIND(" ",A4)-1)** The *Last Name* is a little more involved. You also need to use the LEN function to return the total number of characters in the string: **=RIGHT(A4,LEN(A4)-FIND(" ",A4))** This was covered in: *Lesson 3-21: Extract text from delimited strings using the FIND and LEN functions.*

If you have difficulty with the other questions, here are the lessons that cover the relevant skills:

5   Refer to: *Lesson 3-8: Understand common date functions.*

Session Four: Using Names and the Formula Auditing Tools

> To make no mistakes is not in the power of man; but from their errors and mistakes, the wise and good learn wisdom for the future.
>
> *Plutarch (46 AD - 120 AD)*

This session introduces Excel's ability to apply a name to a range of cells, a single cell, a formula, a constant or a table. Some problems are almost impossible to solve without names. In this session, you'll use name-based techniques to address several common business scenarios.

This session also introduces Excel's superb formula auditing tools. These will allow you to check your work for mistakes or track down errors when you know that something is wrong. As Plutarch asserts, you *will* make errors when working with Excel (assuming that you are human of course).

By the end of this session, you'll be able to use all of the auditing tools to track down and repair workbook errors.

Session Objectives

By the end of this session you will be able to:

- Automatically create single-cell range names
- Manually create single cell range names and named constants
- Use range names to make formulas more readable
- Automatically create range names in two dimensions
- Use intersection range names and the INDIRECT function
- Create dynamic formula-based range names using the OFFSET function
- Create table based dynamic range names
- Create two linked drop-down lists using range names
- Understand the #NUM!, #DIV/0! and #NAME? error values
- Understand the #VALUE!, #REF! and #NULL! error values
- Understand background error checking and error checking rules
- Manually check a worksheet for errors
- Audit a formula by tracing precedents
- Audit a formula by tracing dependents

Lesson 4-1: Automatically create single-cell range names

The sample worksheet for this lesson contains prices that need to be expressed in different currencies. When you have this type of data, a separate exchange rate worksheet makes the exchange rates easy to maintain.

Here's how the exchange rates will be defined:

	A	B
3	GBP/USD	1.45427
4	EUR/USD	1.0923
5	JPY/USD	0.00852

A range name will then be automatically created for each of the values in column B. Excel will choose range names for column B based upon the values in column A. For the exchange rate in cell B3, it will automatically create the range name:

GBP_USD

You can then use the range name to make your formulas more readable.

	A	B	C	D
3	Description	Year	US Dollars	British Pounds
4	Chateau Lafite	1787	$ 160,000.00	=C4/USD_GBP

note

About names

A name can be applied to a range of cells, a single cell, a formula, a constant or a table.

When a name has been applied, it can be referred to within a formula in place of the item that it represents. For example, if the range A5:A45 was given the name *Sales*, the formulas:

=SUM(A5:A45)

and

=SUM(Sales)

…would produce exactly the same result.

tip

You can also bring up the *Create Names* dialog using the keyboard shortcut:

<Cmd>+<Shift>+<Fn>+<F3>

Vintage Wines-1

1 Open *Vintage Wines-1* from your sample files folder.

2 Automatically create range names for each of the exchange rates.

1. Click the *ExchangeRates* worksheet tab.

2. Select the range A3:B5.

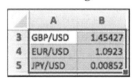

3. Click: Formulas→Defined Names→Create from Selection.

The *Create Names* dialog appears:

Notice that Excel has correctly guessed that the labels for each exchange rate are in the left column.

4. Click the *OK* button.

Nothing seems to have happened, but Excel has actually created a range name for each of the values in cells B3:B5.

note

Syntax rules for Range Names

Range names cannot contain spaces and may only begin with a letter, an underscore character (_), or a backslash (\).

Only letters, numbers, periods, question marks and underscores can be included within a name.

Range names are not case sensitive, so the name **SALES** or **Sales** can be used to reference a range name defined as **sales**.

Range names cannot be the same as any valid cell reference.

Good:
Boeing737
Boeing_737
_Boeing737
\Boeing.737

Bad:
737Boeing (number at start)
Boeing 737 (contains space)
BOE737 (same as a cell reference)

Excel uses range names for some of its own features. For this reason, you should never use any of the following range names:

Print_Area
Sheet_Title
Consolidate_Area
Print_Titles

My preferred naming convention is to always spell out names in full, using mixed case with no underscores:

Good:
SalesTarget

Bad:
Sales_Target (underscore)
SlsTgt (abbreviation)

3   Click the drop-down arrow on the right of the *Name* box to view the range names.

Notice that Excel hasn't used the exact names shown in column A, but has changed each forward slash to an underscore. This is because a forward slash isn't valid syntax for a range name (see sidebar for more on range name syntax).

4   Use formulas containing a range name to calculate prices in Great Britain Pounds, Euros and Japanese Yen.

1.   Click the *Prices* worksheet tab.

2.   Click in cell D4.

3.   Type =**C4/** to begin the formula.

4.   Click: →Insert→Name→Paste.

A dialog appears containing all defined range names.

5.   Click *GBP_USD* and click the *OK* button.

6.   Use the same technique to enter formulas to calculate the *Euro* and *Japanese Yen* prices in cells E4 and F4.

5   AutoFill the formulas in cells D4:F4 to cells D5:F11.

	C	D	E	F
3	US Dollars	British Pounds	Euros	Japanese Yen
4	$ 160,000.00	£ 110,020.84	€ 146,479.90	¥18,779,342.72
5	$ 43,500.00	£ 29,911.91	€ 39,824.22	¥5,105,633.80

6   Save your work as *Vintage Wines-2*.

Lesson 4-2: Manually create single cell range names and named constants

1 Open *Distances-1* from your sample files folder.

2 Manually create a range name for the *Kilometer to Mile* conversion factor using the *Name* box.

    1. Click the *ConversionFactors* worksheet.

	A	B	C
3	From	To	Multiply By
4	Kilometer	Mile	0.621371192
5	Meter	Foot	3.28083

    This time you are unable to automatically create range names because the values in column B are not descriptive enough to easily identify each conversion factor.

    2. Click in cell C4.

    3. Click in the *Name* box and type: **KilometerToMile**

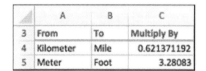

KilometerToMile			× ✓	*fx*	0.6

	A	B	C	D
3	From	To	Multiply By	
4	Kilometer	Mile	0.621371192	
5	Meter	Foot	3.28083	

    4. Press the **<Enter>** key.

3 Manually create a range name for the Meter to Foot conversion factor using the *Define Name* dialog.

    This is an alternative method of defining range names.

    1. Click in cell C5.

    2. Click: Formulas→Defined Names→Define Name.

    The *Define Name* dialog appears.

    3. Type the name **MeterToFoot** into the *Enter a name for the data range* box.

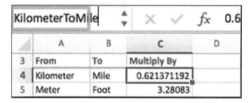

Enter a name for the data range:

MeterToFoot

Select the range of cells:

=ConversionFactors!$C$5

    4. Click the *OK* button.

4 Use formulas containing range names to calculate distances in miles on the *Distances* worksheet.

	A	B	C	D
3	From	To	Km	Miles
4	London	Paris	343	

Distances-1

    1. Click in cell D4 in the *Distances* worksheet.

2. Type: **=C4*KilometerToMile**

Notice that the *KilometerToMile* range name is displayed by the *Formula AutoComplete* menu. You first saw this in: *Lesson 3-2: Use common functions with Formula AutoComplete.*

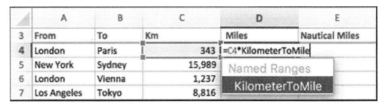

3. Press the **<Enter>** key.

5 AutoFill cell D4 to cells D5:D11.

	A	B	C	D
3	From	To	Km	Miles
4	London	Paris	343	213
5	New York	Sydney	15,989	9,935

6 Given that one Kilometer = 0.539956803 Nautical Miles, create a named constant that will convert Kilometers into Nautical Miles.

Constants are used for values that will rarely change. Named constants are useful because they are difficult to change and are thus less likely to be changed accidentally.

When you create a named constant, there is no cell on the worksheet that contains the constant value.

1. Click: Formulas→Defined Names→Define Name.

2. Type **KilometerToNauticalMile** into the *Enter a name for the data range* box:

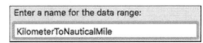

Enter a name for the data range:

KilometerToNauticalMile

3. Type: **=0.539956803** into the *Select the range of cells* box.

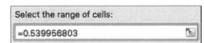

Select the range of cells:

=0.539956803

4. Click the *OK* button.

7 Use the *KilometerToNauticalMile* named constant to add a formula to cell E4 that will calculate the distance from London to Paris in nautical miles.

1. Click in cell E4.

2. Type **=C4*KilometerToNauticalMile**

3. Press the **<Enter>** Key.

8 AutoFill cell E4 to cells E5:E11.

	A	B	C	D	E
3	From	To	Km	Miles	Nautical Miles
4	London	Paris	343	213	185
5	New York	Sydney	15,989	9,935	8,633

9 Save your work as *Distances-2.*

---

tip

You can also use the **<Fn>+<F3>** shortcut key to display a list of all currently defined names.

This is very useful when creating formulas that incorporate names.

note

When to use constants rather than range names

You should use single-cell range names when a value may possibly change in the future.

This was the case in: *Lesson 4-1: Automatically create single-cell range names* because you were dealing with currency exchange rates that fluctuate.

Constants are more appropriate when a value is never expected to change. For this reason, constants would be more appropriate for the conversion factors used in this lesson.

Lesson 4-3: Use range names to make formulas more readable

1   Open *Sales and Profit-1* from your sample files folder.

	A	B
3	Sales	10,000.00
4	Cost	8,000.00
5	Gross Profit	2,000.00
6	Commission	100.00
7	Tax	200.00
8	Net Profit	1,700.00

2   Show formulas instead of values within the worksheet.

Click: Formulas→Formula Auditing→Show Formulas.

	A	B
3	Sales	10000
4	Cost	8000
5	Gross Profit	=B3-B4
6	Commission	=B5*5%
7	Tax	=B5*10%
8	Net Profit	=B5-B6-B7

It is reasonably clear from the formulas that:

Gross Profit = Sales - Cost

... and that five percent commission and ten percent tax are being deducted.

You can make the formulas a lot easier to read by using range names.

3   Create automatic range names for all of the values in cells B3:B8.

This was covered in depth in: *Lesson 4-1: Automatically create single-cell range name.*

1. Select cells A3:B8.

2. Click: Formulas→Defined Names→Create from Selection.

3. Click the *OK* button.

4   View the range names created by Excel.

The easiest way to view the range names is to click the drop-down arrow to the right of the *Name* box:

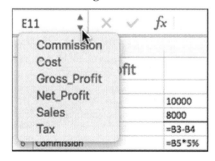

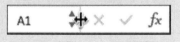

Sales and Profit-1

5 Apply the new range names to the existing formulas.

1. Click: ⚫→Insert→Name→Apply.

   The *Apply Names* dialog appears.

2. Click the *OK* button.

   The formulas now show range names instead of cell references, making them a lot easier to read:

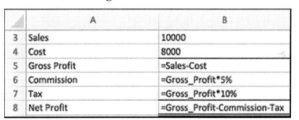

6 Show values instead of formulas within the worksheet.

Click: Formulas→Formula Auditing→Show Formulas.

Values are now displayed rather than formulas:

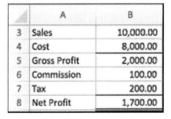

7 Save your work as *Sales and Profit-2.*

Lesson 4-4: Automatically create range names in two dimensions

1   Open *Earnings Summary-2* from your sample files folder.

	A	B	C	D	E	F	G	H	I
8	Name	Sales	Target	Hourly Rate	Hours Worked	Standard Pay	Overtime Pay	Bonus	Total
9	Brad Cruise	22,000	10,000	15.00	40	525.00	112.50	600.00	1,237.50
10	Ian Dean	9,000	8,000	13.00	35	455.00	-	50.00	505.00
11	Paris Smith	10,000	12,000	15.00	42	525.00	157.50	-	682.50
12	Gordon Ramsay	12,000	14,000	17.00	45	595.00	255.00	-	850.00
13	Barack Brown	15,000	9,000	13.00	35	455.00	-	300.00	755.00
14	Johnny Nicholson	18,000	14,000	17.00	40	595.00	127.50	200.00	922.50
15	Tony Blair	9,000	10,000	15.00	42	525.00	157.50	-	682.50
16	Jack Nicholson	10,000	9,000	13.00	30	390.00	-	50.00	440.00
17	Bob Clinton	9,000	11,000	15.00	35	525.00	-	-	525.00
18	Totals:	114,000	97,000		344	4,590.00	810.00	1,200.00	6,600.00

This worksheet was previously created in Session 3.

2   Create automatic range names based upon the labels in column A and row 8.

1.   Select the range A8:I17.

2.   Click: Formulas→Defined Names→Create from Selection.

Excel correctly guesses that the labels are in the *Top row* and *Left column*.

3.   Click the *OK* button.

3   View the range names created using the *Define Name* dialog.

1.   Click: Formulas→Defined Names→Define Name.

The *Define Name* dialog appears.

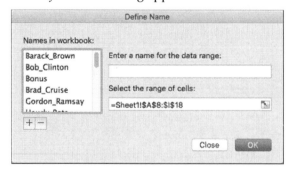

The *Define Name* dialog lists all currently defined names and allows you to edit them.

You can see that you have created a range name for each employee (named in column A) and for each of the columns (named in row 8).

2.   Click the *Close* button.

4   Type **Average Sales** into cell A20.

Earnings Summary-2

5   Type **Average Bonus** into cell A21.

6   Add a formula to cell B20 that uses a range name to calculate the average sales.

This time, you'll use Excel's *formula AutoComplete* feature to insert the range name into an AVERAGE formula.

1.   Click in cell B20 and type:

=AVERAGE(S

Notice that *Formula AutoComplete* shows both functions and defined names beginning with S:

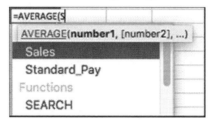

2.   Press the **<Tab>** key to insert the *Sales* range name.

3.   Press the **<Enter>** key (the closing bracket is automatically added).

7   Add a formula to cell B21 that uses a range name to calculate the average bonus.

The correct formula is:

20	Average Sales	22800
21	Average Bonus	=AVERAGE(Bonus)

8   Apply the *Comma Style* to cells B20:B21.

1.   Select cells B20:B21.

2.   Click: Home→Number→Comma Style. [,]

9   Widen column B slightly so that both values are visible.

10   Add a new worksheet (you can leave it at the default name of *Sheet2*).

11   Copy cells A20:B21 from the Sheet1 worksheet and then paste into cells A1:B2 on the *Sheet2* worksheet.

	A	B
1	Average Sales	22,800.00
2	Average Bonus	240.00

You can now appreciate one of the great advantages of range names. The formulas on *Sheet2* are exactly the same as those on *Sheet1* and still work correctly.

Without the use of range names, it wouldn't have been possible to copy and paste the formulas between worksheets. You would have had to re-write the formula as:

=AVERAGE(Sheet1!B9:B17)

12   Save your work as *Earnings Summary-3*.

Lesson 4-5: Use intersection range names and the INDIRECT function

1   Open *Distance Chart-1* from your sample files folder.

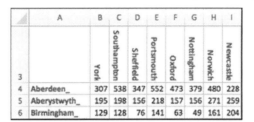

The chart allows you to quickly find the distance between two UK locations. For example, it is clear that the distance from Birmingham to Oxford is 63 miles.

2   Create automatic range names based upon the labels in column A and row 3.

    1.   Select the range A3:X26.

    2.   Click: Formulas→Defined Names→Create from Selection.

        Excel correctly guesses that the labels are in the *Top row* and *Left column*.

    3.   Click the *OK* button.

3   View the range names created using the *Define Name* dialog.

    1.   Click: Formulas→Defined Names→Define Name.

        The *Define Name* dialog appears.

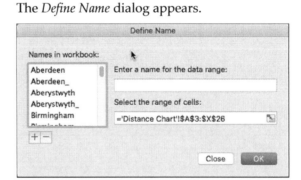

        It is now clear why trailing underscores were used for the labels in column A. Without them, there would have been a naming conflict, as each place name appears for both a row and a column.

    2.   Click the *Close* button.

4   Type **From** into cell A30.

5   Type **To** into cell A31.

6   Type **Miles** into cell A32.

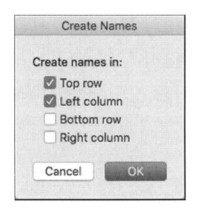

Create Names

Create names in:
- ☑ Top row
- ☑ Left column
- ☐ Bottom row
- ☐ Right column

Cancel   OK

tip

You can also bring up the *Define Name* dialog using the keyboard shortcut:

<Cmd>+<Fn>+<F3>

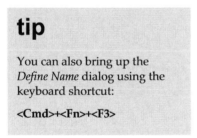

Distance Chart-1

Note

Merging cells

Merging cells is a basic skill covered in depth in *Lesson 4-6* of the *Essential Skills* book in this series.

To merge the cells:

1. Select cells B30:E30.

2. Click:

Home→Alignment→ Merge & Center→ Merge Across

You can also watch this as a video lesson (recorded using Excel 2013) free of charge at:

http://ExcelCentral.com

To do this, click the Excel 2013 and Essential Skills tabs and then navigate to:

Lesson 4-6: Merge cells, wrap text and expand/collapse the formula bar.

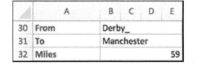

7 Merge cells B30:E30, B31:E31 and B32:E32 (see sidebar if you are unable to do this).

8 Add a list validation to cell B30 that will restrict the cell to the items appearing in cells A4:A26.

This was covered in: *Lesson 2-11: Add a table-based dynamic list validation.*

9 Add a list validation to cell B31 that will restrict the cell to the items appearing in cells B3:X3.

10 Click in cell B30 and choose *Birmingham_* from the drop down list.

11 Click in cell B31 and choose *Oxford* from the drop down list.

Your worksheet should now look like this:

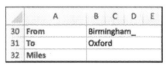

12 Use the intersection operator to create a formula in cell B32 that will show the distance from Birmingham to Oxford.

1. Click in cell B32.

2. Type the formula:

   =Birmingham_ Oxford

   Note that there is a space between the words *Birmingham_* and *Oxford*.

3. Press the **<Enter>** key.

The space is the intersection operator. The correct mileage is displayed in cell B32 (63 miles).

13 Use the INDIRECT function and the intersection operator (space) to show the correct distance in cell B32 based upon the values in cells B30 and B31.

This is more difficult than it first seems. You could be forgiven for thinking that the formula:

=B30 B31

…would work.

Unfortunately, you can't refer to range names in this way. Excel provides the INDIRECT function to solve this problem.

1. Type the following formula into cell B32:

   Note that there is a space between *=INDIRECT(B30)* and *INDIRECT(B31)*.

2. Press the **<Enter>** key.

The correct mileage is now shown in cell B32 for any journey that you select in cells B30 and B31.

14 Save your work as Distance Chart-2.

important

Tables are a better way to implement a dynamic name

You may wonder why I am wasting time teaching a technique that you shouldn't use!

The reason is that there are two scenarios where you may need to use dynamic formula-based range names instead of tables:

1. You may have to create a workbook that will work in pre Excel 2007 versions (the *table* feature was only introduced in Excel 2007).

2. You may need to share a workbook. Tables can't be added after a workbook has been shared. You'll learn about *Shared Workbooks* later, in *Lesson 6-9: Share a workbook on a network*.

Some Excel features (such as validations) are not yet compatible with tables. You still shouldn't waste time using formula-based range names, as it is easier to create a dynamic range name based on a table. This will be covered later in: *Lesson 4-7: Create table-based dynamic range names*.

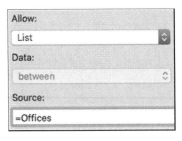

Lesson 4-6: Create dynamic formula-based range names using the OFFSET function

The technique shown in this lesson is a work-around that is rarely needed in Excel 2007, 2010, 2013 or 2016 due to the introduction of the *table* feature (that you learned about in: *Session One: Tables, and Ranges*).

Feel free to skip this lesson if it is not relevant to you (see sidebar).

The range referred to by a range name is already dynamic to a point. If the range has rows or columns added or removed *inside the range,* the range name will automatically adjust. Problems occur when a new value is added to a blank row immediately below a range. In this case, the range name does not automatically adjust.

1   Open *Human Resources-1* from your sample files folder.

     This is a simple workbook containing two worksheets. One worksheet lists employees and the other lists all of the company's current offices and departments.

2   Create automatic range names for cells A4:A6 and C4:C7 on the *Validations* worksheet.

     1.   Select the *Validations* worksheet.

     2.   Select cells A3:A6 (to include the range header).

     3.   Click: Formulas→Defined Names→Create from Selection.

        Note that the actual range name will be A4:A6. Cell A3 was only included in order to define the automatic name: *Offices*.

     4.   Click the *OK* button.

     5.   Repeat for the range C3:C7.

3   Create list validations for columns B and C on the *Employees* worksheet.

     1.   Select all of the cells in column B on the *Employees* worksheet.

     2.   Click: Data→Data Tools→Data Validation.

     3.   Select *List* in the *Allow* drop-down list.

     4.   Type **=Offices** into the *Source* box.

     5.   Click the *OK* button.

     6.   Use the same technique to add a list validation for *Departments* to column C.

4   Use the drop-down lists to add some random *Offices* and *Departments* for Brad Cruise, Ian Dean and Paris Smith.

5   Type **Rome** into cell A7 on the *Validations* worksheet.

6   Select the *Employees* worksheet.

7   Add an office for Gordon Ramsay.

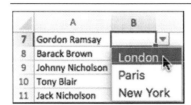

Notice that the new *Rome* office can't be added. That's because the range name does not adjust itself when a new value is added to a blank row immediately below a range.

8 Convert the *Offices* range name into a formula-based range name that is able to automatically re-size.

To do this, you need to use the OFFSET function. This returns a range reference that is a given number of rows or columns from a specified cell.

In this case, the specified cell will be A4 (on the *Validations* worksheet) as this contains the first *Office*, but how can you automatically detect how many offices there are?

The answer is to use the COUNTA function to return the number of cells in column A that are not empty. COUNTA needs a range to examine for non-blank cells. You'll use the range A4:A200 on the basis that you're unlikely to ever have more than 197 offices.

=COUNTA(Validations!$A$4:$A$200) will thus return 4: the current number of offices in the range.

To convert the *Offices* range name into a formula-based range name, you will need to use the *Define Name* dialog.

1. Click: Formulas→Defined Names→Define Name.

2. Click the *Offices* range name.

   Note that this name currently refers to the range:

   > **Select the range of cells:**
   >
   > =Validations!$A$4:$A$6

3. Type the following formula into the *Select the range of cells* box:

   > =OFFSET(Validations!$A$4,0,0,COUNTA(Validations!$A$4:$A$200))

   The four arguments specify where the range will begin, the number of rows to offset the start of the range, the number of columns to offset the start of the range, and the number of rows in the range.

4. Click the *OK* button.

9 Convert the *Departments* range name into a formula-based range name that is able to automatically re-size.

Do this in exactly the same way as for the *Offices* range. This time, the formula in the *Select the range of cells* box will be:

> =OFFSET(Validations!$C$4,0,0,COUNTA(Validations!$C$4:$C$200))

10 Test the validation by adding *Offices* and *Departments*.

When you add a new *Office* or *Department*, the range names now dynamically expand to include the new item.

11 Save your work as *Human Resources-2*.

Lesson 4-7: Create table-based dynamic range names

In the last lesson: *Lesson 4-6: Create dynamic formula-based range names using the OFFSET function,* you used a complex method based on the OFFSET and COUNTA functions to implement a dynamic formula-based range name.

You'll be pleased to know that there is a much simpler way to achieve the same thing using a table-based range name.

You won't be able to use this technique if you need to create workbooks that are compatible with pre-2007 versions of Excel. If you are sure that the workbook will only ever be used with post-2007 versions of Excel, the technique described in this lesson is simpler, more elegant and less prone to error.

1   Open *Human Resources-2* from your sample files folder (if it isn't already open).

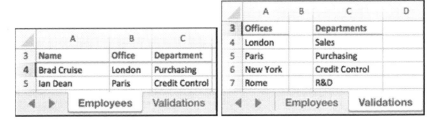

This is a simple worksheet with two tabs. One tab lists employees and the other lists all of the company's current offices and departments.

2   Delete the existing range names for *Departments* and *Offices*.

    1.   Click: Formulas→Defined Names→Define Name.

    2.   Click *Departments* and then click the ☐ button.

    3.   Click *Offices* and then click the ☐ button

    4.   Click the *OK* button to close the dialog.

3   Convert the ranges A3:A7 and C3:C7 on the *Validations* worksheet into tables.

This was covered in depth in: *Lesson 1-11: Convert a range into a table and add a total row.*

    1.   Click anywhere in the range A3:A7 on the *Validations* worksheet.

    2.   Click: Insert→Tables→Table.

    3.   Click the *OK* button.

    4.   Do exactly the same thing for the *Departments* range.

4   Name the two new tables *Office* and *Department*.

    1.   Click anywhere inside the range A3:A7.

    2.   Click: Table→Properties→Table Name.

Human Resources-2

3. Type **Office** into the text box.

4. Do exactly the same thing to name the *Department* table.

5 Create range names called *OfficeTable* and *DepartmentTable* based upon the two new tables.

Unfortunately, Excel doesn't accept a table name for a list validation. Fortunately, it is happy to accept a range name associated with a table.

1. Select all of the values in the *Office* table (cells A4:A7), being careful not to include the header row.

2. Click: Formulas→Defined Names→Define Name.

The *Define Name* dialog appears.

3. Type **OfficeTable** in the *Enter a name for the data range* text box.

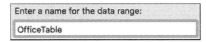

Note that the *Select the range of cells* box now contains a structured reference:

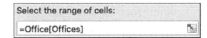

This structured reference refers to all of the data in the *Office* table. In other words, it is a dynamic range name that will shrink and grow with the *Office* table.

4. Click the *OK* button.

5. Create a *DepartmentTable* range name in exactly the same way.

6 Edit the list validation on columns B and C on the *Employees* worksheet to reference the *OfficeTable* and *DepartmentTable* range names.

1. Select column B on the *Employees* worksheet.

2. Click: Data→Data Tools→Data Validation.

3. Delete *=Offices* from the *Source* text box and replace it with: **=OfficeTable**

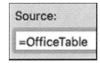

4. Click the *OK* button.

5. Use the same method to edit the list validation for column C.

7 Test the validations.

As items are added to and deleted from the tables in the *Validations* worksheet, the changes are reflected in the contents of the drop-down validation lists on the *Employees* worksheet.

8 Save your work as *Human Resources-3*.

Lesson 4-8: Create two linked drop-down lists using range names

In this lesson, you're going to push Excel's validation features into bold new territory by addressing a common business requirement.

Here's the sample worksheet for this session:

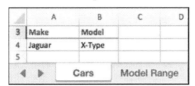

You want to add a validation to columns A and B (to allow users to select a *Make* and *Model*) for each row.

The *Make* validation is easy to implement as a simple list validation.

The *Model* validation is not so simple. The values that are valid need to change depending upon the selected *Make*.

Here's what you want to see:

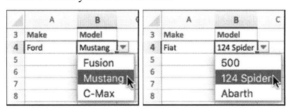

- When the Make is *Ford,* valid models are *Fusion, Mustang* and *C-Max*.

- When the Make is *Fiat,* valid models are *500, 124 Spider* and *Abarth*.

This lesson provides a solution to the problem by dynamically selecting the correct *Model* range name that matches the selected *Make*.

1   Open *New Car Model Range-1* from your sample files folder.

2   Create an automatic range name for the *Make* table on the *Model Range* worksheet.

1.   Select the *Model Range* worksheet.

2.   Select cells A5:A8.

3.   Click: Formulas→Defined Names→Create From Selection.

4.   Click the *OK* button.

3   Create automatic range names for each *Model* on the *Model Range* worksheet.

1.   Select cells A12:C15.

2.   Click Formulas→Defined Names→Create from Selection.

3.   De-select the *Left column* check box, because you only want the range names to use the labels from the *Top row*.

4.   Click the *OK* button.

New Car Model Range-1

4   Apply a list validation to column A of the *Cars* worksheet that uses the *Make* range name as its source.

1. Select column A on the *Cars* worksheet.

2. Click: Data→Data Tools→Data Validation.

3. Enter the following values into the dialog:

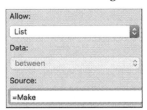

4. Click the *OK* button.

5   Use the drop-down list to select a car make in cell A4.

6   Apply a list validation to cell B4 that will display a list of models based upon the make displayed in cell A4.

1. Click in cell B4.

2. Click: Data→Data Tools→Data Validation.

3. Enter the following values into the dialog:

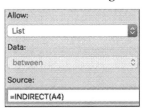

It is very important that the reference to cell A4 is relative (A4) and not absolute ($A$4), because you are going to copy the validation to the other cells in column B in a moment.

4. Click the *OK* button.

7   Copy and paste the validation to all of the cells in column B.

1. Copy the contents of cell B4.

2. Select all of column B.

3. Right-click inside the selected range and click *Paste Special…* from the shortcut menu.

4. Select *Validation* from the *Paste Special* dialog.

5. Click the *OK* button.

8   Test the validation.

The valid choices now change based upon the selected *Make*.

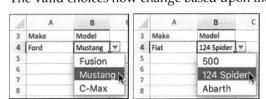

9   Save your work as *New Car Model Range-2*.

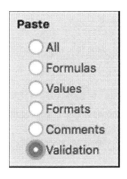

Lesson 4-9: Understand the #NUM!, #DIV/0! and #NAME? error values

note

The #N/A error value

Sometimes Excel can't figure out exactly why an error has occurred.

In this case it displays the:

"I don't know what the specific problem is"

…error value.

#N/A

So why call it #N/A?

The official explanation is that this error displays when a value is *not available* to a function or formula.

Excel has six specific error values that it is able to display in cells containing formulas. It's important that you understand the type of problem that causes Excel to display each of these errors.

The error values are:

#DIV/0!, #NAME?, #NULL!, #NUM!, #REF! and **#VALUE!**

There's also a nonspecific error value called **#N/A** (see sidebar).

The sample worksheet for this lesson has faulty formulas that produce all six errors.

1   Open *Errors-1* from your sample files folder.

This worksheet has a lot of problems. You can see each of the six error messages appearing in different cells.

2   Diagnose and solve the problem causing the #NUM! error in cell D4.

	A	B	C	D
3	Month	Sales	Target	Above/Below Target
4	Jan	$ 5,210.00	$ 3,500.00	#NUM!
5	Feb	$ 5,650.00	$ -	$ 5,650.00

The #NUM! error is usually caused by a formula that returns a number that is too large, or too small for Excel to handle.

Another possible cause is a non-numeric value entered as an argument for a function that expects a numeric value.

1.   Examine the formula in cell D4:

	D
4	=B4^C4

Here lies the problem. Excel is trying to calculate B4 *exponent* C4, which results in a huge number that Excel isn't capable of handling.

2.   Correct the formula.

As you need to calculate how far sales are above or below target you will need to correct the formula to:

The problem vanishes. Notice that the formula in cell D10 now also displays correctly, as it was simply inheriting the #NUM! error from cell D4.

Errors-1

3 Diagnose and solve the problem causing the #DIV/0! error in cell E5.

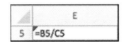

	A	B	C	D	E
				Above/Below Target	% of Target
3	Month	Sales	Target		
4	Jan	$ 5,210.00	$ 3,500.00	$ 1,710.00	149%
5	Feb	$ 5,650.00	$ -	$ 5,650.00	#DIV/0!
6	Mar	$ 6,092.00	$ 4,000.00	$ 2,092.00	152%

Dividing by zero results in an infinite number, causing Excel's "Divide by Zero" error to be displayed.

1. Examine the formula in cell E5.

	E
5	=B5/C5

You know that the zero value must be in cell C5. Sure enough, no sales target was entered for February.

2. Enter a sales target of **3,250** for February.

The problem is solved.

If you didn't know the target for February and wanted to suppress the error message, you could use the IFERROR function as described in: *Lesson 3-23: Use an IFERROR function to suppress error messages.*

4 Diagnose and solve the problem causing the #NAME? error in cell C10.

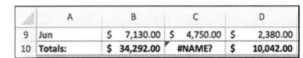

	A	B	C	D
9	Jun	$ 7,130.00	$ 4,750.00	$ 2,380.00
10	Totals:	$ 34,292.00	#NAME?	$ 10,042.00

The #NAME? error means that Excel has encountered a name it doesn't understand. The most likely cause is that you've used a range name that doesn't exist.

1. Examine the formula in cell C10.

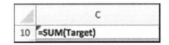

	C
10	=SUM(Target)

Because there was a #NAME? error, you know that there is no range name called *Target*.

2. Select cells C3:C9.

3. Click: Formulas→Defined Names→Create from Selection.

4. Click the *OK* button.

The problem is solved and the error disappears.

5 Save your work as *Errors-2*.

Lesson 4-10: Understand the #VALUE!, #REF! and #NULL! error values

1   Open *Errors-2 from* your sample files folder (if it isn't already open).

2   Diagnose and solve the problem causing the #VALUE! error in cell F8.

	A	B	C	D	E	F
3	Month	Sales	Target	Above/Below Target	% of Target	Exceeded Target?
4	Jan	$ 5,210.00	$ 3,500.00	$ 1,710.00	149%	Yes
5	Feb	$ 5,650.00	$ 3,250.00	$ 2,400.00	174%	Yes
6	Mar	$ 6,092.00	$ 4,000.00	$ 2,092.00	152%	Yes
7	Apr	$ 3,955.00	$ 4,250.00	$ -295.00	93%	No
8	May	$ 6,255.00	$ 4,500.00	$ 1,755.00	139%	#VALUE!

The #VALUE! error means that a function contains an invalid argument.

1.   Examine the formula in cell F8.

fx =IF("B8>C8", "Yes", "No")

The IF function was covered in: *Lesson 3-5: Use the IF logic function.*

The first argument of an IF function demands a logical expression that evaluates TRUE or FALSE.

There's nothing wrong with the logical expression: **B8>C8**. The problem is caused by the quotation marks, which cause Excel to interpret it as text.

2.   Correct the formula in cell F8 by removing the quotation marks from the expression **B8>C8** (the IF function's first argument).

fx =IF(B8>C8, "Yes", "No")

The problem is solved.

3   Diagnose and solve the problem causing the #REF! error in cell B11.

	A	B	C
10	Totals:	$ 34,292.00	$ 24,250.00
11	GBP Totals:	#REF!	

The #REF! error means that a formula refers to a cell that isn't valid. This happens when you reference a cell from a formula and then delete the row or column that used to contain the referenced cell.

Errors-2

1. Examine the formula in cell B11

    fx =B10/#REF!

    Because this cell needs to convert the dollar sales figure in cell B10 to Great Britain Pounds (GBP), the missing reference is the USD/GBP exchange rate.

2. Replace the #REF! part of the formula with **1.62** (the USD/GBP exchange rate when this lesson was written).

    fx =B10/1.62

3. Press the **<Enter>** key.

    The problem is solved.

4   Diagnose and solve the problem causing the #NULL! error in cell B16.

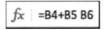

	A	B
15	Period	Sales
16	1st Quarter	#NULL!
17	2nd Quarter	17,340

The #NULL! error occurred because Excel is confused by the use of the intersection (space) operator. It usually simply means that you've incorrectly typed one of the arguments.

1. Examine the formula in cell B16.

    fx =B4+B5 B6

    It is clear that there is a missing addition (+) operator between B5 and B6.

    Excel has interpreted the missing operator as an attempt to reference the intersection of cells B5 and B6. It is, of course, impossible to have an intersection between two single cell references.

    The intersection operator was covered in: *Lesson 4-5: Use intersection range names and the INDIRECT function.*

2. Correct the formula in cell B16 by adding the missing addition operator.

    fx =B4+B5+B6

3. Press the **<Enter>** key.

    The problem is solved.

5   Save your work as *Errors-3*.

Lesson 4-11: Understand background error checking and error checking rules

Excel is constantly working in the background, automatically checking for errors. Whenever Excel thinks you've made a mistake, it will politely let you know. Of course, Excel isn't always correct. It can only guess that you've made a mistake and it is often wrong.

1   Open *Daily Profit Report-1 from* your sample files folder.

This workbook contains two errors. Excel has automatically detected them and indicates each by a small green triangle in the top left hand corner of each cell containing a suspected error.

If you don't see the green triangles on your computer, somebody has switched automatic error checking off. See the sidebar for instructions on how to switch it back on.

note

Why can't I see any green triangles?

If you don't see the green triangles, somebody has switched off automatic error checking.

To switch it back on, check the check box:

⌘→Excel→Preferences→ Error Checking→ Turn on background error checking

	A	B	C	D
3	Date	Sales	Costs	Profit
4	18-Sep-16	20,000	12,000	8,000
5	19-Sep-16	21,000	12,500	8,500
6	20-Sep-16	22,800	12,600	35,400
7	21-Sep-16	23,500	13,000	10,500
8	Total:	87,300	50,100	62,400

2   Understand error checking rules.

1.   Click: ⌘→Excel→Preferences→Error Checking.

Note that Excel monitors for seven different error conditions by default. There's an eighth that is switched off by default, but it can be enabled if required:

Show Errors For
- ☑ Formulas that result in an error
- ☑ Years in 2 digits
- ☑ Numbers formatted as text
- ☑ Formulas that don't match nearby formulas
- ☑ Formulas omitting cells in a region
- ☑ Unlocked cells containing formulas
- ☐ Formulas referring to empty cells
- ☑ Inconsistent calculated column formula in tables

2.   Click the *Close* button.

3   Remove the error warning from cell A5.

1.   Click on cell A5. Notice that an *Error Smart Tag* has appeared to the right of the cell.

2.   Hover the mouse cursor over the *Smart Tag*.

A tip appears, showing the rule that Excel believes has been violated:

5	19-Sep-16	1,000	12,500	8,500
6	20-Sep-16	22,800	12,600	35,400
7	21-Sep-16	This cell contains a date string represented		
8	Total:	with only 2 digits for the year.		

Daily Profit Report-1

3. Click the down arrow on the Smart Tag.

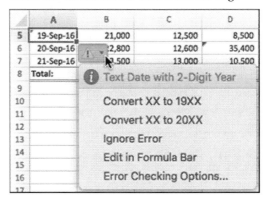

Excel is worried because the date (unlike the other dates in the column) has been entered as a text value with two digits. This is a throw-back to the problems caused in the year 2000 when such dates were predicted to bring about the end of the world (see sidebar).

A date can be entered in this way by preceding the date by an apostrophe to indicate that the entry is a textual value:

'19-Sep-16

Notice that two of the options in the *Smart Tag* list offer to convert the date to 2016 or to 1916.

4. Click *Ignore Error*.

The green triangle vanishes.

4 **Correct the error in cell D6.**

1. Click on cell D6 and hover the mouse cursor over the *Smart Tag*.

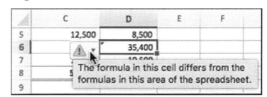

This time Excel has found a real error. It has noticed that the formula in cell D6 is inconsistent with the other formulas in column D. The formula is adding costs to sales when it should be subtracting them.

2. Click the down arrow on the *Smart Tag* and click *Copy Formula from Above* from the shortcut menu.

The error is corrected.

5 **Save your work as *Daily Profit Report-2*.**

Lesson 4-12: Manually check a worksheet for errors

Sometimes those little green triangles can be annoying. Excel often picks up "errors" that are not really errors at all.

Some Excel users would prefer to switch off background error checking and instead run a manual error check when the worksheet is complete.

In this lesson, you'll switch off Excel's background error checking and then manually scan a worksheet for errors.

1   Open *Operating Expenses-1* from your sample files folder.

This workbook contains three errors. Excel has automatically detected them and indicates each by a small green triangle in the top left hand corner of each cell containing a suspected error.

	A	B	C	D
3	Month	Budget	Actual	Variance
4	Jan-16	42,000	45000	3,000
5	Feb-16	45,000	42000	-3,000
6	Mar-16	47,500	46000	-2,500
7	Apr-16	48,000	53000	5,000
8	May-16	47,000	47000	0
9	Jun-16	46,000	45000	-1,000
10	Total	275,500	186000	1,500

2   Switch off background error checking.

1. Click: ➡️ → Excel → Preferences → Error Checking.

2. Clear the *Turn on background error checking* check box:

3. Click the *Close* button.

Notice that the green triangles have now vanished, even though the error conditions remain.

3   Manually check the worksheet for errors.

1. Click: Formulas → Formula Auditing → Error Checking.

Cell D6 is selected (the first cell in the worksheet containing a suspected error) and the *Error Checking* dialog appears:

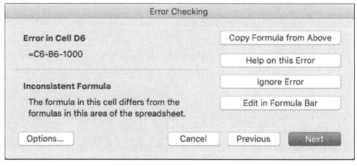

The dialog indicates that Excel has detected an inconsistent formula. This means that the formula in cell D6 is not consistent with the other formulas in column D.

2. Click *Cancel* to close the *Error Checking* dialog.

3. Click: Formulas→Formula Auditing→Show Formulas.

The formulas behind the cells are now displayed:

	D
3	Variance
4	=C4-B4
5	=C5-B5
6	=C6-B6-1000
7	=C7-B7

The error is now apparent. For some reason, an extra 1,000 has been deducted from the variance for March 2016.

4. Click: Formulas→Formula Auditing→Show Formulas.

Values are once again shown in all cells.

5. Click: Formulas→Formula Auditing→Error Checking.

6. Click *Copy Formula from Above* to correct the error.

The error is corrected and the active cell moves to cell C8: the next cell in the worksheet containing a suspected error.

This time, the error is caused by a number being stored as text. This can happen when a numeric cell is formatted as text, or when a value is typed into a cell preceded with an apostrophe like this:

'47000

7. Click *Convert to Number*.

The error is corrected and the active cell moves to cell C10: the next cell in the worksheet containing a suspected error.

This time the error is another inconsistent formula. The formula in cell C10 is incorrectly adding the values in cells C4:C8 instead of C4:C9. Excel has noticed that this is inconsistent with the formulas in cells B10 and D10.

8. Click *Copy Formula from Left* to correct the error.

9. Click the *OK* button to end the error check.

4 Re-enable background error checking.

1. Click: →Excel→Preferences→Error Checking.

2. Check the *Turn on background error checking* check box.

3. Click the *Close* button.

Notice that there are no longer any green triangles, as you've corrected all of the errors.

5 Save your work as *Operating Expenses-2*.

Error in Cell C8

47000

Number Stored as Text

The number in this cell is formatted as text or preceded by an apostrophe.

Error in Cell C10

=SUM(C4:C8)

Inconsistent Formula

The formula in this cell differs from the formulas in this area of the spreadsheet.

Lesson 4-13: Audit a formula by tracing precedents

When you have a worksheet with cross-worksheet formulas and range names, there is a lot of scope for error. Ranges and formulas can often reference the wrong cells.

Excel's *trace precedents* tool provides an easy way to quickly audit cell references in order to confirm the integrity of your workbook.

1   Open *Profit Analysis-1 from* your sample files folder.

This workbook summarizes data from the *January, February* and *March* worksheets into a *First Quarter Summary*. The workbook also makes extensive use of range names.

	A	B	C	D	E	F	G	H
1	First Quarter Summary							
2								
3		Sales	Cost	Profit				
4	Jan	89,199	45,318	43,881				
5	Feb	99,197	42,510	56,687				
6	Mar	87,194	45,025	42,169				
7	Totals:	275,590	132,853	142,737				
8								

◄ ►   First Quarter Summary   January   February   March

2   Audit the formula in cell D7 of the *First Quarter Summary* worksheet using *Trace Precedents*.

1.   Click into cell D7.

Notice that it isn't possible to immediately see which cells are referenced by the *Profit* range name.

fx   =SUM(Profit)

2.   Click: Formulas→Formula Auditing→Trace Precedents.

The cells referenced by the *Profit* range name are now apparent.

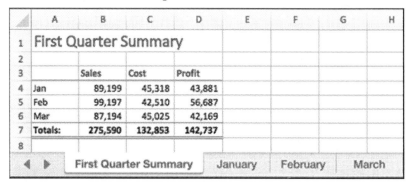

You might think that this isn't very impressive. You could have done the same thing by pressing the **<Fn>+<F2>** keys, or by clicking the word *Profit* in the formula bar. But there's more to come!

3.   Click: Formulas→Formula Auditing→Trace Precedents again.

This time the next level of precedents is shown:

Profit Analysis-1

note

Use Trace Error to quickly find the first error in a chain

When a cell shows an error condition (such as **#DIV/0!**), it is often caused by an error in a precedent cell.

It is possible to click:

Formulas→
Formula Auditing→
Trace Precedents

... several times in order to trace the cell causing the error.

Excel also provides a way of tracing all precedents in a single click when a cell shows an error condition, allowing you to save a few mouse clicks.

When the active cell contains an error condition, you can click:

Formula Auditing→
Error Checking→
Trace Error

This shows all precedents, at all levels, with a single click.

	A	B	C	D
3		Sales	Cost	Profit
4	Jan	●89,199	●45,318	●43,881
5	Feb	●99,197	●42,510	56,687
6	Mar	●87,194	●45,025	42,169
7	Totals:	275,590	132,853	142,737

You can see that the value in cell D4 is calculated from the values in cells B4 and C4. You can also see that the value in cell D7 is calculated from the range D4:D6.

But where are the values in cells B4:C6 coming from?

4. Click: Formulas→Formula Auditing→Trace Precedents again.

	A	B	C	D
2				
3		Sales	Cost	pfit
4	Jan	85,199	45,318	43,881
5	Feb	95,197	42,510	56,687
6	Mar	87,194	45,025	42,169
7	Totals:	275,590	132,853	142,737

The icons pointing to cells B4:C6 indicate that their values come from different worksheets in this (or even another) workbook.

5. Double-click the dotted line joining cell B4 and the icon.

The *Go To* dialog appears, showing the source of the value in cell B4.

6. Select the item shown in the *Go To* window and then click the *OK* button.

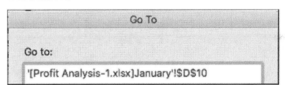

> Go To
>
> Go to:
>
> '[Profit Analysis-1.xlsx]January'!$D$10

You are taken to the cell in the *January* worksheet that provides the value shown in cell B4 on the *First Quarter Summary* worksheet.

7. Click: Formulas→Formula Auditing→Trace Precedents again.

Now you can see the precedents of cell D10 in the *January* worksheet (see sidebar).

8. Click: Formulas→Formula Auditing→Remove Arrows.

The precedent arrows are removed from the *January* worksheet.

9. Select the *First Quarter Summary* worksheet.

10. Click: Formulas→Formula Auditing→Remove Arrows.

The precedent arrows are removed from the *First Quarter Summary* worksheet.

	D	E
3	Sales	Cost
4	16,756	9,431
5	19,437	7,412
6	14,742	7,960
7	15,881	6,214
8	11,835	8,714
9	10,548	5,587
10	89,199	45,318

Lesson 4-14: Audit a formula by tracing dependents

1   Open *Profit Analysis-1* from your sample files folder (if it isn't already open).

2   Select the *January* worksheet.

3   Audit the formula in cell D6 using *Trace Dependents*.

1. Click cell D6 to make it the active cell.

2. Click: Formulas→Formula Auditing→Trace Dependents.

The direct dependents are shown for cell D6. These cells have formulas that directly reference cell D6.

	A	B	C	D	E	F
3	Team	First Name	Last Name	Sales	Cost	Profit
4	Blue	Johnny	Caine	16,756	9,431	7,325
5	Blue	George	Marley	19,437	7,412	12,025
6	Blue	Bill	Spears	14,742	7,960	6,782
7	Red	Gordon	Depp	15,881	6,214	9,667
8	Red	Tom	Marley	11,835	8,714	3,121
9	Red	Charles	Blair	10,548	5,587	4,961
10	Totals:			89,199	45,318	43,881
11						
12	Team			Average Sales	Average Cost	Average Profit
13	Blue			16,978	8,268	8,711
14	Red			12,755	6,838	5,916

You can see that:

*   The *Profit* in cell F6 depends upon *Sales* in D6 (because Profit = Sales-Cost).

*   The *Total Sales* in cell D10 depends upon the *Sales* in D6.

*   The *Average Sales* for the *Blue* team also depends upon the value in D6, because Bill Spears is in the *Blue* team.

3. Click: Formulas→Formula Auditing→Trace Dependents again.

	A	B	C	D	E	F
3	Team	First Name	Last Name	Sales	Cost	Profit
4	Blue	Johnny	Caine	16,756	9,431	7,325
5	Blue	George	Marley	19,437	7,412	12,025
6	Blue	Bill	Spears	14,742	7,960	6,782
7	Red	Gordon	Depp	15,881	6,214	9,667
8	Red	Tom	Marley	11,835	8,714	3,121
9	Red	Charles	Blair	10,548	5,587	4,961
10	Totals:			89,199	45,318	43,881
11						
12	Team			Average Sales	Average Cost	Average Profit
13	Blue			16,978	8,268	8,711
14	Red			12,755	6,838	5,916

The next level of dependents is shown. You can now see that:

*   The *Total* in cell F10 depends upon the *Profit* value in cell F6.

Profit Analysis-1

- The Blue Team's *Average Profit* in cell F13 depends upon the *Average Sales* in cell D13.

There is also an icon pointing to cell D10 indicating that there is a dependent value in a different worksheet in this (or even another) workbook.

4. Double-click the dotted line joining cell D10 and the icon.

   The *Go To* dialog appears, showing the source of the value in cell D10.

5. Select the item shown in the *Go To* window and then click the *OK* button.

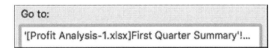

Go to:

'[Profit Analysis-1.xlsx]First Quarter Summary'!...

   You are taken to cell B4 in the *First Quarter Summary* worksheet, as this cell depends upon the value in cell D10 on the *January* worksheet.

6. Click: Formulas→Formula Auditing→Trace Dependents again.

   You can now see the cells whose formulas directly depend upon the value in cell B4.

	A	B	C	D
3		Sales	Cost	Profit
4	Jan	89,199	45,318	43,881
5	Feb	99,197	42,510	56,687
6	Mar	87,194	45,025	42,169
7	Totals:	275,590	132,853	142,737

7. Click: Formulas→Formula Auditing→Trace Dependents again.

   The final level of dependents is shown:

	A	B	C	D
3		Sales	Cost	Profit
4	Jan	89,199	45,318	43,881
5	Feb	99,197	42,510	56,687
6	Mar	87,194	45,025	42,169
7	Totals:	275,590	132,853	142,737

8. Click: Formulas→Formula Auditing→Remove Arrows.

   The dependent arrows are removed from the *First Quarter Summary* worksheet.

9. Select the *January* worksheet.

10. Click: Formulas→Formula Auditing→Remove Arrows.

    The dependent arrows are removed from the *January* worksheet.

Session 4: Exercise

1   Open *Excel Quiz-1* from your sample files folder.

2   Select cells A5:E9 on the *Choices* worksheet.

	A	B	C	D	E
4					
5	1	64,000	128,000	512,000	1,048,576
6	2	1985	1992	1995	1997
7	3	Excel 7	Excel 12	Excel 9	Excel 16
8	4	Lotus 1-2-3	SuperCalc	VisiCalc	Multiplan
9	5	256	512	16,384	22,256

3   Create range names from the selected cells using the value in the left column to name each range.

4   Apply a list validation to cell C4 on the *Quiz* worksheet that will show a list of all valid answers to the first question by referencing the range name matching the value in cell A4 on the *Quiz* worksheet using the INDIRECT function.

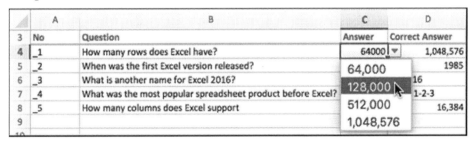

5   Copy and paste the validation from cell C4 to cells C5:C8.

6   Put an IF function into cell E4 that will show the text "CORRECT" if the answer in cell C4 equals the correct answer in cell D4, and a blank space if the answer is not correct.

	C	D	E
3	Answer	Correct Answer	Correct?
4	1048576	1,048,576	CORRECT

7   AutoFill cell E4 down to cells E5:E8.

8   Hide columns A and D.

9   Save your work as *Excel Quiz-2*.

	B	C	E
3	Question	Answer	Correct?
4	How many rows does Excel have?	1048576	CORRECT
5	When was the first Excel version released?	1985	CORRECT
6	What is another name for Excel 2016?		
7	What was the most popular spreadsheet product before Excel?	Excel 7	
8	How many columns does Excel support	Excel 12	
9		Excel 9	
10			
11		Excel 16	

Excel Quiz-1

If you need help slide the page to the left

Session 4: Exercise Answers

These are the four questions that students find the most difficult to answer:

Q 6	Q 5	Q 4	Q 3
The correct function is: **=IF(D4=C4, "CORRECT", "")** This was covered in: *Lesson 3-5: Use the IF logic function.*	1. Click in cell C4. 2. Click: Home→ Clipboard→Copy. 3. Select the range C5:C8. 4. Click: Home→ Clipboard→ Paste→ Paste Special… 5. Select *Validation* in the *Paste Special* dialog. **Paste** ○ All ○ Formulas ○ Values ○ Formats ○ Comments ◉ Validation 6. Click the *OK* button. This was covered in: *Lesson 4-8: Create two linked drop-down lists using range names.*	1. Click in cell C4 on the *Quiz* worksheet. 2. Click: Data→ Data Tools→ Data Validation. 3. Complete the Data Validation dialog like this: **Allow:** List **Data:** between **Source:** =INDIRECT(A4) The INDIRECT function allows you to use the value in column A to reference the range name (with the same name) that contains the correct multiple-choice questions. This was covered in: *Lesson 4-8: Create two linked drop-down lists using range names.*	1. Click: Formulas→ Defined Names→ Create from Selection. 2. Make sure that only the *Left column* is checked in the *Create Names* dialog. **Create names in:** ☐ Top row ☑ Left column ☐ Bottom row ☐ Right column 3. Click the *OK* button. This was covered in: *Lesson 4-1: Automatically create single-cell range names.*

If you have difficulty with the other questions, here are the lessons that cover the relevant skills:

8   In order to hide a column, right-click the column header and select *Hide* from the shortcut menu.

This skill is covered in lesson 5-14 of the *Essential Skills* book in this series.

5

Session Five: What If Analysis and Security

> The superior man, when resting in safety, does not forget that danger may come. When in a state of security, he does not forget the possibility of ruin. When all is orderly, he does not forget that disorder may come. Thus his person is not endangered, and his States and all their clans are preserved.
>
> *Confucius (551 BC - 479 BC)*

The concept of "What If" is very simple. A business may wish to know what will happen in a given set of circumstances (called a scenario). For example, a simple scenario might be: "What if I reduced my profit margins by 5% and my sales increased by 20%?" Excel provides several tools that are geared to more complex scenarios. In this session you'll learn how to use these tools effectively.

Sometimes you'll want to keep the contents of a workbook secure. This session will show you how to prevent unauthorized users from opening or changing your workbooks. You'll also learn how to restrict the cells that a user is able to edit within a workbook. This session will also show you how to hide rows and columns and then create multiple custom views of the worksheet – each view hiding and showing different information.

Session Objectives

By the end of this session you will be able to:

- Create a single-input data table
- Create a two-input data table
- Define scenarios
- Create a scenario summary report
- Use Goal Seek
- Use Solver
- Hide and unhide worksheets, columns and rows
- Create custom views
- Prevent unauthorized users from opening or modifying workbooks
- Control the changes users can make to workbooks
- Restrict the cells users are allowed to change

Lesson 5-1: Create a single-input data table

Don't be fooled by the name. A *data table* has nothing to do with a regular Excel table. Data tables are another of those wonderful Excel features that are a complete mystery to virtually all Excel users.

In this lesson you'll use a data table to list the monthly repayments for a loan at different interest rates.

1 Open *Mortgage-1 from* your sample files folder.

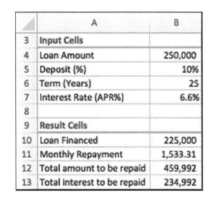

	A	B
3	Input Cells	
4	Loan Amount	250,000
5	Deposit (%)	10%
6	Term (Years)	25
7	Interest Rate (APR%)	6.6%
8		
9	Result Cells	
10	Loan Financed	225,000
11	Monthly Repayment	1,533.31
12	Total amount to be repaid	459,992
13	Total interest to be repaid	234,992

This is a simple worksheet that calculates four result values from four input values. When performing what-if analysis, it is a good idea to separate the input values from the result values on your worksheet.

The worksheet uses the PMT function that was covered in: *Lesson 3-3: Use the Formula Builder task pane and the PMT function.*

During the last 25 years, mortgage interest rates have never dropped below 2.5% or increased to more than 15.5%.

Based upon the assumption that future rates will stay in this range, you will create a data table to show how potential changes in interest rates will affect monthly payments.

2 Create a single input data table to display all result cells for interest rates between 2.5% and 15.5% in half percent increments.

1. Type **Interest %** into cell D3.

2. Type **Monthly Payment** into cell E3.

3. Type **Total Payments** into cell F3.

4. Type **Total Interest** into cell G3.

5. AutoSize columns D, E, F and G so that all of the headers are readable.

6. Select cells D3:G3.

7. Click: Home→Styles→Cell Styles→Heading 3.

8. Type **2.5%** into cell B7.

When you create a data table, you should always put the lowest input value into the relevant input cell. You'll see why in a moment.

9. Add formulas to cells D4:G4 that refer to the relevant input and result cells. The correct formulas are shown below:

	D	E	F	G
3	Interest %	Monthly Payment	Total Payments	Total Interest
4	=B7	=B11	=B12	=B13

10. Type **=D4+0.005** into cell D5 (the formula **D4+0.5%** would produce an identical result).

11. AutoFill cell D5 down to cell D30 (15.5%).

Mortgage-1

trivia

What is the TABLE function?

If you look at the function behind each cell in the data table, you'll see a strange syntax:

{=TABLE(,B7)}

This often confuses users, because you'll find no reference to a TABLE function in the Excel help.

You'll also find that you are unable to manually create a TABLE function.

The TABLE function is simply Excel's "behind the scenes" way of implementing data table functionality. The only way that you can insert a TABLE function into a worksheet is by creating a data table.

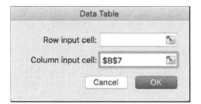

note

Data tables are read only

You cannot change or delete a cell in a data table.

If you try to do this, Excel will produce an error message.

If you need to remove a cell from a data table, you must delete the entire table.

Your worksheet should now look like this:

	D	E	F	G
3	Interest %	Monthly Payment	Total Payments	Total Interest
4	2.5%	1,009.39	302,816	77,816
5	3.0%			

12. Convert cells D4:D30 from formulas to values.

    Excel 2016 data tables have a problem with certain formulas in the left-hand column. For this reason, you need to *Copy* the values in cells D4:D30 and then *Paste Special* them back to the same location as *Values.*

    Another work-around for this limitation is discussed in: *Lesson 7-8: Add a single input data table to a form.*

    You are now ready to create your data table.

13. Select cells D4:G30.

14. Click: Data→Data Tools→What-If Analysis→Data Table...

    The *Data Table* dialog appears.

15. Click once in the *Column input cell* text box.

16. Click on cell B7.

    This sets the *Column input cell* to the absolute cell reference: $B$7.

    Because the interest rates are shown in column D, Excel must change the input value in cell B7 (to each value in column D) in order to calculate result values for columns E, F and G.

17. Click the *OK* button.

    The data table is populated to show all result cells for all interest rates.

18. Select cells E4:G30.

19. Click: Home→Styles→Cell Styles→Comma[0].

	D	E	F	G
3	Interest %	Monthly Payment	Total Payments	Total Interest
4	2.5%	1,009	302,816	77,816
5	3.0%	1,067	320,093	95,093

You are now able to change the *Loan Amount, Deposit* or *Term* input values to update the data table.

3   Save your work as *Mortgage-2.*

Lesson 5-2: Create a two-input data table

A two-input data table is similar to a single-input data table.

However, in a two-input data table, input cells are arranged along both the top and the left-hand side of the table.

In this lesson you'll use a two-input data table to show monthly repayments for different loan amounts and different interest rates.

1 Open *Mortgage-2 from* your sample files folder (if it isn't already open).

2 Create a new worksheet and name it:
Variable Interest and Capital

3 Copy cells A1:B13 from the *Variable Interest* worksheet and paste them into the same cells in the *Variable Interest and Capital* worksheet.

4 AutoSize columns A and B so that they are wide enough to display all values.

5 Create rows for your data table in cells E3:L3, showing capital amounts from 125,000 to 300,000 in increments of 25,000.

1. Type **125,000** into cell E3.

2. Type **150,000** into cell F3.

3. Select cells E3:F3 and AutoFill across to cell L3.

	E	F	G	H
3	125,000	150,000	175,000	200,000

6 Create row labels for your data table in cells D4:D30, showing interest rates from 2.5% to 15.5% in increments of 0.5%.

1. Type **2.5%** into cell D4.

2. Type **3%** into cell D5.

3. Select cells D4:D5 and AutoFill to cell D30 (15.5%).

7 Format cells D4:D30 to show one decimal place.

1. Select cells D4:D30.

2. Click: Home→Number→Decrease Decimal. ⬛

8 Add a formula to cell D3 that will reference the *Monthly Repayment* result cell.

	D	E	F	G
3	=B11	125000	150000	175000

9 If necessary, AutoSize column D so that it is wide enough to display all values.

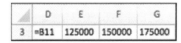
Mortgage-2

10 Apply the *Note* cell style to cells D3:D30 and cells E3:L3.

   1. Select cells D3:D30 and cells E3:L3.

   2. Click: Home→Styles→Cell Styles→Note.

      Your worksheet should now look like this:

	C	D	E	F	G
2					
3		1,009.39	125,000	150,000	175,000
4		2.5%			
5		3.0%			
6		3.5%			
7		4.0%			

      You are now ready to create your two-input data table.

11 Create a two-input data table to show monthly payments for each capital amount and interest rate.

   1. Select cells D3:L30.

   2. Click: Data→Data Tools→What-If Analysis→Data Table...

      The *Data Table* dialog appears.

      The *row input cell* is the *Loan Amount* in cell B4.

      The *column input cell* is the *Interest Rate* in cell B7.

      Note that you could take the view that the amount financed in cell B10 is the correct row input cell. You're using cell B4 as it represents how much capital you would have available if your lender demands a 10% deposit.

   3. Enter these values into the dialog and then click *OK*.

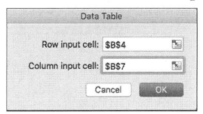

   4. Select cells E4:L30.

   5. Click: Home→Number→Comma Style.

      The numbers are formatted with a thousand comma separator and two decimal places.

      The two-input data table is complete.

	C	D	E	F	G
2					
3		1,009.39	125,000	150,000	175,000
4		2.5%	504.69	605.63	706.57
5		3.0%	533.49	640.19	746.88
6		3.5%	563.20	675.84	788.48
7		4.0%	593.82	712.58	831.34

      The value in cell D3 looks a little untidy. See the sidebar tip if you'd like it to become invisible.

12 Save your work as *Mortgage-3*.

Lesson 5-3: Define scenarios

When you create a set of input values, it is referred to as a scenario.

For example, here's a scenario:

Forecasted sales for next month are: 1,500 Grommets, 4,300 Sprockets, 3,100 Widgets and 2,800 Flugel Valves.

You enter the scenario's values into the input cells:

	A	B
3	Input Cells	Units
4	Grommets	1,500
5	Sprockets	4,300
6	Widgets	3,100
7	Flugel valves	2,800

… and the result cells display the result:

	A	B
15	Result Cells	
16	Sales	842,280.00
17	Cost	643,230.00
18	Profit	199,050.00
19	Gross Profit Pct	23.6%

Sometimes, you will have several different scenarios that you want to compare side-by-side. For example, you may ask your salesmen for *"worst case, expected case* and *best case"* scenarios.

	A	B	C	D
21	Scenarios			
22	Product	Worst Case	Expected Case	Best Case
23	Grommets	750	1,500	2,200
24	Sprockets	4,100	4,300	4,350
25	Widgets	2,000	3,100	3,750
26	Flugel valves	2,400	2,800	2,950

Excel's *Scenario Manager* is designed to enable you to easily compare these scenarios side-by-side.

1   Open *Profit Forecast-1 from* your sample files folder.

Notice that this worksheet has been grouped to show four sets of values:

- Input Cells (referred to as *changing cells* in Excel scenarios).
- Constants (cells that do not, or rarely, change their values).
- Result Cells (cells that change when input cells change).
- Scenarios (values for best, worst and expected case).

2   Create single-cell range names for the input and result cells.

This was covered in depth in: *Lesson 4-1: Automatically create single-cell range names.*

As you'll see later, in: *Lesson 5-4: Create a scenario summary report,* the *Scenario Manager* expects you to define range names for input and result cells in order to correctly display scenario summary reports.

1.   Select cells A4:B7.

note

The scenario manager can only handle 32 changing cells

If you try to define more than 32 changing cells, Excel will display an error message.

Profit Forecast-1

2. Click: Formulas→Defined Names→Create from Selection.

3. Click the *OK* button.

4. Repeat for cells A16:B19.

3 Define the scenarios listed in cells A22:D26.

1. Click: Data→Data Tools→What-If Analysis→ Scenario Manager...

   The *Scenario Manager* dialog appears.

2. Click the ⊞ button to add a new scenario.

3. Type **Worst Case** into the *Scenario name* box.

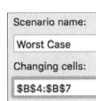

4. Click in the *Changing cells* box and select cells B4:B7 with the mouse.

   The *Scenario Manager* uses the term *Changing cells* to refer to *Input Cells*.

5. Click the *OK* button.

   You're now prompted to enter values for each of the changing cells.

6. Click each of the product names and enter the *Worst Case* values (shown in cells B23:B26).

Grommets:	**750**
Sprockets:	**4100**
Widgets:	**2000**
Flugel_valves:	**2400**

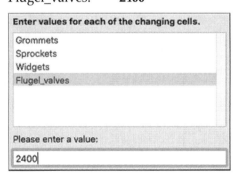

7. Click the *Add* button and then use the same technique to add the *Expected Case* and *Best Case* scenarios.

4 Use the Scenario Manager to view result cells for each scenario.

1. Select one of the cases in the *Scenarios* list.

2. Click the *Show* button to display the scenario on the worksheet.

3. Select a different case and click the *Show* button.

4. Click the *Close* button to close the Scenario Manager.

5 Save your work as *Profit Forecast-2*.

Lesson 5-4: Create a scenario summary report

note

Merging scenarios

Excel allows you to merge scenarios from one or more other workbooks.

Imagine that you send a worksheet out to three salesmen: Tom, Dick and Harry.

Your salesmen are well trained in Excel and know how to define a scenario.

You instruct each of them to forecast their sales by completing the input cells on their worksheet. They then name a scenario with their own name which references the input cells.

When you receive their workbooks, you merge them with your summary workbook like this:

1. Make sure that the *Tom, Dick Harry,* and *Summary* workbooks are open (they are in the sample files if you want to follow through).

2. Make sure that you are viewing the *Summary* workbook.

2. Click: Data→Data Tools→ What-If Analysis→ Scenario Manager.

3. Click the *Merge...* button.

4. Select *Sheet1* of the *Tom* workbook.

5. Click *OK*.

6. Do the same for *Dick* and *Harry*.

The three scenarios *Tom, Dick* and *Harry* are now available in the *Summary* workbook.

When scenarios have been defined, it is possible to display a neatly formatted report or pivot table, showing each scenario side-by-side.

1 Open *Profit Forecast-2 from* your sample files folder (if it isn't already open).

2 Open the Scenario Manager.

Click: Data→Data Tools→What-If Analysis→Scenario Manager...

The *Scenario Manager* dialog is displayed:

3 Create a *Scenario Summary* report.

1. Click the *Summary...* button.

The *Scenario Summary* dialog is displayed.

This dialog asks which result cells should be displayed on the report.

2. Delete the current contents of the *Result cells* box.

3. Select cells B16:B19 with the mouse:

Note that it is possible to show the report as either a *Scenario summary* or as a *Scenario PivotTable* report. You'll learn about PivotTable reports later, in: **Session Eight: Pivot Tables**.

4. Click the *OK* button.

The *Scenario Summary* report is displayed on its own worksheet.

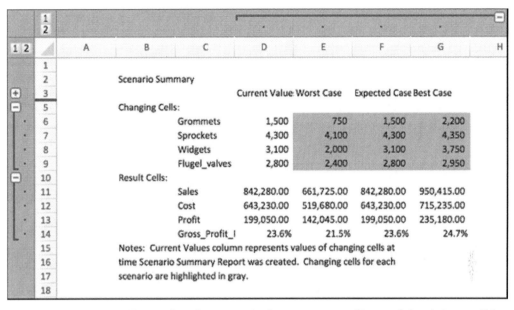

Notice that the report is shown as an outline and that it is possible to collapse and expand the outline by clicking on the plus and minus buttons or on the number buttons in the top left corner.

You can now see how important it was to define named ranges for the input and result cells. Without these, the report would show cell references rather than descriptive names such as *Flugel_valves*.

4   Save your work as *Profit Forecast-3*.

Lesson 5-5: Use Goal Seek

It is very easy to view result values by changing input values. You simply type the new values into the input cells.

	A	B
1	Mortgage	
2		
3	Input Cells	
4	Loan Amount	300,000
5	Deposit (%)	20%
6	Term (Years)	20
7	Interest Rate (APR%)	6.6%
8		
9	Result Cells	
10	Loan Financed	240,000
11	Monthly Repayment	1,803.53
12	Total amount to be repaid	432,848
13	Total interest to be repaid	192,848

In the above worksheet, I wanted to know the monthly repayment for a 300,000 loan with a 20% deposit over 20 years at 6.6% interest. I simply typed the values into the input cells and viewed the results in the result cells.

Consider the case where you want to know the maximum *Loan Amount* if you can only afford a monthly payment of 1,000. This is more difficult because the result cells contain formulas rather than values.

By using Goal Seek, Excel will change one (and only one) input cell so that the desired value is shown in one result cell.

There's a much more complex tool called Solver. You'll learn about this later, in: *Lesson 5-6: Use Solver*. Solver is a more advanced goal seek tool, able to automatically set multiple input cells.

For now, you'll examine the simple and extremely useful Goal Seek tool.

1   Open *Mortgage-3* from your sample files folder.

2   Create a new worksheet called: *Goal Seek*.

3   Copy cells A1:B13 from the *Variable Interest and Capital* worksheet into the same cells on the *Goal Seek* worksheet.

4   Autosize columns A and B so that all text and values are visible.

5   Use *Goal Seek* to find the maximum *Loan Amount* available if you can afford only 1,000 per month.

   1.   Click in cell B11 (the *Monthly Repayment* cell).

   2.   Click: Data→Data Tools→What-If Analysis→Goal Seek…

Mortgage-3

The *Goal Seek* dialog appears:

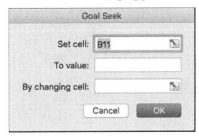

You want to set the *Monthly Repayment* (B11) to the value 1,000 by changing the *Loan Amount* (B4).

3. Complete the dialog as follows:

4. Click the *OK* button.

Goal Seek advises you that it has found a solution:

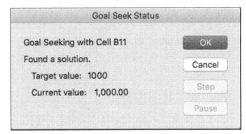

5. Click the *OK* button.

The solution to the problem is shown on the worksheet:

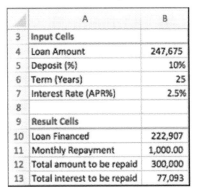

	A	B
3	Input Cells	
4	Loan Amount	247,675
5	Deposit (%)	10%
6	Term (Years)	25
7	Interest Rate (APR%)	2.5%
8		
9	Result Cells	
10	Loan Financed	222,907
11	Monthly Repayment	1,000.00
12	Total amount to be repaid	300,000
13	Total interest to be repaid	77,093

The maximum *Loan Amount* I can raise will be 247,675 if I can only afford 1,000 per month. I could, of course, have also used Goal Seek to change any of the other input cells. The key limitation of Goal Seek is that it can only change one input cell.

6   Save your work as *Mortgage-4*.

Lesson 5-6: Use Solver

What is Solver?

Conceptually, Solver is similar to Goal Seek. While Goal Seek can only change one input cell to set a value in one result cell, Solver can change any number of input cells. This makes the tool a lot more complex.

You can also define a set of rules (called constraints) that Solver needs to observe when finding a solution.

1   Open *Bicycle Manufacturing Schedule-1* from your sample files folder.

This worksheet models a bicycle manufacturing company. The company manufactures four different types of bicycle, but has a limited number of parts available.

- Cells B4:E4 are the input cells (or changing cells) for the worksheet. They define how many bicycles of each model will be manufactured.

- The parts needed to manufacture each type of bicycle are shown in cells B7:E11. For example, a *Street Bike* needs 2 wheels, 1 steel chassis and 1 set of derailleur gears.

- Column I shows how many parts are available.

- Cells B14:F14 show the profit for each bicycle type, along with the total profit for all bicycle types.

Your challenge is to maximize profit by manufacturing the optimum number of each type of bicycle.

2   Install the Solver add-in (if it is not already installed).

1.   Click: ⚲→Tools→Excel Add-ins.

2.   Check the *Solver Add-In* check box and click the *OK* button.

Solver now appears on the ribbon's *Data* tab, in a new *Analysis* group.

Bicycle Manufacturing Schedule-1

note

The SUMPRODUCT function

This worksheet uses the SUMPRODUCT function to calculate the *Parts Needed* in column G and the *Total Profit* in cell F14.

SUMPRODUCT is an array function. Array functions accept ranges as arguments and then perform calculations using each value in the range.

In cell G7 you will find the function:

= SUMPRODUCT($B$4:$E$4, B7:E7)

This will perform the calculation:

B4*B7+C4*C7+D4*D7+E4*E7

trivia

Solver wasn't developed by Microsoft

Solver is a product developed by Frontline Systems, who have now distributed over a billion copies of their product to users.

As well as Excel's Solver, Frontline also developed the solvers included in Lotus 1-2-3 and Quattro Pro.

Every copy of Excel sold since 1990 has included Frontline's Solver.

Frontline also produce a more advanced version of Solver (available at extra cost) called *Premium Solver*. There's also a *Risk Solver* product that enables Excel to model Monte Carlo simulations.

3   Open Solver.

Click: Data→Analysis→Solver.

Solver appears.

4   Let Solver know which are the *Changing* (Input) cells and which is the *Objective* (Result) cell.

Complete the dialog as follows:

You are telling Solver to maximize the profit (shown in cell F14) by changing the *Input Cells* (or *Changing Cells*) B4:E4.

5   Define the constraints for the problem.

1.   Click the *Add* button next to the *Subject to the Constraints* list box.

2.   Complete the dialog as follows:

This tells Solver that it cannot manufacture a negative number of bicycles.

3.   Click the *Add* button.

4.   Set up a second constraint as follows:

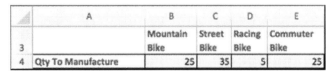

This tells Solver that it cannot use more parts than are available.

5.   Click the *OK* button.

6   Solve the problem.

1.   Click the *Solve* button.

2.   Click the *OK* button.

Solver has solved the problem.

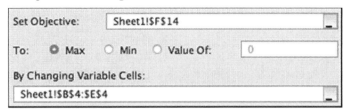

This mix of bicycles maximizes profits to $4,750.

7   Save your work as *Bicycle Manufacturing Schedule-2*.

note

Hiding and unhiding a worksheet using the ribbon

The right-click method is much faster than using the ribbon but here's how it can be done:

To hide a worksheet:

Click: Home➜Cells➜
Format➜
Hide & Unhide➜
Hide Sheet.

To unhide a worksheet:

Click: Home➜Cells➜
Format➜
Hide & Unhide➜
Unhide Sheet.

Then select the sheet that you want to hide/unhide from the dialog and click the *OK* button.

important

Don't rely on hidden worksheets for security

There is no password associated with hiding and unhiding a worksheet, row or column. A knowledgeable user can easily unhide any hidden item.

If you need to hide items more securely, it is possible to protect the structure before distributing a workbook.

When this is done, it isn't possible to unhide and view the hidden items unless you know the password.

Protecting the structure of a workbook will be covered in: *Lesson 5-10: Control the changes users can make to workbooks.*

Human Resources-1

Lesson 5-7: Hide and unhide worksheets, columns and rows

1   Open *Human Resources-1* from your sample files folder.

2   Hide the *Headcount & Salaries* worksheet.

The *Payroll* worksheet depends upon the *Headcount & Salaries* worksheet in order to calculate each employee's hourly rate.

Because this data is sensitive, you may decide to hide the entire *Headcount & Salaries* worksheet.

1. Select the *Headcount & Salaries* worksheet.

2. Right-click the worksheet tab.

3. Click *Hide* from the shortcut menu.

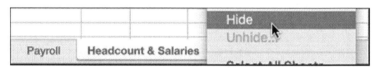

The worksheet disappears.

3   Unhide the *Headcount & Salaries* worksheet.

1. Right-click on any worksheet tab (at the moment the only visible worksheet tab is *Payroll*).

2. Click *Unhide* from the shortcut menu.

    The *Unhide* dialog is displayed, listing all currently hidden worksheets.

3. Click the *OK* button.

    The *Headcount & Salaries* worksheet reappears.

    You can see that this is not a good way to hide confidential information, as any knowledgeable user can simply unhide the worksheet (see sidebar).

4   Hide rows 3:6, rows 19:23 and row 9 on the *Payroll* worksheet.

Perhaps you would like to print out the *Payroll* worksheet for the floor manager so that each employee's hours can be reviewed.

This might be a problem if the salaries had to be kept confidential.

For this reason, you are going to hide the confidential rows on the *Payroll* worksheet before printing.

1. Select the *Payroll* worksheet.

2. Select rows 3 to 6.

3. Right-click anywhere within the selected cells.

4. Click *Hide* from the shortcut menu.

    The rows disappear.

note

Sharing information using screenshots

A screenshot is a little like a photograph of all, or part of a worksheet.

You will often want to paste a read-only depiction of part of a worksheet into an e-mail, Word document, PowerPoint presentation or other Office 2016 document.

To take a screenshot:

1. Select the cells that you want to take a screenshot of.

2. Click:
Home→Clipboard→Copy→
Copy as Picture....

You'll then see the *Copy Picture* dialog:

5. Do the same to hide rows 19:23.

6. Do the same to hide row 9.

The payroll no longer shows any financial values. It would now be possible to print the worksheet (or take a screenshot of the worksheet – see sidebar) without showing the hidden rows.

5 Hide columns E:O on the *Payroll* worksheet.

This is very similar to hiding rows.

1. Select columns E:O.

2. Right-click anywhere in the selected area.

3. Click *Hide* from the shortcut menu.

The columns disappear.

	A	B	C	D
1	Payroll			
8		Johnny Caine	George Marley	Betty Anan
11	Hours Worked			
12	Monday	9	10	10
13	Tuesday	8	9	8
14	Wednesday	10	9	8
15	Thursday	6	8	6
16	Friday	10	7	10
17	Total	43	43	42

6 Unhide columns E:O on the *Payroll* worksheet.

1. Select columns D:P (the columns that are on either side of the hidden columns).

2. Right-click anywhere in the selected area.

3. Click *Unhide* from the shortcut menu.

The columns re-appear.

tip

A faster way to hide a single row or column

A hidden column is simply a column that has its width set to zero.

You can quickly hide a row or column by dragging its border to make it so narrow that it is no longer visible.

7 Unhide all hidden rows on the *Payroll* worksheet.

1. Click the *Select All* button (in the top left corner of the worksheet) to select every cell.

2. Right-click any of the row headers (the numbered buttons on the left of the worksheet).

3. Click *Unhide* from the shortcut menu.

4. All hidden rows re-appear.

There is no need to save this workbook as it has not been changed in any way.

important

Custom views have limitations in Excel 2016 for Windows

Custom views can be created in Excel 2016 for Windows in exactly the same way as shown here for Excel 2016 for Mac, but the Windows version has an important limitation.

In the Windows version, custom views don't work if there is a table anywhere in the workbook.

This won't be a problem if you only use Excel 2016 for Mac, but you should be aware of this limitation if your workbooks need to be usable in the Windows version of Excel.

You can see more about the differences between the Windows and Mac versions of Excel in: *Appendix A: Differences between the Windows and Mac versions of Excel 2016.*

Lesson 5-8: Create custom views

In: *Lesson 5-7: Hide and unhide worksheets, columns and rows*, you learned how useful it can be to hide columns and rows when printing (or taking a screenshot from) a worksheet.

Sometimes you may find that you are continuously hiding and unhiding the same rows and columns in order to print selected parts of a worksheet. When you notice that this is happening, you have an ideal candidate for a custom view.

Custom views allow you to save and recall worksheet layouts that have hidden columns and rows.

1   Open *Human Resources-1* from your sample files folder (if it isn't already open).

2   Select the *Payroll* worksheet.

3   Save the current view as *HR*.

    1.   Click: View→Workbook Views→Custom Views.

       The *Custom Views* dialog appears:

    2.   Click the ⊞ button.

       The *Add View* dialog appears.

    3.   Type **HR** into the *Name* box.

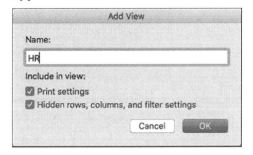

Human Resources-1

Notice that custom views don't only save hidden rows and columns.

Custom views also save all of the following:

- *Print settings*, including any *Page Layout* settings.
- Any filters that are currently applied to the worksheet.
- The zoom factor.
- Window sizes and positions.
- The currently active cell.
- The current worksheet view (*Normal* or *Page Layout*).

4. Click the *OK* button.

Nothing seems to have happened but you have, in fact, stored a view with all rows and columns visible.

4   Hide rows 3:6, rows 19:23 and row 9 on the *Payroll* worksheet.

This was covered in: *Lesson 5-7: Hide and unhide worksheets, columns and rows.*

5   Save the current view as: **Hours Worked**

Do this in the same way that you saved the *HR* custom view earlier.

6   Hide columns B,C,F,G,H,I,J,K,L and N.

7   Save the current view as: **Hours Worked (Female)**

8   Show the *Hours Worked* view.

1. Click: View→Workbook Views→Custom Views.

The *Custom Views* dialog is displayed, showing the three saved views:

2. Click the *Hours Worked* view in the *Views* list.

3. Click the *Show* button.

The worksheet changes to show the *Hours Worked* view.

9   Show the *Hours Worked (Female)* view.

10   Show the *HR* view.

11   Save your work as *Human Resources-2*.

important

Secure passwords

Hacking tools (freely available on the Internet) commonly use five methods to discover passwords:

1. Dictionary attack

In a matter of seconds, the tool tries every word in the dictionary. For this reason, your password should never be a real word such as *London*.

2. Dictionary + numbers

The tool makes several passes through the dictionary, appending a sequential number to the front or back of the password. For this reason, your password should never be a real word with leading or trailing numbers, such as *London99* or *99London*.

3. Reverse words

The tool tries every word in the dictionary spelled backwards.

4. Words with the letter O replaced with a zero

5. *Brute force* attack

The tool tries every possible combination of the letters of the alphabet. It currently takes up to 13 minutes for a dual-core Pentium to crack a seven letter single-case password such as: *xcoekfh*.

For ultimate security against brute force attacks, include upper and lower case letters, numbers, and symbols in your passwords. The best approach is to create a password from a phrase such as: "I like to ride my Honda motorcycle at 100 MPH". This gives the extremely secure password: *IltrmHm@100MPH*

This password would take up to 5 million years to crack with a dual-core Pentium.

Human Resources-2

Lesson 5-9: Prevent unauthorized users from opening or modifying workbooks

There are two levels of password protection available when you save a workbook. You can:

- Prevent users from opening the workbook.

- Prevent users from changing a workbook once they have opened it.

In this lesson you'll implement both types of protection.

1   Open *Human Resources-2* from your sample files folder (if it isn't already open).

2   Protect the workbook with a password that will prevent other users from opening it.

　　1.　Click: ⌘→File→Save As.

　　　　The *Save As* dialog is displayed.

　　2.　Click: *Options* at the bottom of the dialog.

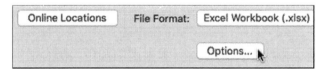

　　3.　Type a password in the *Password to open* box.

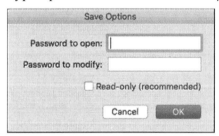

　　　　See the *secure passwords* sidebar for important information about choosing an appropriate password.

　　　　See the facing page sidebar for a discussion of the *Read-only recommended* check box option.

　　4.　Click the *OK* button.

　　　　Excel reminds you not to forget the password and prompts for it again to protect against accidental typing errors.

　　5.　Type the password again.

　　6.　Click the *OK* button.

　　7.　Click the *Save* button.

　　8.　If necessary, click *Replace* to overwrite the existing file.

note

Excel passwords do not provide 100% security

Even if you choose a secure password that is nine or more characters long, there are tools freely available on the Internet that can crack most of the Excel 2016 worksheet protection passwords in minutes. Currently, only the *password to open* is not easily cracked.

The *password to open* is encrypted using the AES 128 standard.

This encryption standard is approved by the US government to encrypt classified documents up to SECRET level. This suggests that it is extremely secure.

note

The Read-only option

If you check the *Read-only (recommended)* check box, the user is presented with a dialog when opening a protected workbook. The dialog suggests that the workbook be opened read-only.

If the user ignores this suggestion, a read/write copy will be opened. As you discovered in this lesson, this copy cannot be used to over-write the protected file, but can be used to create a new file with a different name.

3 Close the *Human Resources-2* workbook and then try to re-open it.

Without the password you are unable to open the workbook.

4 Enter the password and click *OK* to open the workbook.

5 Remove the password from the workbook.

1. Click: ⌘→File→Save As.

2. Click: *Options* at the bottom of the dialog.

3. Remove the password from the *Passsword to open* box.

4. Click *OK*.

5. Click *Save*.

6. Click *Replace* to overwrite the existing file.

6 Protect the workbook with a password that will prevent other users from changing it.

Follow the same procedure as you did when adding a *Password to open*, but this time specify a *Password to modify*.

7 Save and close the workbook.

8 Open *Human Resources-2* read only.

1. Click: ⌘→File→Open Recent→Human Resources-2.

2. The *Password* dialog appears.

3. Click the *Read Only* button without entering a password.

   This doesn't have the effect you might expect. You've opened the workbook without a password and are able to change it.

9 Attempt to save the workbook.

Surprisingly, Excel will only prevent you from saving the workbook with the same name as the password-protected workbook. Excel is quite happy for you to make a copy and even prompts you to do so when you attempt to save the file.

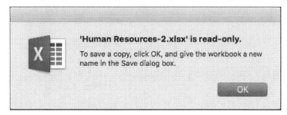

10 Save the workbook as *Human Resources-3*.

This workbook no longer has password protection.

Lesson 5-10: Control the changes users can make to workbooks

Sometimes you are quite happy for any user to open your workbook, but you need to prevent them from inserting, deleting, renaming, moving, hiding or unhiding any of the worksheets or worksheet elements. This is called protecting the *Structure* of a workbook.

Some worksheets are intended to be viewed in a worksheet window that has been set to a specific size. In this case, you need to prevent your users from moving or re-sizing the worksheet windows. This is called protecting the *Windows* of a workbook.

In this lesson, you'll discover how to protect a workbook's structure, windows, or both.

1   Open *Human Resources-3* from your sample files folder (if it isn't already open).

2   Display the *Hours Worked (Female)* custom view.

   This was covered in: *Lesson 5-8: Create custom views.*

3   Hide the *Headcount & Salaries* worksheet.

   This was covered in: *Lesson 5-7: Hide and unhide worksheets, columns and rows.*

4   Exit full screen view.

   If you are viewing the workbook in full-screen view, press the <Escape> key to return to normal view. You need to do this in order to resize the window in the next step.

5   Re-size the Payroll worksheet window so that it fits cells A1:O17 as closely as possible.

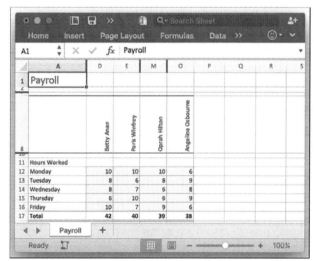

6   Protect the structure and windows of the workbook.

   1.   Click: Review→Changes→Protect Workbook.

      A dialog is displayed.

Human Resources-3

2. Check both of the check boxes and add a password.

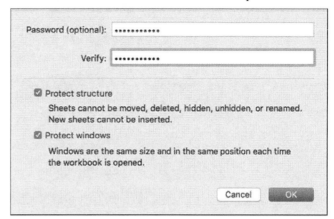

3. Click the *OK* button.

   Because you checked the *Windows* check box, you are now unable to re-size or move the workbook window.

7 Attempt to unhide the Headcount & Salaries worksheet.

   Right-click on the *Payroll* worksheet tab.

   Notice that the *Unhide* option is grayed out and unavailable. This has happened because you have protected the structure of the workbook.

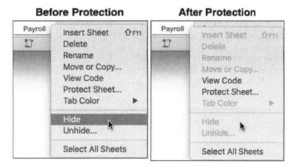

   Notice also that the *Insert Sheet, Delete, Rename, Move or Copy, Tab Color* and *Hide* options are now unavailable.

8 Remove password protection from the structure and windows.

1. Click: Review→Changes→Protect Workbook.

   You are prompted for the password to remove protection:

2. Enter the password and click the OK button.

   Protection is removed.

9 Unhide the *Headcount & Salaries* worksheet.

10 Display the *HR* custom view.

   There's no need to save the workbook as it has not changed.

Lesson 5-11: Restrict the cells users are allowed to change

1   Open *Human Resources-3* from your sample files folder (if it isn't already open).

2   Display the *Hours Worked* custom view.

This was covered in: *Lesson 5-8: Create custom views.*

3   Hide the *Headcount and Salaries* worksheet.

This was covered in: *Lesson 5-7: Hide and unhide worksheets, columns and rows.*

4   Re-size columns B:O so that they are just wide enough to display their contents:

A	B	C	D	E	F	G	H	I	J	K	L	M	N	O
1 Payroll														
8	Johnny Caine	George Marley	Betty Anan	Paris Winfrey	Ozzy Dickens	Johnny Roberts	Charles Monroe	Ronnie Bush	Michal Jolie	JK Spears	Ozzy Rowling	Oprah Hilton	Bill Biggs	Angelina Osbourne
11 Hours Worked														
12 Monday	9	10	10	10	7	7	7	7	7	7	7	10	8	6
13 Tuesday	8	9	8	6	10	10	10	7	6	10	7	8	7	9
14 Wednesday	10	9	8	7	9	8	6	8	7	8	8	6	6	8
15 Thursday	6	8	6	10	9	7	6	6	7	8	8	6	6	9
16 Friday	10	7	10	7	9	10	9	8	8	10	8	9	10	6
17 Total	43	43	42	40	44	42	38	36	35	43	38	39	37	38

The challenge this time will be to prevent the user from changing any value other than those in the yellow shaded cells (cells B12:O16).

You will solve this problem by *unlocking* these cells and then *protecting* the worksheet. This will only allow the user to enter values into the *unlocked* cells.

5   Unlock cells B12:O16.

All cells on a worksheet are (by default) *locked*. You are able to type values into them because the worksheet is not yet *protected*.

In order to prevent the user from changing any cell except cells B12:O16 you need to do two things:

•   Unlock the cells that you want the user to be able to change.

•   Protect the worksheet.

Here's how to unlock the cells:

1.   Select cells B12:O16.

2.   Right click anywhere in the selected area.

3.   Click *Format Cells…* from the shortcut menu.

tip

Use cell locking to make forms more user-friendly

Excel is often used to create forms (such as booking forms). The form is sent to the user by e-mail and the user completes and returns it.

This type of form becomes much easier to use if you do the following:

1. Unlock the cells that the user should type data into.

2. Protect the worksheet making sure that only the *Select unlocked cells* option is checked.

When this is done, the user can use the **<Tab>** key to navigate through all of the cells in the form that need to be completed.

Human Resources-3

note

You can keep your formulas secret with the Hidden attribute

If you set the *Hidden* attribute on the *Format Cells→Protection* tab, users will not be able to see any of your formulas.

Even if a cell is unlocked, the formula does not display in the formula bar when the cell is selected. This could be used if the formula used to calculate a value was a "trade secret".

This will only take effect when the worksheet is protected.

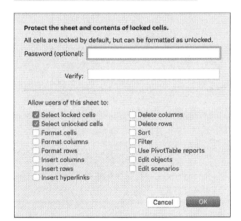

tip

Leave all cells locked to distribute a read-only workbook

If you protect a workbook without unlocking any cells, you have effectively created a read-only workbook.

To prevent the user from copying and pasting the contents, you should also un-check the *Select locked cells* check box. Note that the user will still be able to click:

Insert→Illustrations→Screenshot

...from any another Office application to copy an image of the worksheet.

4. Click the *Protection* tab.

5. Uncheck the *Locked* check box.

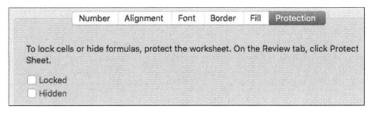

See sidebar for more about the *Hidden* attribute.

6. Click the *OK* button.

6 Protect the *Payroll* worksheet so that the user is unable to change or select any of the locked cells.

When you protect a worksheet, it is no longer possible to change the contents of a *locked* cell.

1. Click: Review→Changes→Protect Sheet.

   A dialog appears

   The default settings allow the user to select (but not change) the contents of locked cells. This normally makes sense, as you want the user to be able to copy and paste any part of the worksheet.

   In this case, however, it creates a huge security problem as the user can easily copy the entire worksheet, paste it into a new worksheet, and then unhide the hidden rows.

   For this reason, you want to prevent the user from selecting locked cells.

2. Uncheck the *Select locked cells* check box.

   Notice that, by default, the user is prevented from doing many more things to the worksheet (such as formatting cells). You can selectively allow these actions by checking the appropriate check boxes.

3. Enter a password.

4. Click the *OK* button.

7 Test the protected worksheet.

You are unable to change (or even select) any of the locked cells but you can select and change any of the unlocked cells.

8 Unprotect the worksheet.

1. Click: Review→Changes→Unprotect Sheet.

2. Enter the password, and then click the *OK* button.

9 Lock cells B12:O16.

Do this in the same way that you unlocked the cells, but this time check the *Locked* check box (instead of un-checking it).

10 Save your work as *Human Resources-4*.

Session 5: Exercise

1 Open *Selling Price Calculator-1* from your sample files folder.

	A	B
3	Input Cells	
4	Cost	$ 4.50
5	Retail Price	$ 17.95
6	Wholesale Discount	60%
7	Annual Units	2,000.00
8		
9	Result Cells	
10	Sales (at wholesale price)	$ 14,360.00
11	Total Cost	$ 9,000.00
12	Gross Profit	$ 5,360.00
13	Gross Profit Percent	37%

2 Create an attractively formatted single input data table in cells D3:F18 to display the *Gross Profit* and *Gross Profit Percent* that would result from a *Retail Price* of $17.95 to $24.95 in increments of $0.50.

	D	E	F
3	Retail Price	Gross Profit	Gross Profit Percent
4	$ 17.95	$ 5,360.00	37%
5	$ 18.45	$ 5,760.00	39%
6	$ 18.95	$ 6,160.00	41%

3 Hide columns D:F.

4 Use *Goal Seek* to calculate the *Retail Price* that would be needed to produce exactly 50% *Gross Profit*.

5 Create range names for cells B4:B7 and cells B10:B13 using the names in cells A4:A7 and A10:A13.

6 Use the scenario manager to create three scenarios:

Worst Case: 2,000 Annual Units
Expected Case: 3,500 Annual Units
Best Case: 5,000 Annual Units

7 Create a *Scenario Summary* report to show *Sales, Total Cost, Gross Profit* and *Gross Profit Percent* values for each scenario.

Scenario Summary		Current Value	Worst Case	Expected Case	Best Case
Changing Cells:					
	Annual_Units	2,000.00	2,000.00	3,500.00	5,000.00
Result Cells:					
	Sales__at_wholesale_price	$ 17,998.98	$ 17,998.98	$ 31,498.22	$ 44,997.45
	Total_Cost	$ 9,000.00	$ 9,000.00	$ 15,750.00	$ 22,500.00
	Gross_Profit	$ 8,998.98	$ 8,998.98	$ 15,748.22	$ 22,497.45
	Gross_Profit_Percent	50%	50%	50%	50%

8 Protect the *Selling Price Calculator* worksheet so that only cells B4:B7 (the cells shaded yellow) can be changed.

9 Save your work as *Selling Price Calculator-2*.

Selling Price Calculator-1

If you need help slide the page to the left

Session 5: Exercise Answers

These are the four questions that students find the most difficult to answer:

Q 6	Q 5	Q 4	Q 2
1. Click: Data→ Data Tools→ What-If Analysis→ Scenario Manager…	1. Select cells A4:B7.	1. Click: Data→ Data Tools→ What-If Analysis→ Goal Seek…	1. Type **Retail Price**, **Gross Profit** and **Gross Profit Percent** into cells D3, E3 and F3.
2. Click the ⊞ button.	2. Click: Formulas→ Defined Names→ Create from Selection.	2. Complete the dialog as follows:	2. AutoSize columns D:F so that all text is visible.
3. Type **Worst Case** into the *Scenario name* box.	3. Click *OK*.	Set cell: $B$13 To value: 50% By changing cell: $B$5	3. Enter the formula: =**B5** into cell D4, =**B12** into cell E4 and =**B13** into cell F4.
Scenario name: Worst Case	4. Repeat for cells A10:B13.	3. Click *OK* and *OK* again.	4. Enter the formula: =**D4+0.5** into cell D5.
4. Click in the *Changing cells* box and then click on cell B7.	This was covered in: *Lesson 4-1: Automatically create single-cell range names.*	This was covered in: *Lesson 5-5: Use Goal Seek.*	5. Autofill cell D5 to cells D6:D18.
Changing cells: $B$7			6. Copy cells D5:D18 and then paste them back into the same location using *Paste Values*.
5. Click the *OK* button.			7. Select cells D4:F18.
6. Type **2000** into the value box.			8. Click: Data→ Data Tools→ What-If Analysis→ Data Table…
Please enter a value: 2000			9. Set the *Column input cell* to: $B$5 and click *OK*.
7. Click the *Add…* button.			10. Use the *Format Painter* to attractively format each column and the column headers.
8. Complete the same steps for the *Expected Case* and *Best Case* scenarios.			This was covered in: *Lesson 5-1: Create a single-input data table.*
This was covered in: *Lesson 5-3: Define scenarios.*			

If you have difficulty with the other questions, here are the lessons that cover the relevant skills:

3   Refer to: *Lesson 5-7: Hide and unhide worksheets, columns and rows.*

7   Refer to: *Lesson 5-4: Create a scenario summary report.*

8   Refer to: *Lesson 5-11: Restrict the cells users are allowed to change.*

Session Six: Working with Hyperlinks, Other Applications and Workgroups

> Teamwork is the ability to work together toward a common vision.
> The ability to direct individual accomplishments toward
> organizational objectives. It is the fuel that allows common people to
> attain uncommon results.
>
> *Andrew Carnegie (1835-1919)*
> *Industrialist, businessman and entrepreneur*

Anybody who opens an Excel workbook these days will have also spent many hours navigating the Internet using a web browser. Navigating web sites by clicking on hyperlinks will feel natural and intuitive to them.

In this session you'll discover how you can also implement a hyperlink based navigation system in large workbooks, so that even users with no Excel skills will immediately feel at home when viewing your work.

This session will also show you how to embed Excel objects into other Office applications such as PowerPoint and Outlook.

Team projects may require several members of a workgroup to open and update a workbook at the same time. By the end of this session you'll be able to use all of Excel's powerful workbook sharing features.

Session Objectives

By the end of this session you will be able to:

- Hyperlink to worksheets and ranges
- Hyperlink to other workbooks and the Internet
- Embed an Excel worksheet object into a Word document
- Link an Excel worksheet to a Word document
- Embed an Excel chart object into a Word document
- Understand the three different ways to share a workbook
- Share a workbook using the lock method
- Share a workbook using the merge method
- Share a workbook on a network
- Accept and reject changes to shared workbooks

Lesson 6-1: Hyperlink to worksheets and ranges

Because just about everybody uses a web browser, the "point and click" method of doing things comes naturally to most users.

It is possible to give users the same browser-like experience by adding hyperlinks to your workbooks in order to mimic web browser navigation. This isn't just a presentational gimmick; hyperlink browsing is the most efficient way to quickly navigate to specific parts of long multi-page documents.

1 Open *Monaco-1* from your sample files folder.

This worksheet has a lot of information about Monaco (the second smallest independent state in the world at only 2 sq km).

2 Create a worksheet hyperlink from cell A5 in the *Main Menu* worksheet to the *Background* worksheet.

1. Select cell A5 on the *Main Menu* worksheet.

2. Click: Insert→Links→Hyperlink.

   The *Insert Hyperlink* dialog appears.

3. Click *This Document* at the top of the dialog.

4. Click *Background* from the *Or select a place in this document* tree view.

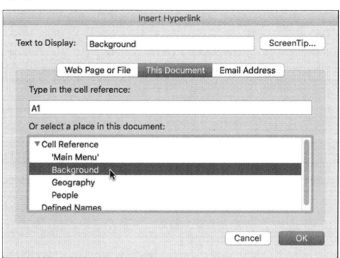

5. Click the *OK* button.

   The text in cell A5 has changed into a hyperlink:

	A
3	**Main Sections**
5	Background
6	Geography
7	People

It is also possible to define a screen tip for the hyperlink (see sidebar).

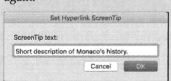
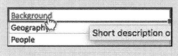
Monaco-1

3   Create worksheet hyperlinks from cells A6 and A7 to the *Geography* and *People* worksheets.

Do this in the same way that you created the *Background* hyperlink.

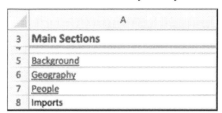

4   Create a range name called *Climate* for cells A32:A33 on the *Geography* worksheet.

    1.   Select cells A32:A33 on the *Geography* worksheet.

    2.   Click: Formulas→Defined Names→Create from Selection.

    3.   Click the *OK* button.

5   Create range names called *Population* and *Life expectancy at birth* for cells A3:A5 and A50:A54 on the *People* worksheet.

Note that the range name: *Life_expectancy_at_birth* will be created with underscores, as range names cannot contain spaces.

6   Make cells A12, A13 and A14 on the *Main Menu* worksheet into hyperlinks pointing to the range names that you created.

    1.   Select cell A12 on the *Main Menu* worksheet.

    2.   Click: Insert→Links→Hyperlink.

    The *Insert Hyperlink* dialog appears.

    3.   Click *This Document* at the top of the dialog.

    4.   Expand the *Defined Names* section in the the *Or select a place in this document* tree view.

    5.   Click *Climate* in the *Defined Names* section.

    6.   Click the *OK* button.

    7.   Do the same for *Population* and *Life Expectancy*.

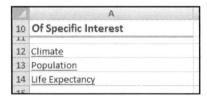

7   Test your hyperlinks.

When you click upon any of the six defined hyperlinks, you are taken to the relevant defined worksheet or range.

8   Save your work as *Monaco-2*.

Lesson 6-2: Hyperlink to other workbooks and the Internet

1   Open *Monaco-2* from your sample files folder (if it isn't already open).

2   Create a hyperlink from cell A8 in the *Main Menu* worksheet to the *Monaco Economy-1* workbook.

  1. Select cell A8.

  2. Click: Insert→Links→Hyperlink.

  3. Click *Web Page or File* at the top of the *Insert Hyperlink* dialog.

  4. Click *Select*, and then the *Monaco Economy-1* file in your sample files folder.

  5. Click the *Open* button and click the *OK* button.

  6. Click the *Imports* hyperlink in cell A8.

  7. The *Monaco Economy-1* workbook opens. Note that the hyperlink took you to cell A1, but the *Imports* data is actually in cells A74:A77.

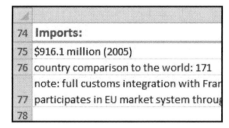

3   Expand the hyperlink to include cells A74:A77.

  Once Excel has done the hard work of constructing a hyperlink to a different workbook it is easy to expand it to point to a range if required.

  1. Click: →Window→Monaco-2.

  You are returned to the *Monaco-2* workbook.

  2. If it's not already selected, move the cursor to cell A8 using the keyboard arrow keys (if you simply click the cell you will execute the hyperlink).

  3. Click: Insert→Links→Hyperlink.

  The hyperlink address is visible in the *Address* box.

  Depending on the version of Excel you are using, you may see a *%20* code in place of spaces. This is normal in hyperlinks.

note

Email hyperlinks

You might have noticed the *Email Address* option in the *Insert Hyperlink* dialog. This allows you to create a hyperlink to an email address.

When you click an email hyperlink, the *Mail* program opens and creates a new message to the specified address.

tip

Selecting a hyperlink cell with the mouse

In this lesson, you used the keyboard arrow keys to select a cell containing a hyperlink.

There's also a way to do this using the mouse.

If you click and hold the mouse button down for a second or two, you can select a hyperlinked cell without activating the hyperlink.

Monaco-2

note

You can also hyperlink to non-Excel files such as Word documents

When you set the *Link to* type to *Existing File or Web Page*, you are able to link to any file on your computer.

Most files know which application opens them, so if you link to a Word document, the document will open in Word when you click the hyperlink.

This opens up a huge range of possibilities. You could create a hyperlink on a worksheet that will:

- Play an MP3 sound file.
- View an MP4 video.
- Open a Word document.

... and do anything else that any application installed on your computer is capable of.

4. Edit the hyperlink to reference the range A74:A77 on the *Economy* worksheet by changing the *Address* to the following:

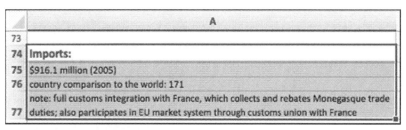

Address: Monaco%20Economy-1.xlsx#Economy!A74:A77

5. Click the *OK* button.

4 Test the hyperlink.

When you click the *Imports* hyperlink, you are taken to the *Economy* worksheet in the *Monaco Economy-1* workbook with cells A74:A77 selected.

	A
73	
74	Imports:
75	$916.1 million (2005)
76	country comparison to the world: 171
77	note: full customs integration with France, which collects and rebates Monegasque trade duties; also participates in EU market system through customs union with France

5 Return to the *Monaco-2* workbook.

Click: ⌘→Window→Monaco-2.

6 Make cell A17 on the *Main Menu* worksheet into a *Web Page* hyperlink pointing to the *Monaco Tourist Office* website at: **www.visitmonaco.com**

1. Select cell A17 on the *Main Menu* worksheet.

2. Click: Insert→Links→Hyperlink.

3. Click *Web Page or File* at the top of the *Insert Hyperlink* dialog.

4. Type **http://www.visitmonaco.com** into the *Address* box.

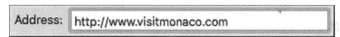

Address: http://www.visitmonaco.com

Excel will add http:// in front of the address automatically if you leave it out.

5. Click the *OK* button.

Cell A17 is converted into a hyperlink pointing to the *Monaco Government Tourist Office* website.

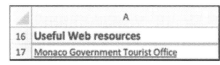

	A
16	Useful Web resources
17	Monaco Government Tourist Office

7 Save your work as *Monaco-3*.

Lesson 6-3: Embed an Excel worksheet object into a Word document

Microsoft Office is an object-orientated application. Simply put, this means that everything you work with in Office is an object.

An Excel cell, an Excel range of cells, an Excel table, an Excel chart, a Word document and a PowerPoint slide are all objects.

The wonderful thing about this object-orientated architecture is that you can freely embed objects inside other objects. For example, you can embed an Excel range into a Word document, or an Excel chart into a PowerPoint presentation.

In this lesson you'll embed an Excel worksheet into a Word document.

1   Open Microsoft Word.

2   Use Word to open *The World's Best Selling Cars-1* (Word document) from your sample files folder.

This file contains the beginning of a Word document:

> The World's Best Selling Cars
>
> Some cars sell well, others hardly sell at all. Once every few years a car comes along that is demonstrably better than its competition. The car may beat the competition on price, performance, reliability, style or a combination of these factors.
>
> Here is a list of the world's most successful cars to date:

3   Embed an Excel worksheet at the end of the word document.

1. Click just to the right of the sentence *"Here is a list of the world's most successful cars to date:"*.

2. Press the **<Enter>** key to move to the next line.

3. Click: Insert→Text→Object→Object… (see sidebar if you can't find the *Text* group).

    The *Object* dialog appears.

4. Select *Microsoft Excel Worksheet* from the *Object type* list.

Object type:
Microsoft Excel 97 - 2004 Worksheet
Microsoft Excel Binary Worksheet
Microsoft Excel Chart
Microsoft Excel Macro-Enabled Worksheet
Microsoft Excel Worksheet

5. Click the *OK* button.

    Excel opens and displays a new, blank worksheet. If you look at the title bar, you can see: *Worksheet in The World's Best Selling Cars-1*.

    > Worksheet in The World's Best Selling Cars-1

note

Displaying ribbon group titles in Word

Just like Excel, Word 2016 for Mac hides the names of ribbon groups by default. You will need to configure Word to display group names in order to follow the instructions in this book.

To display the group titles in Word, follow these steps:

1. Click:
→Word→Preferences.

2. Click the *View* button.

3. In the *Ribbon* group, make sure that *Show group titles* is checked.

The World's Best Selling Cars-1

You are now editing the worksheet that you have inserted into the Word document.

4   Enter the following data into the worksheet:

	A	B	C
1	Make	Model	Sales (Million)
2	Ford	Escort	18
3	Volkswagen	Beetle	23.5
4	Volkswagen	Golf	27.5
5	Ford	F Series	35
6	Toyota	Corolla	40

(When you have entered the data, AutoSize each column so that each is wide enough to display the contents).

5   Return to Word.

Click the Word icon on the Dock to return to the Word window.

Notice that the worksheet looks just as it would in Excel. The worksheet is too big, however, as there are many empty cells.

Here is a list of the world's most successful cars to date:

Make	Model	Sales (Million)		
Ford	Escort	18		
Volkswagen	Beetle	23.5		
Volkswagen	Golf	27.5		
Ford	F Series	35		
Toyota	Corolla	40		

Unfortunately, it isn't possible to resize an embedded Excel worksheet in the Mac version of Word 2016. The only way to make the worksheet shrink to the correct size is to save a copy of it and embed the worksheet again.

6   Save a copy of the worksheet.

1. Double click the worksheet within the Word document.

    You are returned to Excel with the embedded worksheet open.

2. Click: ➜File➜Save Copy As.

3. Save the workbook as: **The World's Best Selling Cars**

You'll link this file back to the Word document in the next lesson.

7   Close Excel.

8   Return to Word.

9   Save your work as *The World's Best Selling Cars-2.*

Lesson 6-4: Link an Excel worksheet to a Word document

1   Open Microsoft Word.

2   Open *The World's Best Selling Cars-2* from your sample files folder.

This file contains the embedded Excel worksheet that you created in the previous lesson.

Here is a list of the world's most successful cars to date:				
Make	Model	Sales (Million)		
Ford	Escort	18		
Volkswagen	Beetle	23.5		
Volkswagen	Golf	27.5		
Ford	F Series	35		
Toyota	Corolla	40		

The worksheet is too big for its contents, and unfortunately there is no way to resize it.

The solution is to delete the worksheet and embed it again, this time as a linked file.

3   Delete the existing embedded worksheet.

Click the worksheet and press the **<Delete>** key.

4   Insert the *The World's Best Selling Cars* Excel workbook as a linked object.

The *World's Best Selling Cars* workbook contains the same data as the worksheet that you just deleted.

1.   Click: Insert→Text→Object→Object.

The *Object* dialog is displayed.

2.   Click the *From File* button.

3.   Click the *Options* button in the bottom left corner of the screen.

Options

4.   Check the *Link to File* check box.

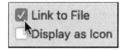

5.   Notice the help text that has appeared:

The World's Best
Selling Cars

Inserts the contents of the file into your document and creates a shortcut to the source file. Changes to the source file will be reflected in your document.

This means that any changes to the Excel worksheet will appear in the linked Excel object.

6. Navigate to the *The World's Best Selling Cars* workbook.

7. Click the *Insert* button.

    The worksheet appears within Word, and is now the perfect size for its contents.

    Here is a list of the world's most successful cars to date:

Make	Model	Sales (Million)
Ford	Escort	18
Volkswagen	Beetle	23.5
Volkswagen	Golf	27.5
Ford	F Series	35
Toyota	Corolla	40

5   Test the link by changing values in the Excel workbook.

Linked objects work in a different way to embedded objects.

If you had not chosen the *Link to file* option, a copy of the workbook would have been embedded into the Word document.

When you double-click a linked object, Excel will open and display the linked file itself (instead of an embedded copy).

1. Double-click the Excel object.

    Excel opens the *The World's Best Selling Cars* workbook.

2. Re-size the Excel and Word windows so that you can see both documents.

3. Change one of the sales figures in the *The World's Best Selling Cars* workbook.

4. Click once in the Word document window to make it the active window.

5. Right-click the Excel linked object in the *The World's Best Selling Cars-2* Word document.

6. Click *Update Link* from the shortcut menu.

    Notice that the values update to match those in the workbook.

    Values are normally only updated when you open the Word document. The *Update Link* command tells Word to refresh the data it is displaying immediately.

6   Close the Excel window without saving.

7   Save the Word document as:
    The World's Best Selling Cars-3.

Lesson 6-5: Embed an Excel chart object into a Word document

1 Open Microsoft Word.

2 Use Word to open *The World's Best Selling Cars-3* (a Word document) from your sample files folder (if it isn't already open).

3 Convert the range into a table.

1. Double-click the Excel object to return to Excel.

   The *The World's Best Selling Cars* workbook opens in Excel.

2. Click inside the range.

3. Click: Insert→Tables→Table.

4. Click the *OK* button to accept the automatically detected range.

   The range is converted into a table.

4 Remove the AutoFilter from the table.

The AutoFilter buttons don't look good in a Word document.

Click: Data→Sort & Filter→Filter.

The filter buttons vanish.

5 Sort the table from bestselling to least selling.

1. Click anywhere in column C.

2. Click: Data→Sort & Filter→Sort Largest to Smallest.

6 Format the values in column C so that they display one decimal place.

1. Select the values in column C.

2. Click Home→Number→Increase Decimal.

7 Return to Word and update the linked workbook.

You saw how to do this in: *Lesson 6-4: Link an Excel worksheet to a Word document.*

8 Add the text **... and here is the same data as a chart** to the end of the document.

1. Click slightly to the right of the table.

2. Press the <Enter> key to move to the next line.

3. Type the text: **... and here is the same data as a chart.**

4. Press the <Enter> key to move to the next line.

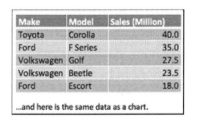

The World's Best Selling Cars-3

9   Copy the Excel object to the end of the document.

1.   Click the Excel object once to select it. Be careful to only click once. If you double-click you will go back into Excel.

2.   Copy the Excel object.

3.   Click on the line after the text: **... and here is the same data as a chart**.

4.   Paste.

An identical Excel object now appears in both places.

10   Convert the duplicated Excel object into a chart.

1.   Double-click the lower Excel object to go back into Excel.

2.   Select cells A1:C6.

3.   Click: Insert→Charts→Pie→Pie.

The worksheet now contains a pie chart.

4.   Right-click just inside the top-left corner of the pie chart.

5.   Click *Move Chart...* from the shortcut menu.

6.   Click the *New sheet* option button.

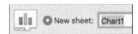

7.   Click the *OK* button.

8.   Click: ⌘→File→Save to save your changes.

11   Return to Word and update the second linked workbook object.

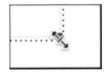

12   Re-size the Excel chart object to an attractive size.

You can resize the chart by clicking and dragging the sizing handles on the corners of the object.

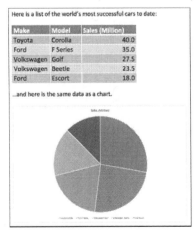

13   Save your work as *The World's Best Selling Cars-4*.

note

Excel Online provides a new way to share documents

Excel Online is an important part of Excel 2016's extensive support for cloud computing.

Cloud computing is extensively covered in the *Essential Skills* book in this series.

Excel Online runs in a web browser and is accessed from the cloud. This provides a completely new way of sharing a document with other users.

If several users all open a workbook that is stored in the cloud (each using Excel Online), any change made by any user will magically, and almost instantly, appear on every other user's screen.

If you want to learn more about sharing workbooks via the cloud using Excel Online, you should read:

Essential Skills Session 8: Cloud Computing

... paying particular attention to:

Lesson 8-8: Edit a workbook simultaneously with other users using Excel Online.

Lesson 6-6: Understand the three different ways to share a workbook

> When an undertaking hath been committed to many, it caused but confusion, and therefore it is a saying... too many cooks spoils the broth.
>
> *B Gerbier, Principles of Building 24 (1662)*

Workbook sharing is one of the most confusing and complex Excel features.

To use workbook sharing properly, you need to understand the real-world problems that workbook sharing must overcome.

In order to understand the three different sharing methods Excel provides, consider how you might have shared paper documents in the pre-computer age.

The lock method

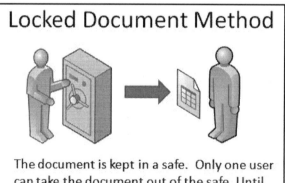

This is the simplest (and easiest) method to use. The feature is covered in: *Lesson 6-7: Share a workbook using the lock method.*

The merge method

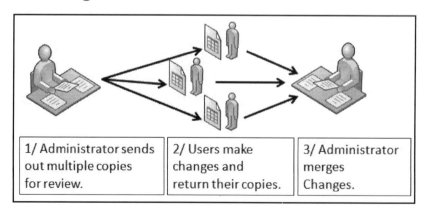

Excel allows you to send out multiple copies of a workbook by e-mail, and then merge all of the workbooks back into a master workbook when they are sent back with revisions. This feature is covered in: *Lesson 6-8: Share a workbook using the merge method.*

Sharing workbooks on a network

If you have a network, it is better to save the workbook onto a shared drive, and then to have many different people work on it *at the same time.*

This method will be explained in: *Lesson 6-9: Share a workbook on a network.*

Using a network makes the process far easier, as you don't need to manually merge the changes.

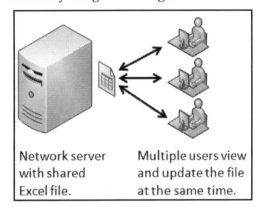

Network server with shared Excel file.   Multiple users view and update the file at the same time.

This method presents Excel with several challenges:

- If two users change the same cell at the same time – which change should succeed? In Excel terminology, you'd say: "which change should *win*"?

- How can you implement an audit trail so that you know which user changed which piece of data? In Excel terminology, you'd like to be able to *track changes.*

- How can a manager approve changes that users have made?

Excel rises to all three challenges and provides comprehensive tools to cater for each of these requirements.

By the end of this session you'll completely understand how to use all of Excel's shared workbook features.

Lesson 6-7: Share a workbook using the lock method

This is the easiest method of sharing, because it is outrageously simple to implement. You don't have to do anything at all other than to place your workbook onto a shared drive.

Sometimes you will have a single workbook that must be viewed and updated by many different people. To do this, the workbook is placed on a shared network drive so that many different people can view and update it.

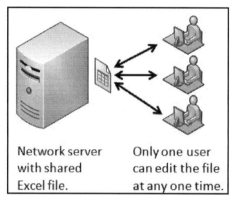

Network server with shared Excel file.

Only one user can edit the file at any one time.

Here's how things could go wrong if more than one user was allowed to edit the file at the same time:

1. Mike opens a workbook and makes some changes.

2. Before Mike has saved and closed the workbook, Mary opens the same workbook, makes some changes, saves, and closes the workbook.

3. Mike now saves his workbook, over-writing Mary's changes.

Excel avoids this problem by preventing two users from opening the same workbook, in read/write mode, at the same time. Here's how it works:

1. Mike opens a workbook and makes some changes.

2. Mary tries to open the same workbook. The Excel policeman says:

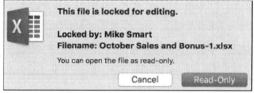

This file is locked for editing.

Locked by: Mike Smart
Filename: October Sales and Bonus-1.xlsx

You can open the file as read-only.

Cancel   Read-Only

3. Mary really wants to change the workbook, so she clicks *Read-Only*.

   The workbook still opens, but in *Read-Only* mode. She is able to read it but cannot save any changes (unless she saves a copy by changing the name of the workbook).

4. Mike saves and closes his workbook.

5. A message pops up on Mary's desktop advising her that the file is now available for editing (it's the Excel policeman again):

October Sales and Bonus-1

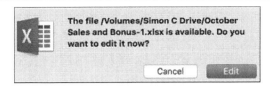

6. Mary clicks the *Edit* button to open the workbook, makes her changes, saves, and closes the workbook.

In this lesson, you'll see Excel manage document locking to make sure that only one user is able to edit a workbook at any one time.

You will only be able to follow through with this lesson if you have access to a network. It isn't possible to simulate two users accessing the same file if the file is located on your Mac.

You'll also need to open two separate instances of Excel (see sidebar for instructions on how to do this).

note

How to simulate two different Excel users on one computer by opening two different Excel instances

Excel for Mac is only designed to run as a single instance, but you can open a second instance by using the *Terminal*.

1. Open the Launchpad by clicking its icon on the Dock.

2. Type: **Terminal**

The *Terminal* icon should appear.

3. Click the *Terminal* icon.

The Terminal window opens.

4. Type the following command:

open –n –a "Microsoft Excel"

5. Press the <Enter> key.

A second instance of Excel opens, and a second Excel icon appears on the Dock.

1 Copy *October Sales and Bonus-1* from your sample files folder into a folder on your network.

2 Open *October Sales and Bonus-1* from your network.

3 Open a second instance of Excel (see sidebar).

4 Attempt to open the same copy of *October Sales and Bonus-1* in the second Excel instance.

A warning dialog is displayed:

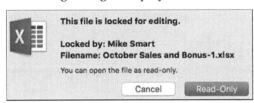

5 Click the *Read-Only* button.

The file opens in *Read Only* mode. In this mode you are unable to save any changes to the workbook. The title bar at the top of the window changes to inform you that you are in *Read-Only* mode.

6 Close the file in the first Excel instance

Eventually a dialog will appear in the second Excel instance. Be patient! It happened almost immediately on my computer, but may take a lot longer on yours.

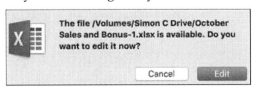

7 Click *Edit* to open the file for editing.

8 Close the second Excel instance.

You don't have to save the file as you haven't changed it in any way.

Lesson 6-8: Share a workbook using the merge method

In *Lesson 6-7: Share a workbook using the lock method,* you explored Excel's default way of handling workbook sharing.

This method works, but is very primitive. There are four problems:

1. There's no history to let you know which user made each change.

2. There's no review process to allow you to approve changes before they are applied.

3. Only one user can edit the document at the same time.

4. Every user must be connected to the network.

If all of the reviewers are connected to the same network, you wouldn't want to use the merge method described in this lesson. It would be more efficient to share the workbook on the network (you'll learn about this in: *Lesson 6-9: Share a workbook on a network*).

In this lesson, it is assumed that all of the reviewers are not connected to a network. In this case, you would need to send review copies by e-mail and then merge any changes made when they were returned.

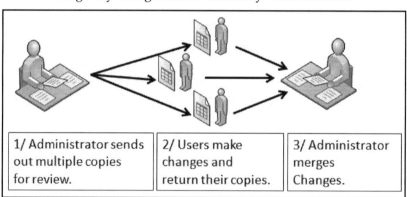

| 1/ Administrator sends out multiple copies for review. | 2/ Users make changes and return their copies. | 3/ Administrator merges Changes. |

1 Open *October Sales and Bonus-1* from your sample files folder (if it isn't already open).

2 Save the file as *October Sales and Bonus-2*.

In a moment, this workbook will be converted into a shared workbook. When you do this, it will demand to be saved.

By saving it with a new name you will avoid over-writing the original file, enabling you to repeat this lesson and the following two lessons at a later date if required.

3 Enable workbook merging by converting the workbook into a shared workbook.

1. Click: Review→Changes→Share Workbook.

The *Share Workbook* dialog appears.

2. Check the *Allow changes by more than one user at the same time* check box.

☑ Allow changes by more than one user at the same time.
This also allows workbook merging.

3. Click the *OK* button.

    You are now prompted to save the workbook.

4. Click the *OK* button.

    Notice that the title bar at the top of the Excel window now advises you that this is a shared file.

    October Sales and Bonus-2 [Shared]

4   Make a copy of the workbook to send to your reviewer.

    Save the workbook as: *Harry–October Sales and Bonus-2.*

    This is the file that you would e-mail to Harry for review. You could also make more copies to send to other employees.

5   In Harry's review copy of the workbook change *Lucille Ashe's* sales to **23,200** and *John Bradshaw's* Sales to **27,500**.

    1. Change *Lucille Ashe's* sales (cell C8) to **23,200**.

    2. Change *John Bradshaw's* sales (Cell C10) to **27,500**.

6   Save the *Harry-October Sales and Bonus-2* workbook.

7   Merge the changes from the *Harry-October Sales and Bonus-2* workbook into the *October Sales and Bonus-2* workbook.

    1. Close the *Harry-October Sales and Bonus-2* workbook.

        A workbook cannot be merged from unless it is closed.

    2. Open the *October Sales and Bonus-2* workbook.

    3. Click: ≰→Tools→Merge Workbooks.

    4. Select the *Harry-October Sales and Bonus-2* workbook and click the *OK* button.

        Notice that cells C8 and C10 are highlighted to show that they have been changed.

    5. Hover the mouse cursor over cell C8 and notice that you are able to view the change history.

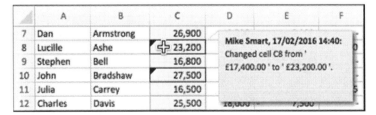

8   Save the workbook but keep it open for the next lesson.

Lesson 6-9: Share a workbook on a network

In *Lesson 6-8: Share a workbook using the merge method*, you explored a way of distributing multiple copies of a workbook via e-mail for review.

If all reviewers are connected to the same network, there is a much better way of sharing a workbook that will avoid the need to manually merge workbooks.

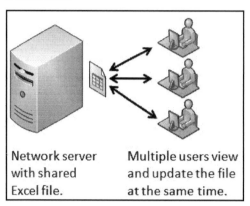

Network server with shared Excel file.   Multiple users view and update the file at the same time.

Because several users may edit the same workbook, there is a possibility that two users will change the same cell at the same time. This is called a *conflict*. When this happens, Excel must decide which user will "win" (their change is accepted) and which will "lose" (their change is rejected).

Excel also provides reviewing tools to allow Excel's decision to be changed later. (Reviewing is covered in: *Lesson 6-10: Accept and reject changes to shared workbooks*).

To follow through with this lesson, you'll need to open two separate instances of Excel (see sidebar in: *Lesson 6-7: Share a workbook using the lock method*, for instructions on how to do this). Excel will then regard each instance as having a different user.

note

How to find out who else has the workbook open

You can view a list of the other users who are currently working with a shared workbook.

1. Click:

Review→Changes→Share Workbook.

The *Share Workbook* dialog is displayed.

2. Click the *Editing* tab.

A list of all users who currently have the workbook open is displayed.

1   You should still have *October Sales and Bonus-2* open from the last lesson.

The three lessons beginning with: *Lesson 6-8: Share a workbook using the merge method* must be completed sequentially.

2   Open *October Sales and Bonus-2* again in a second Excel instance.

Excel now believes that two different users have Excel open at the same time, each viewing the same workbook.

For the rest of this lesson, I will call the first user *User 1* and the second user *User 2*.

If you find that the *User2* workbook has opened read-only, see sidebar for the cause of the problem.

You must begin this sequence of three lessons at: Lesson 6-8

3   Change Jane Anderson's sales (cell C6) to 22,000 on the *User 1* computer.

note

Automatically update changes made to a shared workbook

In an ideal world, all users of a shared workbook would see changes as soon as any user typed a value into a cell.

This is only possible when the workbook is saved in the cloud and accessed with Excel Online. See: *Lesson 6-6: Understand the three different ways to share a workbook – sidebar,* for more information about cloud computing.

Without using Excel Online it is still possible to show you all changes made in the last five minutes using auto-refresh.

Here's how to switch on auto-refresh:

1. Click: Review→Changes→ Share Workbook.

2. Click the *Advanced* tab.

3. In the *Update Changes* section, click the *Automatically every* option.

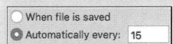

Note that the minimum automatic refresh is 15 minutes, but you can change it to a higher number if you wish.

Note also that you will only see other users' changes *when they save their workbook.*

Because you (and other users) may forget to save your changes, there's also an option to automatically save.

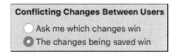

User 1			User 2		
	B	C		B	C
6	Anderson	22,000	6	Anderson	20,000
7	Armstrong	26,900	7	Armstrong	26,900

Notice that you cannot yet see the change on the *User 2* computer.

4 Change Jane Anderson's sales (cell C6) to 24,000 on the *User 2* computer.

User 1			User 2		
	B	C		B	C
6	Anderson	22,000	6	Anderson	24,000
7	Armstrong	26,900	7	Armstrong	26,900

You now have a classic conflict. Both users have changed cell C6 but, until they save their changes, Excel doesn't yet have to resolve the conflict.

5 Save the workbook on the *User 1* computer.

Excel still cannot see a conflict because it doesn't yet know whether *User-2* will ever save their changes. You still cannot see *User-1's* change on the *User 2* computer.

6 Save the workbook on the *User 2* computer.

Excel now detects the conflict and asks how it should be resolved.

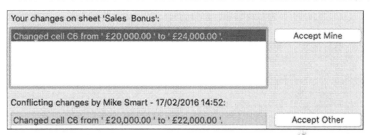

7 Click *Accept Mine* to accept *24,000* as the correct value.

8 Close Excel on the *User-2* computer.

9 Change the conflict options so that the most recent save always wins.

A moment ago, Excel asked you which change should win. This is the default way of handling conflicts. It is possible to change this behavior so that Excel simply saves the most recent change without bothering you.

1. Click: Review→Changes→Share Workbook.

2. Click the *Advanced* tab.

3. Click the *The changes being saved win* option button.

Conflicting Changes Between Users
○ Ask me which changes win
● The changes being saved win

4. Click the *OK* button.

10 Save the workbook (on the *User-1* computer), but keep it open for the next lesson.

Notice that Excel advises that a value has been changed by another user and updates the value in cell C6 to 24,000.

Lesson 6-10: Accept and reject changes to shared workbooks

Excel maintains an audit trail of every change made to a shared workbook. This is called the *change history*. Change history is useful for two reasons:

1. It allows you to review changes made by other users and reverse them if needed.

2. It provides an audit trail that can be automatically added to a *History* tab in the shared workbook (see sidebar on facing page).

1 You should still have *October Sales and Bonus-2* open from the last lesson.

The three lessons beginning with: *Lesson 6-8: Share a workbook using the merge method* must be completed sequentially.

2 Review and accept all changes made to the workbook to date.

1. Click: Review→Changes→Track Changes→ Accept/Reject Changes.

2. The *Select Changes to Accept or Reject* dialog is displayed.

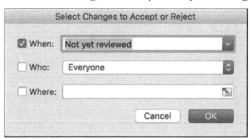

3. Click the *OK* button.

You are presented with details of the single edit made to cell C8.

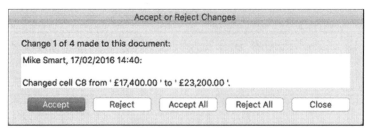

4. Click *Accept* to accept the edit.

5. Click *Accept* to accept the next change (to cell C10).

You now see a different dialog showing details of all edits to cell C6. This is a different dialog because cell C6 has been changed three times.

Select a value for cell C6:

£20,000.00 (Original Value)
£22,000.00 (Mike Smart 17/02/2016 14:52)
£24,000.00 (Mike Smart 17/02/2016 14:53)

note

Change history options

Because the history saves every single change to the workbook, a shared Excel file can get very large.

If file size is an issue, and if you can do without the history features, you may wish to switch it off.

History is maintained for 30 days by default, but you are able to increase or decrease this period.

To edit the *change history* options:

1. Click: Review→Changes→ Share Workbook.

2. Click the *Advanced* tab.

The *Track Changes* section allows you to edit the change history options.

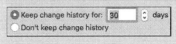
You must begin this sequence of three lessons at: Lesson 6-8

The change history is displayed in a dialog so that you can decide which of the three edits to accept.

6.   Select the second item in the list (when the value in cell C6 was changed to 22,000).

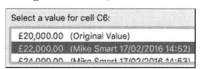

7.   Click the *Accept* button to accept the previous value of 22,000.

Notice that the value in cell C6 reverts to 22,000.

3   Understand *Track Changes* options.

Click: Review→Changes→Track Changes→Highlight Changes…

The *Highlight Changes* dialog is displayed, showing several options that may be set when reviewing changes.

As is so often the case, the default options are nearly always what you need, but here's how you can use the other options.

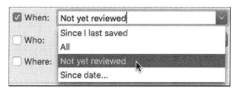

The *When* options allow you to filter the change history based upon time. *Not yet reviewed* is the one you'll use most, as you probably won't want to review the same changes twice.

The *Who* options allow you to focus upon a particular user, or to filter out your own changes, as you do not normally need to review your own edits.

The *Where* option allows you to view changes on a selected range of cells. This could be useful if you wanted to know which users have edited a specific cell or cells.

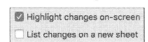

Highlight changes on screen will surround each changed cell with a box and place a triangle in the top left corner. This allows you to view all changes by hovering the mouse cursor over the cell.

See sidebar for more information about the last option: *List changes on a new sheet*.

4   Save your work as *October Sales and Bonus-3*.

Session 6: Exercise

1 Open the *Spectrum Car Sales-1* Excel workbook from your sample files folder.

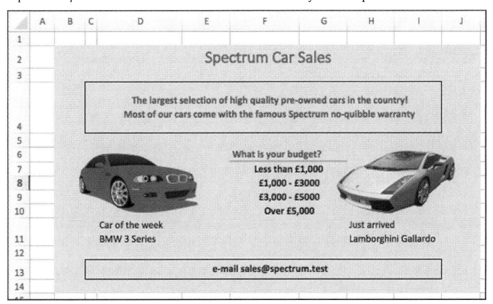

2 Hyperlink the *What is your budget?* cells (F7, F8, F9 and F10) to the relevant worksheets.

3 Hyperlink the *Car of the week BMW 3 Series* text (cell D11) to the £1,000 - £3,000 worksheet.

4 Hyperlink the *Just arrived Lamborghini Gallardo* text (cell H11) to the *Over £5,000* worksheet.

5 Make the *e-mail sales@spectrum.test* text in cell D13 into an e-mail hyperlink that will send an e-mail to the e-mail address: *sales@spectrum.test* with the subject: *Car sales enquiry*.

6 Save the workbook as *Spectrum Car Sales-2* and close Excel.

7 Open the *Stock List-1* sample file in Microsoft Word.

8 Place a linked object after the text in the *Stock List-1* Word document that will show the contents of the *Over £5,000* worksheet in the *Spectrum Car Sales-2* workbook.

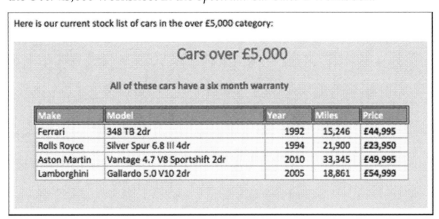

9 Save the Word document as *Stock List-2*.

Spectrum Car Sales-1

Stock List-1

If you need help slide the page to the left

Session 6: Exercise Answers

These are the five questions that students find the most difficult to answer:

Q 8	Q 5	Q 2, 3, 4

1. Open the *Spectrum Car Sales-2 workbook* in Excel.
 	
2. Select the *Over £5,000* worksheet.
 	
3. Save and close the *Spectrum Car Sales-2* workbook.
 	
4. Open the *Stock List-1* document in Microsoft Word.
 	
5. Click just to the right of the ... *£5,000 category:* text.
 	
6. Press the **<Enter>** key to move to the next line.
 	
7. Click: Insert→Text→Object→Object.
 	
8. Click *From File*.
 	
9. Click *Options* and make sure that *Link to File* is checked.
 	
10. Select the *Spectrum Car Sales-2* workbook.
 	
11. Click the *Insert* button.
 	
This was covered in: *Lesson 6-4: Link an Excel worksheet to a Word document.*
	1. Select cell D13 on the *Home* worksheet.
	
	2. Click: Insert→Links→Hyperlink.
	
	3. Click the *Email Address* tab on the left-hand selection bar.
	
	4. Complete the dialog as follows:
	
	Email address:
	sales@spectrum.test
	
	Subject:
	Car sales enquiry.
	
	5. Click the *OK* button.
	
	This was covered in: *Lesson 6-2: Hyperlink to other workbooks and the Internet.*
		1. Click in Cell F7.
		
		2. Click:
		
		Insert→Links→Hyperlink
		
		3. Click: *This Document* at the top of the dialog.
		
		4. Click *Under £1,000* in the *Or select a place in this document* pane.
		
		Or select a place in this document:
		▼ Cell Reference
		  Home
		  'Under £1,000'
		  '£1,000-£3,000'
		
		5. Repeat the same steps to add hyperlinks to cells F8, F9, F10, D11 and H11.
		
		This was covered in: *Lesson 6-1: Hyperlink to worksheets and ranges.*

Session Seven: Forms and Macros

> You don't need to know how an engine works to drive a car.
>
> *Proverb, unknown authors*

You can design Excel applications for users who have no Excel skills.

When you create this type of application, you need to provide a simple and intuitive form-based user interface. The user interface should be so simple that the application can be used without any training or assumed Excel skills.

In this session you'll create a powerful, form-based, Excel application with a simple and intuitive user interface.

You'll also learn how to record and run macros. Macros allow you to provide users with simple form controls that execute a complex sequence of Excel actions.

Session Objectives

By the end of this session you will be able to:

- Add group box and option button controls to a worksheet form
- Add a combo box control to a worksheet form
- Set form control cell links
- Connect result cells to a form
- Add a check box control to a worksheet form
- Use check box data in result cells
- Add a temperature gauge chart to a form
- Add a single input data table to a form
- Improve form appearance and usability
- Understand macros and VBA
- Record a macro
- Understand macro security
- Use shapes to run macros
- Run a macro from a button control

Lesson 7-1: Add group box and option button controls to a worksheet form

1 Open *Mortgage Calculator-1* from your sample files folder.

2 Add the *Developer* tab to the ribbon.

Because form controls are an advanced feature of Excel, Microsoft hides them from normal users. You must add the *Developer* tab to the ribbon in order to reveal them.

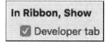

1. Click: ⌘→Excel→Preferences→View.

2. In the *In Ribbon, Show* group, make sure that *Developer tab* is checked.

3. Click the *Close* button.

The *Developer* tab appears on the ribbon.

3 Delete row 5 and then insert two new blank rows so that there are four blank rows between *Property Price* and *Arrangement Fee*.

4 Add a *Group Box* control so that it completely fills cells B5:D6.

1. Click: Developer→Controls→Group Box.

2. Hold down the **<Cmd>** key. This will make the group box snap to the corners of the selected cells.

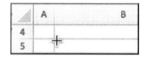

3. Carefully position the black cross cursor near the top left corner of cell B5.

4. Click and drag to the bottom right corner of cell D6 and release the mouse button.

If a contextual menu appears, click away from it.

A group box appears.

5 Change the caption of the group box to: **Deposit:**

1. Click on a blank area of the worksheet to de-select the group box.

2. Double click the *Group Box 1* caption on the border of the group box.

3. Delete the existing *Group Box 1* text and then type: **Deposit:**

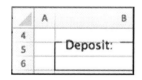

6 Add six option button controls to the group box.

1. Click: Developer→Controls→Option Button.

2. Click and drag inside the group box to add an option button. Keep the button small, as you need space for six buttons and they should not overlap. Be careful to keep the border of each option button inside the group box.

Mortgage Calculator-1

3. Repeat for the other five buttons. It is important that you add them in sequence from left to right.

7   Change the option button captions to **5%** to **30%** (reading left to right).

1. Right-click the first option button to select it.

   A box appears around the option button, along with a shortcut menu.

2. Press the **<Esc>** key or click once again inside the control to close the shortcut menu (an even faster way to do steps one and two in a single operation is to double right-click the control).

3. Double-click the text next to the option button.

4. Delete the existing text and type: **5%**

5. Do the same for the **10%** to **30%** option buttons.

8   Move and re-size the option buttons so that they are evenly spaced inside the group box.

1. Select an option button and close the shortcut menu.

2. Use the arrow keys on the keyboard to move the option button to its new position.

3. Click and drag one of the white squares (sizing handles) on the border of the option button to re-size if necessary.

4. Hover over the border of the selected option button control (but not on one of the white squares) until you see the four-headed arrow cursor shape.

5. Click and drag to move the option button control.

6. Your option group should now look like this:

9   Add another set of option buttons to show terms from 5 to 30 years.

1. Delete row 12 and then insert three new rows.

2. Add a group box form control so that it completely fills cells B12:D14.

3. Add the caption and option buttons. It is important that you add them in sequence (in ascending order).

10   Save your work as *Mortgage Calculator-2*.

Lesson 7-2: Add a combo box control to a worksheet form

1 Open *Mortgage Calculator-2* from your sample files folder (if it isn't already open).

2 Delete the contents of cell D16.

3 Remove the black border from cell D16.

 1. Select cell D16.

 2. Click: Home→Font→Borders→No Border.

4 Place a combo box control in cell D16.

 1. Select cell D16.

 2. Click: Developer→Controls→Combo Box.

 3. Hold down the **<Cmd>** key. This will make the control fit perfectly in the cell.

 4. Click just inside the top left border of cell D16 and drag to just inside the bottom right border.

 5. Release the mouse button and click away from the drop-down menu.

 The control is inserted into the cell, but the cell's a little too small for the control's minimum size.

 6. Resize row 16 so that the combo box fits perfectly in cell D16.

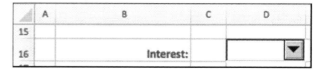

5 Create a new worksheet called *Data* to provide interest rate data from 2% to 15% in increments of 0.5%.

 1. Create a new worksheet called *Data.*

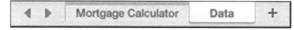

 2. Select the *Data* worksheet.

 3. Type: **Interest Rates** into cell A1.

 4. Type: **2.0%** into cell A2.

 5. Type the formula: **=A2+0.5%** into cell A3.

 6. AutoFill cell A3 into cells A4:A28.

6 Format cells A2:A28 so that only one decimal place is shown.

 1. Select cells A2:A28.

 2. Click: Home→Number→Decrease Decimal.

Mortgage Calculator-2

	A	B
1	Interest Rates	
2	2.0%	
3	2.5%	
4	3.0%	

7 Create a range name for the interest rate values in cells A2:A28.

Range names were extensively covered in: *Session Four: Using Names and the Formula Auditing Tools.*

1. Select cells A1:A28.

2. Click: Formulas→Defined Names→Create from Selection.

3. Click the *OK* button.

8 Set the combo box's *Input Range* to reference the interest rate data.

1. Select the *Mortgage Calculator* worksheet.

2. Right-click inside the combo box control.

3. Click *Format Control...* from the shortcut menu.

4. Select the *Control* tab.

5. Click in the *Input range* box.

6. Type **Interest_Rates** into the *Input Range* box.

7. Click the *OK* button.

9 Test the combo box control.

1. Click away from the control to de-select it.

2. Click and hold on the drop-down arrow on the combo box.

Notice that the combo box displays all of the interest rates defined by the *Interest_Rates* range name.

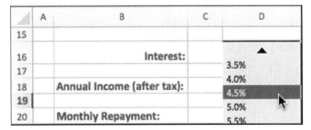

10 Save your work as *Mortgage Calculator-3.*

Lesson 7-3: Set form control cell links

When working with forms, it is useful to separate the user interface from the input and result cells. The user interface is the part of the worksheet where the user enters values and views results. In this lesson's worksheet the user interface comprises of cells B3:D20.

Calculations are done in a different section of the worksheet where you will define *Input Cells* and *Result Cells*. You'll recognize this method of working from the lessons in: *Session Five: What If Analysis and Security.*

In this lesson's worksheet, the *Input Cells* and *Result Cells* are shown in cells B23:D36. You will hide these rows from the user later.

In this lesson you'll connect the *User Interface* with the *Input Cells*.

1   Open *Mortgage Calculator-3* from your sample files folder (if it isn't already open).

2   Link the user interface's *Property Price, Arrangement Fee,* and *Annual Income (after tax)* cells to the relevant *Input Cells.*

This is extremely easy, as it can be done using simple cell references:

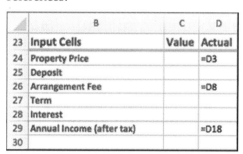

	B	C	D
23	Input Cells	Value	Actual
24	Property Price		=D3
25	Deposit		
26	Arrangement Fee		=D8
27	Term		
28	Interest		
29	Annual Income (after tax)		=D18
30			

3   Connect the data from the *Deposit* group box to cell C25.

1. Right-click the *5% Deposit* option button.

2. Click *Format Control...* from the shortcut menu.

3. Click the *Control* tab.

4. Click in the *Cell link* box.

5. Click in cell C25.

6. Click the *OK* button.

4   Test the cell link.

1. Click away from the option buttons to de-select.

2. Left-click each option button in turn.

3. Notice that numbers from 1 to 6 appear in cell C25 as each option button is clicked. Option 5% results in 1, option 10% results in 2... and so on.

Mortgage Calculator-3

If you find that the wrong numbers are appearing, it is because you added the option buttons in the wrong order. In this case you'll have to move the buttons around and change their captions, until you have the correct number associated with each button.

5 Add a formula to cell D25 so that it displays the correct percentage for each option.

1. Type **=C25*0.05** into cell D25.

2. Test again. This time the actual percentage of the selected option button should display in cell D25.

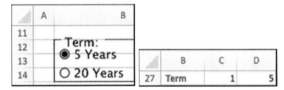

6 Connect the data from the *Term* group box to cell C27.

Do this in exactly the same way that you connected the *Deposit* group box to cell C25.

7 Add a formula to cell D27 to show the actual term.

1. Type **=C27*5** into cell D27.

2. Test the *Term* option buttons.

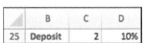

8 Connect the data from the *Interest* combo box to cell C28.

1. Right-click the combo box control.

2. Click *Format Control...* from the shortcut menu.

3. Click the *Control* Tab.

4. Click in the *Cell link* box.

5. Click in cell C28.

6. Click the *OK* button.

9 Test the *Interest* combo box cell link.

Just like the option button controls, the value returned from the combo box is a number representing which option was selected. 2% returns the number 1, 2.5% returns the number 2... and so on.

10 Add a formula to cell D28 so that it displays the correct interest rate.

Type the formula **=(C28*0.5+1.5)/100** into cell D28.

11 Test the combo box.

12 Save your work as *Mortgage Calculator-4.*

Lesson 7-4: Connect result cells to a form

In the previous lessons you created a user interface using Excel's form controls.

The form now collects data from the user, and uses this data to update the input cells.

In this lesson you'll use the input cells to calculate the result cells, and then use the result cells to update the form.

1 Open *Mortgage Calculator-4 from* your sample files folder (if it isn't already open).

2 Add a formula to cell D32 that will calculate the *Amount Financed.*

Amount Financed = Property Price – Deposit + Arrangement Fee

To perform this calculation, you need to type the following formula into cell D32:

=D24-(D24*D25)+D26

3 Add a formula to cell D33 to calculate the *Monthly Repayment.*

For this calculation you will use the PMT function that was covered in: *Lesson 3-3: Use the Formula Builder task pane and the PMT function.*

The function arguments will be:

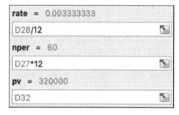

4 Convert the negative *Monthly Repayment* into a positive value.

The easiest way to do this is to place a minus operator in front of the function:

5 Add a formula to cell D34 to calculate the *Total Repaid.*

Total Repaid = Monthly Repayment * 12 * Term

To perform this calculation, you need to type the following formula into cell D34:

=D33*12*D27

6 Add a formula to cell D35 to calculate the *Total Interest.*

Total Interest = Total Repaid – Amount Financed

Mortgage Calculator-4

To perform this calculation, you need to type the following formula into cell D35:

=D34-D32

7   Add a formula to cell D36 to calculate the *Repayment as % of Income*.

Repayment as % of Income =
Monthly Repayment * 12/Annual Income (after tax)

To perform this calculation, you need to type the following formula into cell D36:

=D33*12/D29

8   Connect the *Amount Financed* result cell (D32) to the *Amount Financed* form cell (D10).

Enter the following formula into cell D10:

=D32

9   Connect the *Monthly Repayment* result cell (D33) to the *Monthly Repayment* form cell (D20).

Enter the following formula into cell D20:

=D33

10   Test the form.

Enter the values shown below into the form. The result cells should match those shown:

11   Save your work as *Mortgage Calculator-5*.

Lesson 7-5: Add a check box control to a worksheet form

In this lesson you will improve the form to model interest-only mortgages.

1   Open *Mortgage Calculator-5* from your sample files folder (if it isn't already open).

2   Left-align the text in cell B16.

    1.   Select cell B16.

    2.   Click: Home→Alignment→Align Left.

3   Move the combo box so that it appears directly after the *Interest:* text in cell B16.

    1.   Right-click the combo box.

        If a shortcut menu appears, either press the **<Esc>** key or click once again inside the control to close it.

    2.   Use the arrow keys on the keyboard to move the combo box to its new position.

        Your combo box should now look like this:

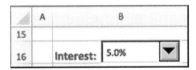

4   Add a check box control so that it completely fills cells C16:D16.

    1.   Click: Developer→Controls→Check Box.

    2.   Hold down the **<Cmd>** key. This will make the control fit perfectly in the cells.

    3.   Click just inside the top left border of cell C16 and drag to just inside the bottom right border of cell D16.

    4.   Release the mouse button and click away from the drop-down menu.

        The control is inserted into the cells (and aligns perfectly).

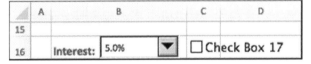

        Your check box may have a different caption, such as *Check Box 20,* as the control number is not consistently applied.

5   Change the check box caption to *Interest Only Loan*.

        Change this in the same way that you changed the option button captions in: *Lesson 7-1: Add group box and option button controls to a worksheet form.*

Mortgage Calculator-5

	A	B	C	D
15				
16		Interest:	5.0% ▼	☐ Interest only loan

6   Add an input cell to link to the new check box.

    1.   Insert a row above row 29.

    2.   Type the text **Interest Only?** into cell B29.

	B	C	D
28	Interest	7	5.0%
29	Interest Only?		
30	Annual Income (after tax)		38,000

7   Connect the data from the *Interest Only Loan* check box to cell D29.

    1.   Right-click the *Interest Only Loan* check box.

    2.   Click *Format Control...* from the shortcut menu.

    3.   Click the *Control* tab.

    4.   Click in the *Cell link* box.

    5.   Click in cell D29.

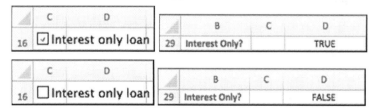

    6.   Click the *OK* button.

8   Test the cell link.

    1.   Click away from the check box to de-select it.

    2.   Click the *Interest Only Loan* check box a few times.

       When the box is checked, TRUE appears in cell D29. When the box is unchecked, FALSE appears in cell D29.

	C	D			B	C	D
16	☑ Interest only loan			29	Interest Only?		TRUE

	C	D			B	C	D
16	☐ Interest only loan			29	Interest Only?		FALSE

9   Save your work as *Mortgage Calculator-6*.

Lesson 7-6: Use check box data in result cells

1   Open *Mortgage Calculator-6* from your sample files folder (if it isn't already open).

2   Correct the formula in the *Monthly Repayment* result cell (D34) to allow for interest only loans.

   1.   Click in cell D34.

   2.   Click the *Insert Function* button to the left of the formula bar.

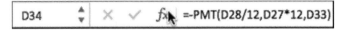

   3.   The *Formula Builder* task pane appears.

       The capital owed at the end of an interest only loan (Excel's terminology for this is: *Future Value*) will be a negative number that is the same as the *Amount Financed.* The *Future Value* will thus be:

       Amount Financed * -1

       A normal capital and repayment loan will have been fully repaid by the end of the term, so there will be no future value.

       In order to make the PMT function return the correct value for both types of loan, you will have to use an IF logic function to set the future value. The IF function was covered in: *Lesson 3-5: Use the IF logic function.*

   4.   Type the following formula into the *fv* argument box:

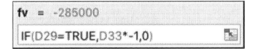

       This will set the *Future Value* to be the same as the **Amount Financed * -1** for an interest only loan, and to **zero** for a capital and repayment loan.

   5.   Click the *Done* button.

3   Correct the *Total Interest* result cell (D36) to allow for interest only loans.

   A capital and repayment loan will incur interest of:

   Total Repaid – Amount Financed.

   Every payment in an *interest only* loan consists only of interest. This means that the *Total Interest* will be the same as the *Total Repaid.*

   In order to correct the *Total Interest* result cell, you will, once again, have to use an IF logic function.

   1.   Click in cell D36.

   2.   Delete the previous formula.

   3.   Add an IF function. The function arguments are:

Mortgage Calculator-6

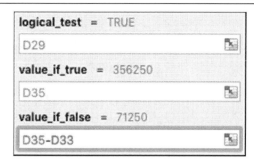

logical_test	=	TRUE
D29		
value_if_true	=	356250
D35		
value_if_false	=	71250
D35-D33		

4   Test the check box.

I tested with the following form values:

	B	C	D
1	Mortgage Calculator		
2			
3	Property Price:		350,000
4			
5	Deposit:		
6	○ 5% ○ 10% ○ 15% ● 20% ○ 25% ○ 30%		
7			
8	Arrangement Fee:		5,000
9			
10	Amount Financed:		285,000
11			
12	Term:		
13	○ 5 Years ○ 10 Years ○ 15 Years		
14	● 20 Years ○ 25 Years ○ 30 Years		
15			
16	Interest: 5.0% ▼	☐ Interest only loan	
17			
18	Annual Income (after tax):		38,000
19			
20	Monthly Repayment:		1,880.87

When the *Interest Only Loan* box was unchecked, the *Result Cells* were:

	B	C	D
32	Result Cells		
33	Amount Financed		285,000
34	Monthly Repayment		1,880.87
35	Total Repaid		451,410
36	Total Interest		166,410
37	Repayment as % of Income		59%

When the *Interest Only Loan* box was checked, the *Result Cells* were:

	B	C	D
32	Result Cells		
33	Amount Financed		285,000
34	Monthly Repayment		1,187.50
35	Total Repaid		285,000
36	Total Interest		285,000
37	Repayment as % of Income		38%

5   Save your work as *Mortgage Calculator-7*.

Lesson 7-7: Add a temperature gauge chart to a form

Charting is covered in depth in session 5 of the *Essential Skills* book in this series. Excel doesn't have a temperature gauge chart in its pre-defined range of charts. It is possible, however, to create this type of chart by formatting a regular column chart in a special way.

1 Open *Mortgage Calculator-7* from your sample files folder.

2 Add a column chart to the worksheet with the single data value of *Repayment as % of Income*.

   1. Select cell D37.

   2. Click: Insert→Charts→Column→Clustered Column.

   3. Right-click the center of the chart and then click *Select Data...* from the shortcut menu.

   4. Remove all of the text from the *Chart data range* box.

   5. Click in the *Chart data range* box and then click cell D37.

   6. Click the *OK* button.

      You now have a chart with a single bar showing the loan affordability as a percentage of income (see sidebar if the percentages do not display correctly).

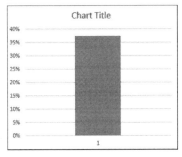

3 Change the vertical axis so that it begins at 0% and ends at 100%.

   1. Click the chart to activate it.

   2. Right click on the *Vertical (Value Axis)* (one of the percentages).

   3. Click *Format Axis* from the shortcut menu.

   4. Set the *Minimum* and *Maximum* values to **0** and **1**.

4 Remove the gap from the left hand side of the column.

   1. Right-click on the chart column and then click *Format Data Series...* from the shortcut menu.

      The *Format Data Series* task pane appears.

   2. Change the *Gap Width* to 0%.

5 Remove the *Horizontal Axis* and *Chart Title* elements from the chart.

   1. Click on the chart to activate it.

---

note

If the vertical axis does not show percentages

It's possible that the chart will fail to detect that the vertical axis values should be displayed as percentages.

If this happens:

1. Right-click the vertical axis and click *Format Axis* from the shortcut menu.

2. Click the *Number* fly-out menu.

3. Click the *Category* drop-down menu and select *Percentage*.

Bounds	
Minimum	0.0
Maximum	1.0

Mortgage Calculator-7

---

2. Click: Chart Design→Chart Layouts→
   Add Chart Element→Chart Title→None.

3. Click: Chart Design→Chart Layouts→
   Add Chart Element→Axes→Primary Horizontal.

6   Apply a thin black line around the Plot Area.

1. Right-click in the center of the chart (but not on the bar or a gridline).

2. Click *Format Plot Area...* from the shortcut menu.

   The *Format Plot Area* task pane appears.

3. Click on the *Border* fly-out menu.

4. Click the *Solid Line* option button.

5. Click the *Color* button and select *Black.*

7   Re-size the chart so that it resembles a temperature gauge that is the same height as the form.

1. Click on the chart to select it.

2. Click and drag the bottom right-hand corner sizing handle to size as required.

3. Click and drag anywhere on the border of the chart that is not a sizing handle to move it to the required position (see the cover of this book for a rough idea of where that should be).

8   Remove the border around the chart.

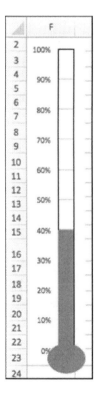

1. Click on the chart to select it.

2. Right-click on the border of the chart.

3. Click *Format Chart Area...* from the shortcut menu.

   The *Format Chart Area* task pane appears.

4. Click: Border→No Line.

9   Add an oval shape to mimic the bulb at the bottom of a thermometer.

1. Click away from the chart to de-select it.

2. Click: Insert→Illustrations→Shapes→Basic Shapes→Oval.

3. Click and drag to draw an oval at the bottom of the chart.

4. Right-click the oval shape and click *Format Shape...* from the shortcut menu.

5. Click Line→No Line in the *Format Shape* task pane.

6. Click the *Close* button ⊚ at the top right of the *Format Shape* task pane.

   Your chart should now look similar to the sidebar.

10   Save your work as *Mortgage Calculator-8.*

Lesson 7-8: Add a single input data table to a form

You covered single-input data tables in: *Lesson 5-1: Create a single-input data table*. In this lesson you'll recap this skill by adding a single-input data table to the form to show how repayments could increase if interest rates were to rise by up to 4% more than the current rate.

1   Open *Mortgage Calculator-8* from your sample files folder (if it isn't already open).

2   Add titles for each of the data table's columns.

Type labels into cells H2:L2 so that they are the same as the following:

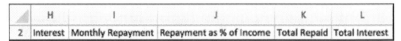

3   Merge cells H1:H2, I1:I2, J1:J2, K1:K2 and L1:L2.

   1.   Select cells H1:H2.

   2.   Click: Home→Alignment→Merge and Center→Merge Cells.

   3.   Repeat for the other cell pairs.

4   Switch text wrapping on for cells H1:L1.

   1.   Select cells H1:L1.

   2.   Click: Home→Alignment→Wrap Text.

5   Arrange the labels so that they appear on two lines where necessary.

   1.   Double-click just before the word *Repayment* in cell I1 (*Monthly Repayment*).

   2.   Hold down the **<Alt>** key.

   3.   Press the **<Enter>** key.

   4.   Repeat for the other column labels.

   5.   Re-size each column.

   Your column headers should now look like this:

	H	I	J	K	L
1		Monthly	Repayment	Total	Total
2	Interest	Repayment	as % of Income	Repaid	Interest

6   Add a formula to cell H3 that will show the interest rate selected on the form.

   1.   Click in cell H3.

   2.   Add the formula: **=(C28*0.5+1.5)/100**

   You need to refer to cell C28 rather than D28 to work-around an odd quirk in Excel data tables (see sidebar).

7   Add a formula to cell H4 that will show an interest rate 1% higher than the rate in cell H3.

     1. Click in cell H4.

     2. Add the formula: **=H3+0.01**

8 AutoFill the formula in cell H4 to cells H5:H7.

9 Format the formulas in cells H3:H7 so that they are formatted as percentages and display one decimal place.

     1. Select cells H3:H7 and click: Home→Number→Percent Style.

     2. Click: Home→Number→Increase Decimal.

10 Add formulas to cells I3:L3 that will reference the relative result cells.

The correct formulas are:

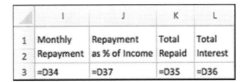

	I	J	K	L
1	Monthly	Repayment	Total	Total
2	Repayment	as % of Income	Repaid	Interest
3	=D34	=D37	=D35	=D36

11 Add a single input data table to cells H3:L7.

     1. Select cells H3:L7.

     2. Click: Data→Data Tools→What-If Analysis→Data Table...

        The *Data Table* dialog appears.

     3. Click in the *Column input cell* box.

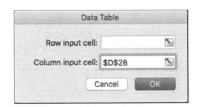

     4. Click in cell D28.

     5. Click the *OK* button.

12 Copy the formats from cells I3:L3 to cells I4:L7.

     1. Select cells I3:L3.

     2. Click: Home→Clipboard→Copy.

     3. Select cells I4:L7.

     4. Click: Home→Clipboard→Paste→Paste Special...

     5. Select the *Formats* option button.

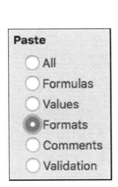

     6. Click the *OK* button.

13 Resize the columns if necessary.

Your data table should now look like this:

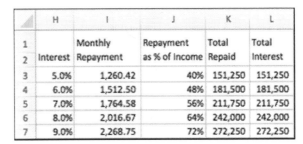

	H	I	J	K	L
1		Monthly	Repayment	Total	Total
2	Interest	Repayment	as % of Income	Repaid	Interest
3	5.0%	1,260.42	40%	151,250	151,250
4	6.0%	1,512.50	48%	181,500	181,500
5	7.0%	1,764.58	56%	211,750	211,750
6	8.0%	2,016.67	64%	242,000	242,000
7	9.0%	2,268.75	72%	272,250	272,250

The actual values shown on your worksheet may differ depending upon the values selected in your form.

14 Save your work as *Mortgage Calculator-9*.

Lesson 7-9: Improve form appearance and usability

An elegant form-based user interface enables you to create utilities for users with no Excel skills. The form should be so intuitive that staff training is not needed. In its present form, the Mortgage Calculator might intimidate non-technical users. You need to do a few more things to make this into a really professional form. They are:

- Improve the appearance of the form.

- Hide irrelevant worksheets and cells. In this case you need to hide the *Input Cells, Result Cells* and the *Data* worksheet.

- Protect the form so that users cannot alter the functionality or layout.

1 Open *Mortgage Calculator-9* from your sample files folder.

2 Add a pie chart to show the *Amount Financed* and *Total Interest*.

1. Click in cell D33, hold down the **<Cmd>** key and click cell D36.

2. Click: Insert→Charts→Pie→3-D Pie.

3. Move and re-size the chart so that it fills cells H9:L20.

4. Right-click on the center of the pie chart.

5. Click *Select Data...* from the shortcut menu.

6. Click in the *Horizontal (Category) axis labels* box.

7. Click on cell B33, hold down the **<Cmd>** key and click on cell B36.

8. Click the *OK* button.

3 Surround the form area with two narrow padding columns.

It is useful for a form to be clearly delineated from the worksheet. This is best achieved by adding two narrow padding columns to each border of the form (see the screen grab on the front cover of this book).

The borders can then be shaded to clearly mark the form edges.

1. Add two narrow columns (about 9 pixels wide) to the left of column A.

2. Add two narrow rows (about 9 pixels deep) above row 1.

3. Add two narrow rows (about 9 pixels deep) above row 24.

4. Resize columns P and Q so that they are about 9 pixels wide).

4 Shade the form area (excluding controls and cells that the user will enter data into) light yellow.

1. Click in cell D22.

2. Set the background color to very light yellow.

3. Double-click: Home→Clipboard→Format Painter.

Mortgage Calculator-9

4. Click once in each cell in the range: C4:G23 that should be yellow (see cover of this book for guidance).

    You may have to move the checkbox control in order to shade the cells behind it, and then move it back again.

5. Click: Home→Clipboard→Format Painter to switch the format painter off.

5 Use similar techniques to format the worksheet to match the design shown (in color) on the cover of this book.

You will have to add a padding column to the left of the temperature gauge chart.

Sample file *Mortgage Calculator-10* has the end result as shown on the book cover. You can use different formatting and colors if you think that they look better.

6 Switch off the gridlines.

The gridlines are spoiling the appearance of the group boxes.

Click: View→Show→Gridlines.

7 Unlock cells F5, F10, F20, E29, E31, E32 and F33.

In a moment you will protect the workbook. At this point it will only be possible to change unlocked cells.

Notice that you have to unlock cells E29, E31, E32 and F33 because a control cannot change a value in a locked cell.

1. Select all of the cells to be unlocked.

2. Right-click one of the selected cells.

3. Click *Format Cells...* from the shortcut menu.

4. Click the *Protection* tab and clear the *Locked* check box.

    Cell locking and protection were covered in: *Lesson 5-11: Restrict the cells users are allowed to change.*

8 Configure the charts to use data in hidden rows and columns.

See sidebar if you are unsure how to do this.

9 Hide the *Data* worksheet, *Input Cells* and *Result Cells* (rows 27:41).

1. Right-click the *Data* tab and click *Hide* from the shortcut menu.

2. Select rows 27:41, right-click in the selected area and click *Hide* from the shortcut menu.

10 Protect the worksheet.

1. Click: Review→Changes→Protect Sheet.

2. Add a password if you want greater security.

3. Check the *Select unlocked cells* check box.

4. Uncheck the *Select locked cells* check box.

5. Click the *OK* button.

11 Save your work as *Mortgage Calculator-10.*

---

note

Charting data in hidden rows and columns

By default, a chart cannot use source data that is in a hidden row or column.

To chart data in hidden rows and columns:

1. Right-click in the center of the chart.

2. Click *Select Data...* from the shortcut menu.

4. Check the *Show data in hidden rows and columns check box.*

☑ Show data in hidden rows and columns

5. Click the *OK* button.

Charting was covered in depth in the *Essential Skills* book in this series.

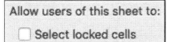

note

VBA is a programming language that can be used to write custom extensions to Excel

Microsoft Office is written in a very special way. It consists of several hundred objects all "glued" together with programming code. In: *Lesson 6 5: Embed an Excel chart object into a Word document,* you saw how easy it was to place one object inside another object.

Microsoft has documented all of the objects that make up Office, so that programmers can use Office objects in their own applications.

I regularly use Excel chart objects when I write accounting applications and need to display data as a graph. The users don't even know that I "borrowed" the functionality from Excel, and Microsoft don't mind a bit (as long as each computer has an Office license).

Because all of the objects that make up Excel can be used in other computer programs, it is possible to add new features to Excel that Microsoft didn't anticipate you would want.

Here's an example:

Commodity and Foreign Exchange traders often want a live data feed (showing up to date prices) connected to an Excel worksheet. Excel can't do that "out of the box", but a competent VBA programmer can connect the feed into the worksheet in a matter of minutes.

VBA isn't an Excel-specific skill. The Visual Basic language can be used to add functionality to Excel, Word, PowerPoint, Visio, Project... and many other Microsoft and third party applications.

Lesson 7-10: Understand macros and VBA

Macros are a very misunderstood concept. Most books cause terrible confusion by mixing up the twin subjects of macros and the VBA (Visual Basic for Applications) programming language.

You don't need to know anything about the VBA programming language to use macros.

Macros record keystrokes and mouse-clicks

The macro recorder is able to record (and play back) every mouse click or key stroke that you make. Here's how I would record a simple macro:

1. Start the recorder to record a macro called *TypeMikeIntoCellA5.*

2. Click into cell A5 to make it the active cell.

3. Type: **Mike** into cell A5.

4. Press the **<Enter>** key.

5. Stop the recorder.

This would record a macro that I would be able to play back in future. The macro recorded the following key presses:

Move to cell A5, Press the **<M>** key, press the **<i>** key, press the **<k>** key, press the **<e>** key, press the **<Enter>** key.

If I wanted to play back the *Mike* macro in the future, I would simply run the *TypeMikeIntoCellA5* macro.

The word *Mike* would then magically appear in cell A5 and the cursor would move down to cell A6. The macro would have effectively pressed all of the keys for me automatically.

The actual method that Excel uses to save and play back your key presses and mouse clicks is to automatically write VBA code, but you don't need to know anything about those technicalities in order to record and play macros.

1   Open a new blank workbook.

2   Begin recording a macro called *MyName* with a shortcut key of **<Alt>+<Cmd>+<t>**.

     1. Click: View→Macros→Record Macro.

     2. Type **MyName** into the *Macro name* box.

        Note that macro names cannot contain spaces.

     3. Type a lower case **t** into the *Option+Cmd+* box.

     4. Select *This Workbook* from the *Store macro in* drop-down list.

The other options for this setting will be explained later.

5. Describe your macro in the *Description* box.

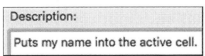

6. Click the *OK* button – but do nothing else!

   You are now recording your macro. There's no time element to a macro recording, so you can be relaxed. The macro will record every key press and every mouse click, so it is important that you do not press any keys or click anywhere with the mouse.

3 Record a macro that will put your name into the active cell.

Remember that every click and keystroke are recorded, so be careful not to move to any other cell. If you did, your name would always appear in the cell you had moved to when the macro was played.

1. Type your name into the currently active cell.

2. Press **<Cmd>+<Enter>**.

   When you press **<Cmd>+<Enter>** you save the value into the cell without moving to the next line. This keystroke combination is very useful when recording macros.

4 Stop the macro recording.

You can do this in two ways:

Click: View→Macros→Stop Recording.

OR

Click the *Stop* button at the bottom left of the screen.

It is a common error to forget to stop a macro recording. I've seen Excel crash in my classes when a student had forgotten and then accidentally continued to record for a long period.

5 Test the macro.

1. Click in any blank cell.

2. Click: View→Macros→View Macros.

   The macro dialog appears, listing only the *MyName* macro (as you have only recorded one macro so far).

3. Click the *Run* button.

   Your name appears in the currently active cell.

4. Click in another blank cell and press: **<Alt>+<Cmd>+<t>**

   Once again, your name appears in the currently active cell.

6 Close the workbook without saving.

note

Choosing where to store your macros

There are three possible places to store a macro:

> Personal Macro Workbook
> New Workbook
> ✓ This Workbook

Macros stored in *This Workbook* are also available to other workbooks – but only if the workbook containing the macro is open!

The *Personal Macro Workbook* is a special workbook called *Personal.xlsb*. This is stored in a folder called XLSTART buried deep in the file system where nobody is likely to find and change it.

Whenever you open Excel, the Personal Macro Workbook opens in the background (but it is hidden so you never see it). Because it is always open, every workbook has access to its macros at all times. The only purpose of the Personal Macro Workbook is to act as a container to store macros that you want to be available to every workbook.

Remember that if you store macros in the Personal Macro Workbook, they will only work on your machine. If you e-mail a workbook that depends upon one of these macros, it will not work on the recipient's machine. In this type of scenario, you'd want to store the macro in *This Workbook*.

You'll rarely want to use the *New Workbook* option. If you record a macro in a new workbook, you would have to always make sure that it was open before you could access its macros.

Lesson 7-11: Record a macro

1 Open *Expenses Claim-1* from your sample files folder.

Imagine this is a form that you need to fill in every week. Every time you make an expenses claim, you have to add your *Employee Number* and other details. This isn't very efficient, so you decide to record a macro that will automatically complete part of the form.

2 Begin recording a macro.

Click: View→Macros→Record Macro.

The *Record Macro* dialog appears.

3 Name the macro *FillInExpenseForm*.

Type **FillInExpenseForm** into the *Macro name* box.

Note that macro names cannot contain spaces. Always use mixed case for macro names and do not abbreviate. (For example, don't use names such as **FillExpFrm** – they will only confuse).

4 Assign a shortcut key of **<Alt>+<Cmd>+<e>** to the macro.

Type a lower case **e** into the *Option+Cmd+* box.

See the sidebar on facing page for more about choosing macro shortcut keys.

5 Store the macro in *This Workbook*.

Note that there are three possible places to store a macro.

> Personal Macro Workbook
> New Workbook
> ✓ This Workbook

Normally you'll simply want to choose between *This Workbook* (when the macro is only useful in one workbook) and the *Personal Macro Workbook* (when the macro may be used by all workbooks). See the sidebar for more details.

This macro will only ever be used in the *Expenses Claim-1* workbook, so the most appropriate location is in *This Workbook*.

> Store macro in:
> This Workbook

If there were many expense claim forms that all had the same data in cells B3, B5, B7, B9 and B11, you'd want to store the macro in the *Personal Macro Workbook* to make it available to all workbooks on your computer.

6 Add a *Description* to the macro.

It is good practice to describe your macros so that other users will understand what they are used for. The description is displayed in the *Macro* dialog when the user runs the macro.

Describe your macro in the *Description* box.

Expenses Claim-1

important

Choosing macro shortcut keys

OS X has many built-in shortcut keys (such as <Alt>+<Cmd>+<m> to minimize windows).

If you tried to define <Alt>+<Cmd>+<m> as your macro shortcut key, an error message would appear, informing you that you cannot do this.

> **The Operating System has reserved that keyboard shortcut.**
> You should assign a different keyboard shortcut.

There are several strategies to avoid causing clashes with the built-in shortcut keys:

1. Use capital letters for shortcut keys. This will result in a shortcut key of:

<Alt>+<Cmd>+<Shift>+<m>

2. Only run macros from the ribbon.

Click: View→Macros→View Macros.

You can also use the shortcut key: <Alt>+<Fn>+<F8>

This is quite an awkward way to access your macros.

3. Provide the user with buttons to run macros. You'll learn how to do this in: *Lesson 7-14: Run a macro from a button control.*

note

Relative references

Excel 2016 for Mac always uses *absolute references* when recording macros. This means, for example, that if you record a macro that moves up one cell to cell A3, it will *always* move to cell A3, instead of moving relative to the active cell.

It isn't possible to change this behavior in the Mac version of Excel 2016.

> Description:
> Fill in the Name, Department, Employee Number, Bank Account No and Sort Code in the Expenses Claim form

7 Record the macro.

1. Click the *OK* button.

2. Make cell B3 the active cell.

    This is a potential pitfall. If B3 is already the active cell (when you begin recording the macro) and you simply type your name, the recorder will place your name into whichever cell is the active cell when the macro is run. This may not be B3.

    For this reason, if B3 was active when you began recording you would have to click into a different cell, and then back again into cell B3 to explicitly record your intention to move the cursor to cell B3.

3. Fill in each box (with fictitious details). Here's the ones I used:

	A	B
3	Name:	Elvis Presley
5	Department:	Rock and Roll
7	Employee Number:	EP999
9	Bank Account No:	398724789A
11	Sort Code:	32-77-63

4. Click in cell A16, as this is the most likely cell that the user would want to enter text into after the macro has run.

5. Click: View→Macros→Stop Recording.

8 Test the macro.

1. Delete the contents of cells B3:B11.

2. Click: View→Macros→View Macros.

    The macro dialog appears, listing only the *FillInExpenseForm* macro (as you have only recorded one macro so far).

3. Click the *Run* button.

    All of the details that you previously recorded appear in the relevant cells.

4. Delete the contents of cells B3:B11.

5. Press <Alt>+<Cmd>+<e>

    Once again the form is completed with the recorded details.

9 Don't save your work yet, but keep the workbook open.

You need to understand more about security and workbook formats before you can save. You'll save this workbook in the next lesson: *Lesson 7-12: Understand macro security.*

You must begin this sequence of two lessons at: Lesson 7-11

Lesson 7-12: Understand macro security

Why is security needed?

Macros are a wonderful Excel feature but they can also be dangerous. It is possible to record a macro that will damage your computer in many ways.

Macro security provides several methods to identify which macros you can trust and which you can't.

You shouldn't trust any macro enabled workbook that is sent to you across the Internet. It is extremely easy to send an e-mail with a forged name and e-mail address.

The Excel Workbook and Excel Macro-Enabled Workbook formats.

There are two commonly used Excel formats:

- Excel Workbook (.xlsx file extension).

  This type of workbook can always be trusted, because it is incapable of storing a macro.

- Excel Macro-Enabled Workbook (.xlsm file extension).

  You must ensure that you can trust the origin of this type of workbook, as it is capable of carrying destructive macro viruses.

Opening a macro enabled workbook.

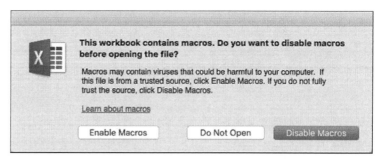

Whenever you attempt to open a workbook that contains macros, Excel warns you about the possible security risk and asks whether you wish to enable them.

If you don't trust the source of the file, you can chose to open it with macros disabled.

You can disable this warning by going to:
→Excel→Preferences→Security & Privacy→
Warn me before opening a file that contains macros.

…but I'd strongly recommend leaving the warning enabled.

1   *Expenses Claim-1* should still be open from the previous lesson.

In the previous lesson, you recorded a macro within this workbook.

The workbook is currently an anomaly – a regular Excel Workbook that contains a macro. Excel cannot allow such a workbook to be saved.

2   Attempt to save the workbook.

Excel warns you (in a rather cryptic way) that you cannot save this workbook as a regular (macro free) workbook.

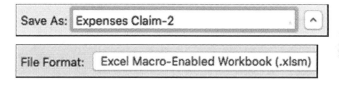

3   Click the *Cancel* button to close the dialog.

The *Save As* dialog appears.

4   Save the workbook as an *Excel Macro-Enabled* Workbook named *Expenses Claim-2*.

1.   Navigate to the folder that you wish to save the file to.

2.   Change the *File Format* to: *Excel Macro-Enabled Workbook.*

3.   Change the file name to: **Expenses Claim-2**

4.   Click the *Save* button.

You have now saved your first macro enabled workbook.

5   Close *Expenses Claim-2*.

6   Reopen *Expenses Claim-2*.

A warning message appears.

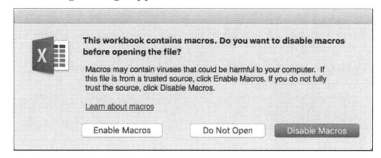

7   Click *Enable Macros* to open the workbook with macros enabled.

8   Close *Expenses Claim-2*.

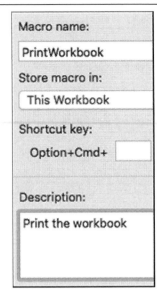

Macro name:

PrintWorkbook

Store macro in:

This Workbook

Shortcut key:

Option+Cmd+

Description:

Print the workbook

Lesson 7-13: Use shapes to run macros

1 Open *Mortgage Calculator-10 from* your sample files folder.

2 Record a macro in *This Workbook* called *PrintWorkbook.*

1. Click: View→Macros→Record Macro.

2. Type **PrintWorkbook** into the *Macro name* box.

3. Describe what the macro does in the *Description* box (see sidebar).

4. Click the *OK* button.

5. Click: ▲→File→Print and click the *Print* button.

   The worksheet will print out on your default printer.

6. Click: View→Macros→Stop Recording.

3 Save the workbook as a macro enabled workbook called *Mortgage Calculator-11.*

1. Click: ▲→File→Save As.

2. Navigate to the folder that you wish to save the file in.

3. Select *Excel Macro-Enabled Workbook* from the *File Format* dropdown list.

4. Type: **Mortgage Calculator-11** into the *Save As* box.

5. Click the *Save* button.

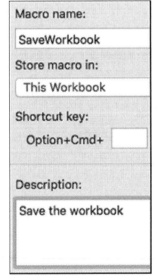

Macro name:

SaveWorkbook

Store macro in:

This Workbook

Shortcut key:

Option+Cmd+

Description:

Save the workbook

4 Record a macro in *This Workbook* called *SaveWorkbook.*

1. Click: View→Macros→Record Macro.

2. Type **SaveWorkbook** into the *Macro name* box.

3. Describe what the macro does in the *Description* box (see sidebar).

4. Click the *OK* button.

5. Click: ▲→File→Save.

6. Click: View→Macros→Stop Recording.

5 Add three shape controls to the worksheet.

1. Click: Review→Changes→Unprotect Sheet (if the worksheet is protected).

2. Re-size the pie chart to make space for a row of buttons underneath.

3. Click: Insert→Illustrations→Shapes→Rectangles→ Rounded Rectangle.

4. Click and drag on the worksheet to draw the button.

5. Click: Shape Format→Shape Styles→ Shape Style Gallery→Intense Effect – Blue, Accent 1.

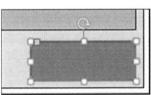

Mortgage Calculator-10

6. Click: Shape Format→Shape Styles→ Shape Effects→Bevel→Circle.

7. Right-click on the button and click *Edit Text* from the shortcut menu.

8. Type: **Save Quote** to add a caption to the shape.

9. Click: Home→Alignment→Middle Align.

10. Click: Home→Alignment→Center Align.

11. Copy and paste the shape twice.

12. Change the captions on the other two shapes to read **Print Quote** and **Go To Website**.

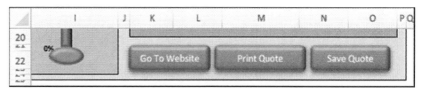

6 Connect the *Save Quote* and *Print Quote* shapes to the *SaveWorkbook* and *PrintWorkbook* macros.

1. Right-click the *Save Quote* shape.

2. Click *Assign Macro…* from the shortcut menu.

3. Select the *SaveWorkbook* macro.

4. Click the *OK* button.

5. Follow the same procedure to assign the *PrintWorkbook* macro to the *Print Quote* shape.

7 Connect the *Go To Website* shape to the ExcelCentral.com website.

1. Right-click the *Go To Website* shape.

2. Click *Hyperlink…* from the shortcut menu.

3. Click *Web Page or File* at the top of the dialog.

4. Type **http://ExcelCentral.com** into the *Address* box.

5. Click the *OK* button.

8 Protect the worksheet.

1. Click: Review→Changes→Protect Sheet.

2. Click the *OK* button.

9 Save your work as *Mortgage Calculator-11*.

10 Test the shapes.

1. Close and re-open the workbook.

   Note that you will need to enable macros after re-opening (see: *Lesson 7-12: Understand macro security*).

2. Click upon each shape.

   The relevant macro or hyperlink executes.

Lesson 7-14: Run a macro from a button control

1   Open *Human Resources-2 from* your sample files folder.

This is the workbook created in: *Lesson 5-8: Create custom views.* The workbook contains three custom views:

- Hours Worked

- Hours Worked (Female)

- HR

It is not obvious that the workbook contains custom views. You can make users more aware of the feature, and make the feature easier to use, by adding button controls to move between the custom views.

2   Record macros in *This Workbook* that will show each custom view.

1. Click: View→Macros→Record Macro.

2. Type **ShowHoursWorkedView** in the *Macro name* box.

3. Describe what the macro does in the *Description* box.

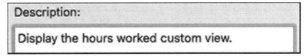

4. Click the *OK* button to begin recording the macro.

5. Click: View→Workbook Views→Custom Views.

6. Select the *Hours Worked* view.

7. Click the *Show* button.

8. Click: View→Macros→Stop Recording.

9. Create a **ShowHoursWorkedFemaleView** macro that will display the *Hours Worked (Female)* custom view.

10. Create a **ShowHRView** macro that will display the *HR* custom view.

3   Add a button control to cell A8 with the caption *Hours Worked* that will run the *ShowHoursWorkedView* macro.

1. If the *Developer* tab is not shown on the ribbon, click: →Excel→Preferences→View and check the *Developer tab* check box at the bottom of the window.

2. Click: Developer→Controls→Button.

3. Click and drag in the top of cell A8 to add a button.

4. The *Assign Macro* dialog appears.

Human Resources-2

note

Create a macro that runs automatically when a workbook is opened

In this lesson's workbook you might want the opening view to always be the HR view, no matter which view was selected when the workbook was last saved.

You are able to do this by creating a macro that automatically runs when the workbook is opened.

To do this, simply record a macro named *Auto_open* that selects the HR view.

The name of the macro tells Excel to run it automatically when the workbook is opened.

5. Select the *ShowHoursWorkedView* macro.

6. Click the *OK* button.

7. Click on the face of the button, delete the existing text and type: **Hours Worked**

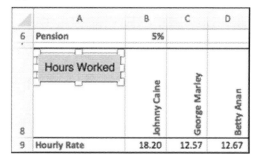

4   Add another button control to cell A8 with the caption *Hours Worked (Female)* that will run the *ShowHoursWorkedFemaleView* macro.

5   Add another button control to cell A8 with the caption *HR* that will run the *ShowHRView* macro.

	A	B	C	D	E	F	G
1	Payroll						
	Hours Worked	Johnny Caine	George Marley	Betty Anan	Paris Winfrey	Ozzy Dickens	Johnny Roberts
8	Hours Worked (Female)						
	HR						
11	Hours Worked						
12	Monday	9	10	10	10	7	7
13	Tuesday	8	9	8	6	10	10

6   Test the workbook.

Click on each of the buttons. The workbook should display each custom view as the buttons are clicked.

7   Save your work as a macro-enabled workbook with the name *Human Resources-3*.

Session 7: Exercise

1   Open *Gala Dinner-1* from your sample files folder.

2   Add combo box, group box, option button and check box form controls, so that the user interface looks like this:

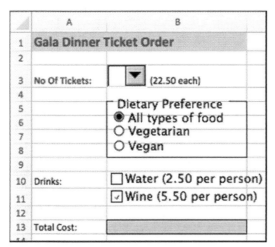

3   Add a new worksheet called *Data*.

4   Add a named range to the *Data* worksheet called *Tickets*, containing the numbers 1-10.

5   Set the *Input range* of the combo box control to the *Tickets* range name.

6   Link the combo box and check box controls to the input cells (B19, B20 and B21).

7   Add formulas to the result cells (B24, B25, B26 and B27) to calculate the total cost of the order.

8   Add a formula to cell B13 so that it displays the same value as cell B27 and hide rows 18 to 27.

9   Record a macro named *PrintOrder* in *This Worksheet* that will print the worksheet.

10   Add a button control to the form that will run the *PrintOrder* macro.

11   Save your work as a *Macro-Enabled Workbook* named *Gala Dinner-2*.

Gala Dinner-1

If you need help slide the page to the left ▶

Session 7: Exercise Answers

These are the four questions that students find the most difficult to answer:

Q 9	Q 7	Q 6	Q 3 & 4
1. Click: View→Macros→Macros→Record Macro…	The correct formulas are:	1. Right-click the combo box.	1. Click the *New Sheet* button at the bottom left of the screen to insert a new worksheet.
2. Type **PrintOrder** into the *Macro name* box.	*Ticket Cost* (B24): **=B19*22.5**	2. Click *Format Control…* from the shortcut menu.	2. Double-click on the new tab and change the worksheet name to: **Data**
3. Select *This Workbook* from the *Store macro in* drop-down list.	*Water Cost* (B25): **=IF(B20=TRUE, B19*2.5,0)**	3. Click the *Control* tab.	3. Select the *Data* worksheet and type **Tickets** into cell A1.
4. Click the *OK* button.	*Wine Cost* (B26): **=IF(B21=TRUE, B19*5.5,0)**	4. Click in the *Cell Link* box.	4. Type the numbers 1 to 10 in cells A2:A11.
5. Click: ⌘→File→Print.	*Total Cost* (B27): **=SUM(B24:B26)**	5. Click in cell B19.	5. Select cells A1:A11.
6. Click the *Print* button.	This was covered in: *Lesson 7-6: Use check box data in result cells.*	6. Click the *OK* button.	6. Click: Formulas→Defined Names→Create from Selection.
7. Click: View→Macros→Stop Recording.		7. Follow the same steps for the check boxes, linking the *Water* check box to cell B20 and the *Wine* check box to cell B21.	7. Click the *OK* button.
This was covered in: *Lesson 7-13: Use shapes to run macros.*		This was covered in: *Lesson 7-3: Set form control cell links.*	You have now created a named range called *Tickets* that references cells A2:A11.
			This was covered in: *Lesson 4-1: Automatically create single-cell range names.*

If you have difficulty with the other questions, here are the lessons that cover the relevant skills:

2   Refer to: *Lesson 7-1: Add group box and option button controls to a worksheet form, Lesson 7-2: Add a combo box control to a worksheet form* and *Lesson 7-5: Add a check box control to a worksheet form.*

5   Refer to: *Lesson 7-2: Add a combo box control to a worksheet form.*

8   The correct formula is: **=B27**. To hide the rows, select them, right-click inside the selected range and click *Hide* from the shortcut menu.

10   Refer to: *Lesson 7-14: Run a macro from a button control.*

Session Eight: Pivot Tables

> If the only tool you have is a hammer, you tend to see every problem as a nail.
>
> *Abraham Maslow (1908 - 1970)*

I'm constantly amazed at how many highly experienced Excel users are unable to understand pivot tables.

I've seen many cases where a user has spent hours creating a worksheet-based solution that could have been addressed in a few seconds using a pivot table. This session will empower you with a complete mastery of this powerful Excel feature.

Session Objectives

By the end of this session you will be able to:

- Create a one dimensional pivot table report from a table
- Create a grouped pivot table report
- Understand pivot table rows and columns
- Understand the pivot table data cache
- Apply a simple filter and sort to a pivot table
- Use report filter fields
- Filter a pivot table visually using slicers
- Use slicers to create a custom timeline
- Use report filter fields to automatically create multiple pages
- Format a pivot table using pivot table styles
- Create a custom pivot table style
- Understand pivot table report layouts
- Add/remove subtotals and apply cell styles to pivot table fields
- Display multiple summations within a single pivot table
- Add a calculated field to a pivot table
- Add a calculated item to a pivot table
- Group by Text, Date and numeric value ranges
- Show row data by percentage of total rather than value
- Use pivot table values in simple formulas
- Use the GETPIVOTDATA function
- Embed multiple pivot tables into a worksheet
- Use slicers to filter multiple pivot tables

trivia

Only 10% of Excel users can create a pivot table

An extensive survey of Excel users suggested that only 10% of all Excel users are able to create a pivot table.

Lesson 8-1: Create a one dimensional pivot table report from a table

In this lesson, you'll create a simple one-dimensional pivot table. There's a huge amount to learn about pivot tables, but it will be fun to do some useful work with one straight away.

Here's the sample file that you'll use in this lesson:

	A	B	C	D	E	F	G	H
1	Order No	Order Date	Customer	Employee	Title	Genre	Qty	Total
2	136438	02-Oct-14	Silver Screen Video	Lee,Frank	Lawrence of Arabia	Biography	15	122.76
3	136438	02-Oct-14	Silver Screen Video	Lee,Frank	The Discreet Charm of the Bourgeoisie	Comedy	9	67.46
4	136438	02-Oct-14	Silver Screen Video	Lee,Frank	Berlin Alexanderplatz	Drama	25	250.60
5	136438	02-Oct-14	Silver Screen Video	Lee,Frank	Gone With The Wind	Drama	14	107.72
6	136439	03-Oct-14	Cinefocus DVD	Diamond,Elizabeth	Mouchette	Drama	5	31.77

This is the type of worksheet that pivot tables can work well with because the columns contain repeating data.

The sample file contains over 2,000 rows of transactional data, listing sales during the 18-month period from October 2014 to March 2016 inclusive.

You can see from the data that the worksheet contains details of orders sold by a DVD wholesaler, along with the titles supplied on each order. Order *136438* was placed on *2nd-Oct-14* and was ordered by *Silver Screen Video*. The order was sold by *Frank Lee* and there were four items on the order. Two of the films ordered were in the *Drama* genre and the other two were in the *Biography* and *Comedy* genres.

A business may wish to ask several questions about sales during this period, such as:

- What were my sales by *Genre*?

- How many units did each *Employee* sell?

In this lesson, you'll use a simple pivot table to answer both questions in less than 10 seconds!

1   Open *Transactions-1* from your sample files folder.

   This worksheet contains a large table named *Data* (see sidebar for more on using tables with pivot tables).

   The table looks like a regular range because the *Filter* buttons have been switched off and the *Table Style* has been set to *None*.

2   Click anywhere inside the table.

3   Click Insert→Tables→PivotTable.

   The *Create PivotTable* dialog appears.

   Notice that, because you clicked inside the table, the dialog has automatically detected the table's name of *Data*.

important

Pivot Tables, Ranges, Named Ranges and Tables

You can create a pivot table that is associated with a *Range*, a *Named Range* or a *Table*. In Excel 2016 it is best practice to always associate pivot tables with *Tables*.

Ranges and *Named Ranges* share a common problem. If rows are added to either, the pivot table will not be aware of the added rows when it is refreshed. It would be necessary to click:

PivotTable Analyze→Data→ Change Data Source

... every time a row or column was added to the source data.

Tables are wonderful to use as a data source for pivot tables because you can add and remove rows without affecting the integrity of the pivot table.

You learned everything there is to know about tables in: *Session One: Tables, and Ranges.*

Transactions-1

note

You can also create a pivot table using Recommended PivotTables

Instead of creating your pivot table manually (as taught in this lesson), Excel can create a pivot table automatically from a template.

In this lesson you clicked:

Insert→Tables→PivotTable

This created an empty pivot table.

You could also have clicked:

Insert→Tables→ Recommended PivotTables

This option tries to automatically create a useful pivot table based on the data.

note

Help – my PivotTable Builder dialog isn't visible

Pivot tables are a little like charts in that you cannot work upon their design unless they are activated. To activate, you simply click anywhere inside the pivot table.

When the pivot table is activated, the *PivotTable Builder* dialog appears, along with the *PivotTable Analyze* and *Design* tabs on the ribbon.

You can also explicitly close the *PivotTable Builder* dialog (by clicking the close button in the top left-hand corner of the dialog). If you do this, it will remain hidden even when the pivot table is activated. To bring back the task pane you will need to:

1. Click inside the pivot table to activate it.

2. Click: PivotTable Analyze→ Show→Field List.

4   Click the *OK* button.

An empty pivot table is shown on screen and the *PivotTable Builder* dialog appears (see sidebar if it doesn't).

5   Create a pivot table to show sales by genre.

1. Check the *Qty* and *Total* check boxes in the *PivotTable Builder*.

2. Drag *Genre* from the *Field Name* box into the *Rows* box.

You have now answered the first question:

- What were my sales by *Genre*?

6   Format the values shown in column C of the pivot table so that they show two decimal places with a comma separator.

1.   Right-click on any value in column C.

2.   Click *Field Settings* from the shortcut menu.

3.   Click the *Number* button.

4.   Click *Number* in the *Category* list.

5.   Click the *Use 1000 Separator* check box.

6.   Click the *OK* button twice to close both dialogs.

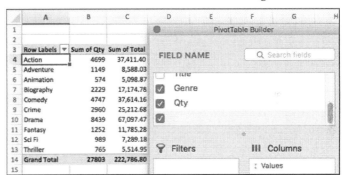

7   Clear all check boxes, then check the *Qty* check box and drag *Employee* into the *Rows* box.

Once again, with very little effort, you have answered the second question:

- How many units did each *Employee* sell?

8   Name the pivot table: *Transactions*.

1.   Click inside the pivot table.

2.   Click: PivotTable Analyze→PivotTable→PivotTable Name.

3.   Type **Transactions** into the *PivotTable Name* box.

9   Name the pivot table worksheet tab: **Pivot Table**

10   Save your work as *Transactions-2*.

Lesson 8-2: Create a grouped pivot table report

1 Open *Transactions-2* from your sample files folder (if it isn't already open).

2 Select the *Pivot Table* worksheet (if it isn't already selected).

3 Click inside the pivot table to show the *PivotTable Builder* dialog.

If the *PivotTable Builder* doesn't appear, click: PivotTable Analyze→Show→Field List.

4 Drag *Genre* into the *Rows* box.

Each employee's sales for each genre are now shown in the report.

5 Add *Title* information to the pivot table.

Drag *Title* into the *Rows* box in the *PivotTable Builder* dialog.

The report now breaks sales down by *Employee, Genre* and *Title*.

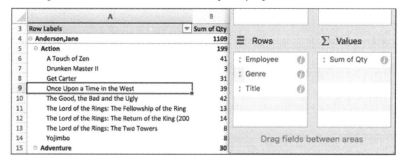

6 Collapse the outline to show only sales by *Employee*.

1. Right-click in cell A4.

2. Click: Group and Outline→Hide Detail.

Transactions-2

trivia

PivotTable or Pivot Table?

The term *Pivot Table* has been used for a long time to describe the general concept of summarizing data.

One of the earliest implementations of pivot tables was introduced in *Lotus Improv* (released in 1991).

Pivot tables also featured in the 1992 release of *Quattro Pro*. Quattro called this feature *DataPivot*.

Pivot tables first appeared in Excel in the 1994 *Excel 5* release. The Excel pivot table feature was called *PivotTable* (without a space). This name was registered as a trademark by Microsoft in December 1994.

In the ribbon, and in most Microsoft documentation, you'll see 'pivot table' spelled as *PivotTable* rather than *pivot table*.

It would be correct to refer to an Excel pivot table both in the more general way (*pivot table*) and also using the Microsoft trademark (*PivotTable*).

In this book I try to consistently use the *PivotTable* terminology only when referring to a feature within the user interface where this spelling is used. At all other times I find *pivot table* (with a space) to be more elegant.

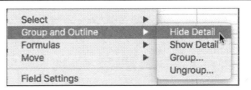

The pivot table collapses to the level of *Employee*.

	A	B
3	Row Labels ▼	Sum of Qty
4	⊞ Anderson,Jane	1109
5	⊞ Armstrong,Dan	1000
6	⊞ Ashe,Lucille	1116
7	⊞ Bell,Stephen	1409

7 Expand Dan Armstrong's sales to show full details.

Click the small + sign to the left of cell A5.

	A	B
5	⊞ Armstrong,Dan	1000
6	⊞ Ashe,Lucille	1116

Sales are expanded to show full details of Dan's sales.

	A	B
5	⊟ Armstrong,Dan	1000
6	⊟ Action	136
7	A Touch of Zen	24
8	Drunken Master II	22

8 Collapse the outline so that Dan's sales by *Genre* are shown without *Title* details.

1. Right-click in cell A6.

   A shortcut menu appears.

2. Click: Group and Outline→Hide Detail.

   The *Title* level of the pivot table collapses to show Dan's sales by *Genre* but not by *Title*.

	A	B
5	⊟ Armstrong,Dan	1000
6	⊞ Action	136
7	⊞ Adventure	26
8	⊞ Animation	22

9 Collapse the outline to only show sales by *Employee*.

Click the small minus sign to the left of cell A5.

The outline collapses to show only the *Employee* level.

	A	B
5	⊞ Armstrong,Dan	1000
6	⊞ Ashe,Lucille	1116
7	⊞ Bell,Stephen	1409

10 Save your work as *Transactions-3*.

Lesson 8-3: Understand pivot table rows and columns

1   Open *Transactions-3* from your sample files folder (if it isn't already open).

2   Select the *Pivot Table* worksheet (if it isn't already selected).

3   Click inside the pivot table to display the *PivotTable Builder* dialog.

If the *PivotTable Builder* doesn't appear, click: PivotTable Analyze→Show→Field List.

At the bottom of the dialog, you can see four panes:

At the moment, you have three columns in the *Rows* list and one in the *Values* list. This creates a pivot table that shows sales grouped first by *Employee,* then grouped by *Genre* and then grouped by *Title.*

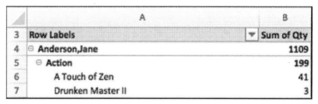

4   Remove the *Genre* and *Title* rows from the *Rows* list.

    1.   Drag *Genre* from the *Rows* pane of the *PivotTable Builder* dialog to any point on the screen that is outside the dialog.

    2.   In the same way, drag *Title* out of the *Rows* pane to remove it.

5   Add the *Genre* to the pivot table as a *Column Label.*

Instead of dragging *Genre* into the *Rows* pane, you need to drag it into the *Columns* pane.

Transactions-3

The pivot table now shows sales for each employee by genre with the genres listed along the top row as column labels:

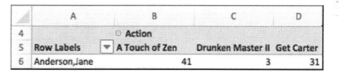

	A	B	C	D	E
4	Row Labels ▼	Action	Adventure	Animation	Biography
5	Anderson,Jane	199	30		134
6	Armstrong,Dan	136	26	22	79
7	Ashe,Lucille	176	42	23	54

6   Add the *Title* field to the *Columns* list.

Drag the *Title* field into the *Columns* pane list.

Make sure that you place *Title* below *Genre*.

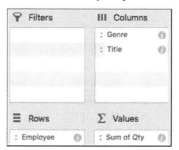

▼ Filters	III Columns
	⦂ Genre ⓘ
	⦂ Title ⓘ
≡ Rows	Σ Values
⦂ Employee ⓘ	⦂ Sum of Qty ⓘ

A small + sign is now displayed next to each genre:

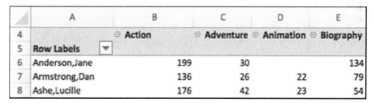

	A	B	C	D	E
4		⊞ Action	⊞ Adventure	⊞ Animation	⊞ Biography
5	Row Labels ▼				
6	Anderson,Jane	199	30		134
7	Armstrong,Dan	136	26	22	79
8	Ashe,Lucille	176	42	23	54

7   Expand and collapse the *Action* genre.

1.   Click the small + sign to the left of *Action* in cell B4.

The field expands to show each title within the *Action* genre:

	A	B	C	D
4		⊟ Action		
5	Row Labels ▼	A Touch of Zen	Drunken Master II	Get Carter
6	Anderson,Jane	41	3	31

2.   Click the small – sign that has now appeared to the left of *Action* in cell B4.

The outline collapses back to the genre level:

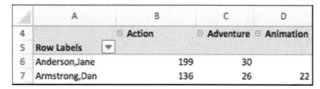

	A	B	C	D
4		⊟ Action	⊟ Adventure	⊟ Animation
5	Row Labels ▼			
6	Anderson,Jane	199	30	
7	Armstrong,Dan	136	26	22

8   Save your work as *Transactions-4.*

note

External data sources

It's possible to create a pivot table that uses an external data source, such as an Access, Oracle or SQL Server database. Unfortunately, this is only possible by downloading a 3rd party database driver.

Excel 2016 for Windows does not have this restriction, and is able to connection to external data sources without downloading add-ons.

You can see more about the differences between the Mac and Windows versions of Excel 2016 in: *Appendix A: Differences between the Windows and Mac versions of Excel 2016.*

Lesson 8-4: Understand the pivot table data cache

Data sources

Your data source will typically be a single table on a single worksheet.

This the most common data source for a pivot table and is the type of data source you've been using up until now (see sidebar for other types of data source).

Pivot tables do not directly use the data source

When you first create a pivot table, a hidden copy of the data source (called the *pivot table data cache*) is created and held in the computer's memory. This is a specially structured version of the data source that includes many pre-computed subtotals as well as all of the source data.

If you change the data source (for example by adding a new row to a table) the change does not appear in the pivot table until you refresh (create a new copy of) the *pivot table data cache.* You'll see how to refresh the cache later in this lesson.

I'm often asked whether Excel has an option to automatically refresh the pivot table whenever the source data changes. Unfortunately this isn't possible, but (as you will see later) you can ask Excel to refresh the cache whenever a workbook is opened.

Pivot tables can work without the data source

When you save a workbook containing a pivot table, the *pivot table data cache* is saved along with the workbook, meaning that the pivot table will still work perfectly even if the worksheet it is based on is deleted.

The downside is that workbooks containing both the source data and the *pivot table data cache* can have huge file sizes, as all data is effectively stored twice. For this reason, it is possible to ask Excel not to save the *pivot table data cache* with the workbook in the *PivotTable Options* (as you will see later in this lesson).

1   Open *Transactions-4* from your sample files folder.

> This pivot table uses the *Data* table on the *Data* worksheet as its data source. Notice that Frank Lee has sold a total of 157 videos in the *Biography* genre.

2   Change the source data to add ten more sales for Frank Lee in the Biography genre.

> 1.   Click the *Data* worksheet tab.
>
> 2.   Increase Frank Lee's sales (in row 2) from 15 units to 25 units.

	A	E
4		⊞ Biography
5	Row Labels ▾	
18	Lee,Frank	157

1	Title	Genre	Qty	Total
2	Lawrence of Arabia	Biography	25	122.76

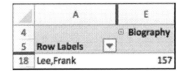

Transactions-4

3 Notice that the pivot table does not show any change.

Click the *Pivot Table* worksheet tab. Notice that Frank Lee's *Biography* genre sales remain the same at 157.

4 Refresh the pivot table data cache and observe the change.

1. Click inside the pivot table to activate it.

2. Click: PivotTable Analyze→Data→Refresh.

   Notice that Frank Lee's sales have now updated.

5 Restore Frank Lee's sales (on row 2 of the *Data* table) to the original value (of 15 units) and refresh the pivot table data cache.

6 Examine options relating to the pivot table data cache.

1. Click inside the pivot table to activate it.

2. Click: PivotTable Analyze→PivotTable→Options→Options.

3. Click the *Data* tab.

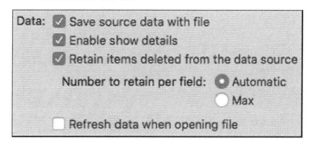

Save source data with file: Disabling this option prevents Excel from saving the *pivot table data cache*. If it is disabled, it can result in greatly reduced file sizes.

Enable show details: This option controls whether you can drill-down to see the transactions that were used to calculate any total. For more on this, see: *Lesson 8-2: Create a grouped pivot table report* (*sidebar*).

Retain items deleted from the data source: This option is a little confusing. This setting will have no effect on the numbers that are displayed within the pivot table, but actually controls how filters and slicers are refreshed.

If this setting is enabled (the default), filters and slicers will 'remember' all filtering options that have ever existed, even if they are deleted from the data source. This could be useful if you expected more data to be added later, or if you wanted to preserve a complete list of categories in your filters.

You'll learn about slicers later, in: *Lesson 8-7: Filter a pivot table visually using slicers.*

Refresh data when opening the file: Selecting this option refreshes the pivot table data cache when the workbook is opened.

tip

You can refresh a pivot table more quickly using the right-click method

In this lesson you refreshed the pivot table using the ribbon.

If you right-click inside a pivot table, you'll also see a *Refresh Data* option on the shortcut menu.

Lesson 8-5: Apply a simple filter and sort to a pivot table

1 Open *Transactions-4* from your sample files folder (if it isn't already open).

2 Select the *Pivot Table* worksheet (if it isn't already selected).

3 Click inside the pivot table to display the *PivotTable Builder* dialog.

4 Remove the *Genre* and *Title* column fields.

This was covered in: *Lesson 8-3: Understand pivot table rows and columns.*

5 Click the drop-down arrow next to *Row Labels* in cell A3.

Filter options appear.

These are very similar to the options that you learned how to use in: *Lesson 1-5: Apply a simple filter to a range* and *Lesson 1-6: Apply a top 10 and custom filter to a range.*

6 Filter the pivot table so that only female employees are shown.

1. Uncheck the check boxes next to each male employee (see sidebar).

2. Click away from the filter dialog to close it.

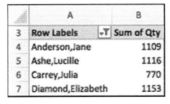

Notice the filter icon in cell A3 has changed to indicate that the pivot table has been filtered. 🔽

This is a very long winded way to filter out the male employees.

In a real-world workbook, you'd probably create a *Gender* column in the source data containing the values **M** or **F**.

You could then filter by gender with a single check box.

7 Sort *Employee* names in Z-A order.

At the moment, the names are sorted in A-Z order.

1. Right-click on any of the employee names in column A.

2. Click: Sort→Sort Z to A from the shortcut menu.

The pivot table is sorted in Z-A order.

Sidebar:

- ⊟ (Select All)
- ☑ Anderson,Jane
- ☐ Armstrong,Dan
- ☑ Ashe,Lucille
- ☐ Bell,Stephen
- ☐ Bradshaw,John
- ☑ Carrey,Julia
- ☐ Davis,Charles
- ☑ Diamond,Elizabeth
- ☐ Goodman,Paul
- ☐ Hawking,Alfred
- ☐ Hicks,Michael
- ☐ Jennings,John
- ☐ Lee,Frank
- ☑ Manning,Marilyn
- ☑ Newhart,Anna
- ☑ Putin,Julia
- ☐ Richards,Andy
- ☑ Sagan,Jessica
- ☑ Silverstone,Gloria
- ☐ Simpson,Howard
- ☑ Simpson,Meryl
- ☑ Spears,Julie
- ☑ Streep,Margaret
- ☐ West,Chuck

Transactions-4

	A	B
3	Row Labels ▾Ṯ	Sum of Qty
4	Streep,Margaret	1772
5	Spears,Julie	1314
6	Simpson,Meryl	822
7	Silverstone,Gloria	1040
8	Sagan,Jessica	1407
9	Putin,Julia	1054
10	Newhart,Anna	1081

note

Filters are not inherited from source data

If the data associated with a pivot table (whether a table, range or named range) has a filter applied to it (or contains subtotals) this will not be carried forward into the pivot table.

If you need the same filter in your pivot table, you must first create the pivot table and then apply the same filter.

Another way to achieve this is to copy the (filtered) data to a new worksheet and then create the pivot table from this subset of the actual data.

A useful technique for copying and pasting filtered data (visible cells) is described in: *Lesson 2-3: Automatically subtotal a range* (sidebar).

8 Manually sort *Employee* names by first name.

It isn't possible to automatically sort by first name. To do this, you would need *First Name* to be a different field to *Last Name*.

If there were a lot of names, you could attend to this in the source data by splitting the *Employee Name* column into two. (You learned how to do this in: *Lesson 2-1: Split fixed width data using Text to Columns* and in *Lesson 3-21: Extract text from delimited strings using the FIND and LEN functions*).

Because there are only twelve names, it will be quicker to manually sort the list.

1. Click in cell A10 (*Newhart,Anna*).

2. Move the mouse cursor to the border of the cell so that the hand cursor appears:

3. Click and drag to move Anna Newhart to the top of the list.

4. Repeat to sort the employees by their first names as shown:

	A	B
3	Row Labels ▾Ṯ	Sum of Qty
4	Newhart,Anna	1081
5	Diamond,Elizabeth	1153
6	Silverstone,Gloria	1040
7	Anderson,Jane	1109
8	Sagan,Jessica	1407
9	Carrey,Julia	770
10	Putin,Julia	1054
11	Spears,Julie	1314
12	Ashe,Lucille	1116
13	Streep,Margaret	1772
14	Manning,Marilyn	1161
15	Simpson,Meryl	822
16	Grand Total	13799

9 Remove the filter.

1. Click the filter button at the top right of cell A3.

2. Check the *Select All* check box at the top of the list of names.

3. Close the filter dialog.

10 Save your work as *Transactions-5*.

Lesson 8-6: Use report filter fields

In pre-2007 versions of Excel, report filters were called *Page Fields*.

1   Open *Transactions-5* from your sample files folder (if it isn't already open).

2   Select the *Pivot Table* worksheet (if it isn't already selected).

3   Click inside the pivot table to display the *PivotTable Builder* dialog.

4   Drag the *Genre* field from the field list at the top of the dialog to the *Filters* list below.

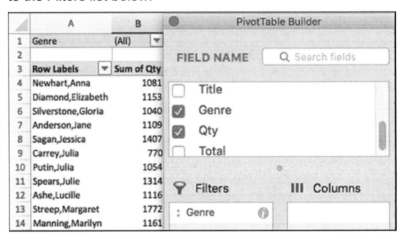

Notice that a filter has appeared at the top left of the pivot table (in cells A1 and B1):

The filter currently shows all sales for all genres.

5   Use the report filter field to display sales for the *Comedy* genre.

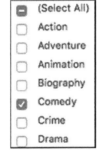

1. Click the drop-down list arrow in cell B1.

2. Uncheck the *Select All* box and check the *Comedy* box.

3. Click away from the filter dialog to close it.

    Notice that the *Sum of Qty* values now change to only show quantities sold in the *Comedy* genre.

6   Use a report filter field to show sales in the *Comedy* genre for June 2015.

1. Click in the pivot table to open the *PivotTable Builder* dialog.

2. Drag the *Order Date* field into the *Filters* list.

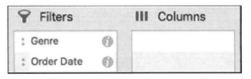

Transactions-5

3. Click the drop-down arrow in cell B2.

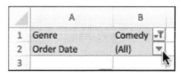

4. Type **jun-15** into the *Search* box.

(The search text is not case sensitive, so exactly the same results would be displayed if you had typed *JUN-15*).

The *Search* box filters the entries in the list to dates containing the text *jun-15.*

5. Uncheck *Select All* and check all of the checkboxes for June 2015.

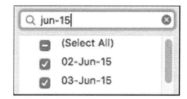

You'll discover an easier way to filter by month in: *Lesson 8-8: Use slicers to create a custom timeline.*

6. Click away from the filter dialog.

7. The total quantities of goods sold in the *Comedy* genre during *June 2015* are now displayed.

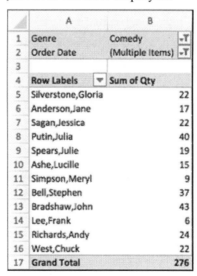

Notice that the filter information in cell B2 *(Multiple Items)* gives no information to the user about the filter currently in place. In *Lesson 8-7: Filter a pivot table visually using slicers* you'll discover a much better way of showing the user which multiple item filters are currently active.

7   Save your work as *Transactions-6.*

Lesson 8-7: Filter a pivot table visually using slicers

Unlike report filter fields, slicers show which filters are in place when a multiple-item filter is applied.

Slicers are also very useful for designing touch-screen user interfaces for tablet personal computers.

1   Open *Transactions-6* from your sample files folder (if it isn't already open).

2   Remove all existing fields and filters from the pivot table.

Sometimes you will want to completely clear all filters and fields from a pivot table.

1.   Click inside the pivot table to activate it.

2.   Click PivotTable Analyze→Actions→Clear→Clear All.

3   Display the *Total* and *Qty* values for each genre.

In the *PivotTable Builder* dialog, click the check-boxes for *Qty* and *Total* and then drag *Genre* into the *Rows* box.

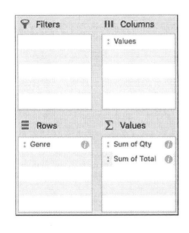

4   Change the number format for the values shown in column C to show two decimal places with a comma thousand separator.

You learned how to do this in: *Lesson 8-1: Create a one dimensional pivot table report from a table.*

5   Change the number format for the values shown in column B to show no decimal places and a comma thousand separator.

You learned how to do this in: *Lesson 8-1: Create a one dimensional pivot table report from a table.*

6   Change the text in cell A4 to **Genre**, in cell B4 to **Sales Qty** and in cell C4 to **Total Sales**.

Click in each cell and type the new text.

Your pivot table should now look like this:

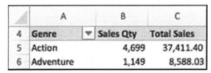

	A	B	C
4	Genre	Sales Qty	Total Sales
5	Action	4,699	37,411.40
6	Adventure	1,149	8,588.03

7   Add slicers to filter by Genre and Customer.

In *Lesson 8-6: Use report filter fields,* you saw how filtering could be done using report filter fields. This time you'll implement the filters using slicers.

1.   Click anywhere in the pivot table to activate it.

2.   Click: PivotTable Analyze→Filter→Insert Slicer.

The *Insert Slicers* dialog appears.

Transactions-6

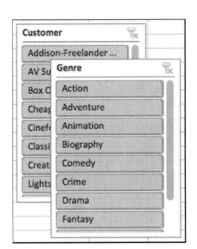

3. Check the *Genre* and *Customer* check boxes.

4. Click the *OK* button.

Two slicers appear on the worksheet.

8 **Move and format the slicers so that they have an attractive appearance.**

1. Click on the *Genre* slicer to select it and then click and drag the border to move it next to the pivot table.

2. Click: Slicer→Buttons→Columns and type **6** into the text box.

3. Re-size the slicer so that all genre names are visible.

4. Click: Slicer→Slicer Styles and select an attractive style.

5. Do the same for the *Customer* slicer, setting the *Columns* to 3.

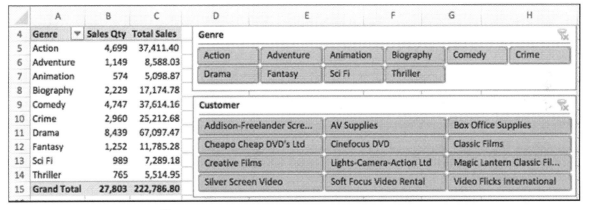

9 **Test the slicers.**

1. Click the *Action* button on the *Genre* slicer.

Notice that the pivot table is filtered to only show sales values for the *Action* genre.

2. Click the *Cinefocus DVD* button on the *Customer* slicer and then hold down the **<Cmd>** key and click the *Classic Films* button.

Notice that only sales to the selected customers for the *Action* genre are now shown.

3. Clear the slicer filters by clicking the *Clear Filter* buttons in each slicer's top right corner.

10 **Save your work as *Transactions-7*.**

note

Creating Years, Months, Days and Quarters from a date value

Year

The YEAR function is covered in: *Lesson 3-8: Understand common date functions.*

Month as a string

The TEXT function is covered in *Lesson 3-19: Use the TEXT function to format numerical values as strings.*

The custom format code: "mmm" formats a date as a three character text value (such as *Jan*). The *Essential Skills* book in this series extensively covers the (rather cryptic) formatting codes available in Excel.

Day

The DAY function is covered in: *Lesson 3-8: Understand common date functions.*

Quarter

1. The Month is first returned as a number (1-12) using the MONTH function (covered in: *Lesson 3-8: Understand common date functions*).

2. The number of the month returned is then divided by three. For example, May would return 5/3 = 2.666.

3. The ROUNDUP function is used to round the number up to the nearest whole number. This returns the correct quarter (1-4).

The completed formula can be seen in the *Data* worksheet:

=ROUNDUP(MONTH([@Date])/3,0)

Lesson 8-8: Use slicers to create a custom timeline

The Windows version of Excel 2016 offers a timeline control that works in a similar way to a slicer. The timeline control offers a quick and convenient way to filter by date, but you are unable to significantly customize its appearance. In this lesson, you'll create the same timeline functionality using slicers to provide a more elegant user interface.

Before you can add a date-driven interface to a pivot table you will need to create fields in the underlying data table for *Year, Month, Day* and *Quarter*. This has already been done in the sample file for this lesson:

	B	C	D	E	F
1	Date	Year	Month	Day	Quarter
2	02-Jan-15	2015	Jan	2	1
3	01-Jan-15	2015	Jan	1	1

Before beginning this lesson, you may find it useful to study the formulas used to create these fields from the *Date* field. If you do not understand how these formulas work, refer to the sidebar for more information.

1 Open *Executive Summary-1 from* your sample files folder.

2 Add slicers to the pivot table for *Year, Quarter, Month* and *Day*.

   You learned how to do this in: *Lesson 8-7: Filter a pivot table visually using slicers.*

3 Format the slicers so that they look the same as the screen grab at the bottom of the facing page.

   You learned how to do this in: *Lesson 8-7: Filter a pivot table visually using slicers.*

   Notice that a *Year* slicer has been included even though the underlying data only has a single year (2015).

   When you use slicers to create a timeline, it is good practice to always include a *Year* slicer because you can never be sure that more data will not be added to the underlying data table.

   For example, if 2016 sales data were added to the table, selecting *Jan* would show sales for both Jan 2015 and Jan 2016 if the *Year* slicer was not included.

4 Use the slicers to show sales for the first two quarters of 2015 in the *Action, Animation and Comedy* genres.

   1. Click the *1* button in the *Quarter* slicer and then hold down the **<Cmd>** key and click the *2* button.

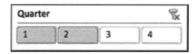

   Notice that the months Jan-Jun are now selected in the *Month* slicer.

   OR

Click the *Jan* button in the *Month* slicer and then hold down the **<Shift>** key and click the *Jun* button.

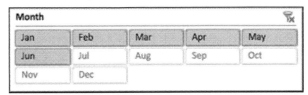

Notice that the 1 and 2 buttons are now selected in the *Quarter* slicer

2. Click the *Action* button in the *Genre* slicer and then hold down the **<Cmd>** key and click the *Animation* and *Comedy* buttons.

Sales are now shown for the first two quarters of 2015 in the *Action, Comedy* and *Animation* genres.

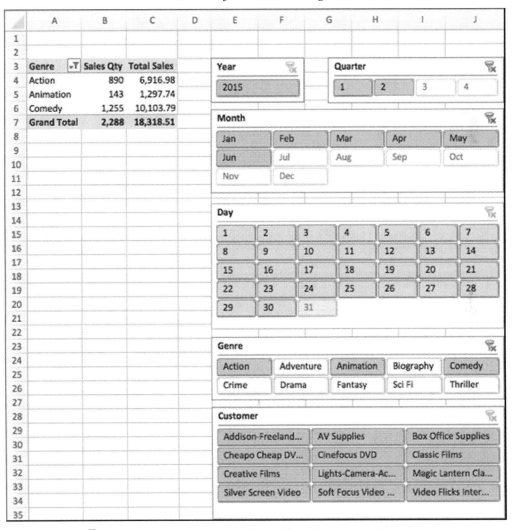

5 Save your work as *Executive Summary-2*.

Lesson 8-9: Use report filter fields to automatically create multiple pages

In this lesson, you will cater for the following scenario:

You have been asked to print out a sales listing for each employee. This involves printing a total of 23 separate reports.

It is easy, but time consuming, to print each sheet manually. You would need to perform 23 filter and print operations. Surely there's a better way?

Of course there is. You can use a report filter to automate the whole task and print all 23 reports in one operation.

1   Open *Transactions-7* from your sample files folder.

2   Select the *Pivot Table* worksheet (if it isn't already selected).

3   Remove all filters and fields from the pivot table.

There's a quick way to remove all filters and fields from a pivot table. This is very useful when you want to start again with an empty pivot table.

1.   Click inside the pivot table to activate it.

2.   Click: PivotTable Analyze→Actions→Clear→Clear All.

4   Change the fields displayed by the pivot table so that they match the following:

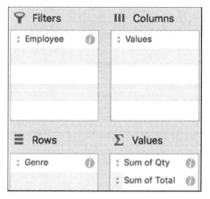

You learned how to do this in: *Lesson 8-3: Understand pivot table rows and columns.* Note that the ⦂ Values field automatically appears in the *Columns* list when you add more than one field to the *Values* list.

Your pivot table now looks like this:

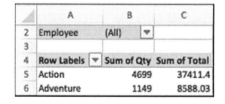

5 Create separate worksheets detailing each employee's sales.

1. Click anywhere within the pivot table.

2. Click: PivotTable Analyze→PivotTable→Options→ Show Report Filter Pages…

   The *Show Pages* dialog appears.

   Because there is only one report filter, there's only one choice.

   If you had multiple filters, you could choose which filter you wanted to use.

3. Click the *OK* button.

   Something amazing happens.

   24 worksheets are instantly created, one for each employee.

   Here's Jane Anderson's sheet:

   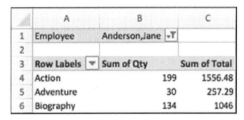

   You can see that it contains a copy of the original pivot table with a filter set for *Anderson, Jane.*

6 Print preview all worksheets.

1. Click on the first employee's tab (Anderson, Jane).

2. Use the worksheet scroll bar buttons so that the last employee's tab (West, Chuck) is visible.

3. Hold down the **<Shift>** key.

4. Click on the last employee's tab (West, Chuck).

   You have now selected all of the employee worksheets (you don't want to print the *Pivot Table* or *Data* worksheets).

5. Click: ⌘→File→Print.

   Notice that *Print Active Sheets* is selected by default.

   Notice the preview pane. All 24 employee sheets will be printed.

6. Click the *Cancel* button to return to the worksheet.

7 Save your work as *Multiple Sheets-1.*

Lesson 8-10: Format a pivot table using pivot table styles

In: *Lesson 1-12: Format a table using table styles and convert a table into a range,* you learned how to use a built-in style to format an Excel table. Pivot table styles are used in a similar way.

1 Open *Transactions-7* from your sample files folder.

2 Remove all existing fields and filters from the pivot table.

    1. Select the *Pivot Table* worksheet.

    2. Click inside the pivot table to activate it.

    3. Click: PivotTable Analyze→Actions→Clear→Clear All.

3 Delete the slicers from the pivot table.

Click on each slicer and then press the **<Delete>** key.

4 Select the fields shown below.

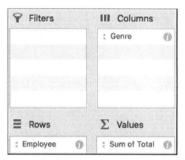

5 Filter to only show the genres: *Action, Adventure* and *Animation* for employees: *Dan Armstrong, Julie Spears* and *Chuck West*.

You learned how to do this in: *Lesson 8-5: Apply a simple filter and sort to a pivot table.*

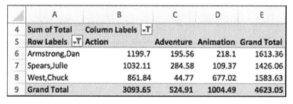

	A	B	C	D	E
4	Sum of Total	Column Labels ▾T			
5	Row Labels ▾T	Action	Adventure	Animation	Grand Total
6	Armstrong,Dan	1199.7	195.56	218.1	1613.36
7	Spears,Julie	1032.11	284.58	109.37	1426.06
8	West,Chuck	861.84	44.77	677.02	1583.63
9	Grand Total	3093.65	524.91	1004.49	4623.05

6 Apply the PivotTable style: *Light 17.*

Click: Design→PivotTable Styles→Light→Pivot Style Light 17.

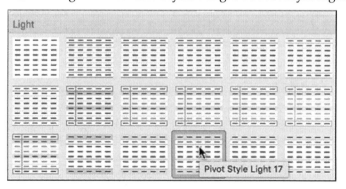

Transactions-7

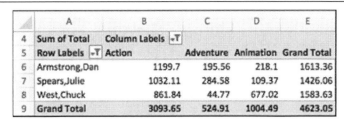

	A	B	C	D	E
4	Sum of Total	Column Labels ▾T			
5	Row Labels ▾T	Action	Adventure	Animation	Grand Total
6	Armstrong,Dan	1199.7	195.56	218.1	1613.36
7	Spears,Julie	1032.11	284.58	109.37	1426.06
8	West,Chuck	861.84	44.77	677.02	1583.63
9	Grand Total	3093.65	524.91	1004.49	4623.05

7   Enable *Banded Rows.*

Check: Design→PivotTable Style Options→Banded Rows.

The pivot table changes to show colored shading on alternate rows.

	A	B	C	D	E
4	Sum of Total	Column Labels ▾T			
5	Row Labels ▾T	Action	Adventure	Animation	Grand Total
6	Armstrong,Dan	1199.7	195.56	218.1	1613.36
7	Spears,Julie	1032.11	284.58	109.37	1426.06
8	West,Chuck	861.84	44.77	677.02	1583.63
9	Grand Total	3093.65	524.91	1004.49	4623.05

The colored bands can help the eye to track across rows, especially when a pivot table is printed.

8   Disable *Banded Rows* and enable *Banded Columns.*

Uncheck: Design→PivotTable Style Options→Banded Rows.

Check: Design→PivotTable Style Options→Banded Columns.

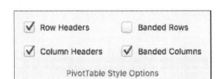

	A	B	C	D	E
4	Sum of Total	Column Labels ▾T			
5	Row Labels ▾T	Action	Adventure	Animation	Grand Total
6	Armstrong,Dan	1199.7	195.56	218.1	1613.36
7	Spears,Julie	1032.11	284.58	109.37	1426.06
8	West,Chuck	861.84	44.77	677.02	1583.63
9	Grand Total	3093.65	524.91	1004.49	4623.05

9   Disable *Banded Columns.*

Clear the *Banded Columns* check box.

10   Understand the two other *PivotTable Style Options.*

The other two options in the *PivotTable Style Options* group are: *Row Headers* and *Column Headers.*

In the *Light 17* style, the column headers are shown in a contrasting color. The *Column Headers* check box allows you to switch this color off.

Some of the other styles also show row headers (cells A6:A8) in a contrasting color. If you were using this type of style, you could switch this color off with the *Row Headers* check box.

11   Save your work as *Transactions-8.*

Lesson 8-11: Create a custom pivot table style

In: *Lesson 1-13: Create a custom table style,* you learned how to create a custom style for an Excel table. Pivot table custom styles are applied in a similar way.

1   Open *Transactions-8* from your sample files folder (if it isn't already open).

2   Remove the existing style.

   1.   Click the pivot table to activate it.

   2.   Click: Design→PivotTable Styles→Light→None.

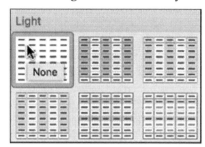

3   Create a custom pivot table style called *Corporate* by duplicating the *Medium8* built in style.

You'll usually find that modifying a duplicate of an existing style is easier than creating a style from scratch.

   1.   Right-click on:

      Design→PivotTable Styles→Medium→Pivot Style Medium 8

   2.   Click *Duplicate...* from the shortcut menu.

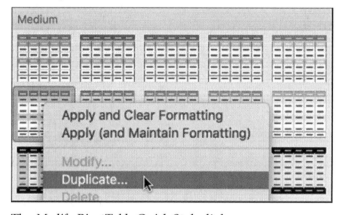

The *Modify PivotTable Quick Style* dialog appears:

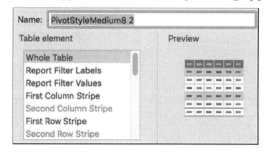

Transactions-8

Elements that aren't affected by this style are grayed out.

3. Type the name **Corporate** into the *Name* text box.

4. Click the *OK* button to dismiss the dialog.

4 Apply the new *Corporate* style to the pivot table.

Click: Design→PivotTable Styles→Custom→Corporate.

You'll see the new *Corporate* style at the top of the *PivotTable Styles* gallery in a new group called *Custom*.

5 Modify the *Corporate* style so that it shows the *Grand Total* column in bold face.

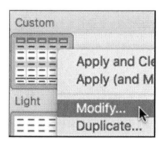

1. Right-click on:

    Design→PivotTable Styles→Custom→Corporate.

2. Click *Modify...* from the shortcut menu.

3. Select *Grand Total Column* from the *Table element* list.

    Grand Total Column is not shown in bold, indicating that the style isn't currently applying any formatting to the grand total column.

4. Click the *Format* button.

5. Select the *Font* tab.

6. Select the *Font style:* Bold.

7. Click the *OK* button.

8. Click the *OK* button again.

    The *Grand Total* column is now shown in bold face.

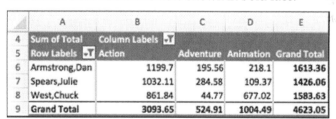

	A	B	C	D	E
4	Sum of Total	Column Labels			
5	Row Labels	Action	Adventure	Animation	Grand Total
6	Armstrong,Dan	1199.7	195.56	218.1	1613.36
7	Spears,Julie	1032.11	284.58	109.37	1426.06
8	West,Chuck	861.84	44.77	677.02	1583.63
9	Grand Total	3093.65	524.91	1004.49	4623.05

6 Save your work as *Transactions-9*.

Lesson 8-12: Understand pivot table report layouts

1   Open *Transactions-9* from your sample files folder (if it isn't already open).

2   Remove all existing fields from the pivot table by dragging them up into the field list.

This is another way to remove selected fields.

It's important to realize that when you drag a field back to the field list, you do not clear any filter conditions associated with the field.

3   Select the fields shown below.

You learned how to do this in: *Lesson 8-3: Understand pivot table rows and columns.*

The pivot table is shown in *compact form layout*. This is the default layout.

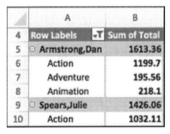

This layout is useful when you need the report to take up the minimum amount of space on screen or paper.

Subsidiary fields are only slightly indented from their parent field.

Transactions-9

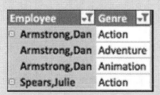
4 Change the report layout to *Outline Form*.

Click:

Design→Layout→Report Layout→Show in Outline Form

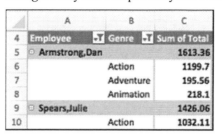

Outline Form is the classic pivot table layout that was the default in pre-2007 versions of Excel.

Outline Form takes up more space but is more readable, as each field has its own column label.

5 Change the report layout to *Tabular Form*.

Click:

Design→Layout→Report Layout→Show in Tabular Form

	A	B	C
4	Employee ⊤	Genre ⊤	Sum of Total
5	Armstrong,Dan	Action	1199.7
6		Adventure	195.56
7		Animation	218.1
8	Armstrong,Dan Total		1613.36
9	Spears,Julie	Action	1032.11
10		Adventure	284.58
11		Animation	109.37
12	Spears,Julie Total		1426.06
13	West,Chuck	Action	861.84
14		Adventure	44.77
15		Animation	677.02
16	West,Chuck Total		1583.63
17	Grand Total		4623.05

This layout is very easy to read because it is similar to a regular Excel table with totals shown at the bottom of each column.

This layout is also very useful when you want to copy the values in a pivot table into a regular range (especially when combined with the *Repeat All Item Labels option* – see sidebar).

6 Save your work as *Transactions-10.*

Lesson 8-13: Add/remove subtotals and apply cell styles to pivot table fields

1   Open *Transactions-10 from* your sample files folder (if it isn't already open).

2   Apply a filter to show only the *Biography* and *Thriller* genres.

You learned how to do this in: *Lesson 8-5: Apply a simple filter and sort to a pivot table.*

3   Add the *Title* field to the pivot table as a third-level row label.

Drag the *Title* field into to the *Rows* list.

4   If necessary, expand all of the *Genre* fields to show all *Titles.*

You learned how to do this in: *Lesson 8-2: Create a grouped pivot table report.*

Because the pivot table layout is set to *Tabular Form,* subtotals are displayed for all subsidiary groups. Both *Employee* and *Genre* are showing subtotals.

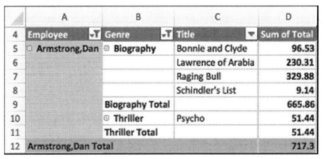

	A	B	C	D
4	Employee	Genre	Title	Sum of Total
5	Armstrong,Dan	Biography	Bonnie and Clyde	96.53
6			Lawrence of Arabia	230.31
7			Raging Bull	329.88
8			Schindler's List	9.14
9		Biography Total		665.86
10		Thriller	Psycho	51.44
11		Thriller Total		51.44
12	Armstrong,Dan Total			717.3

5   Format the *Genre* subtotal fields using the *Total* cell style.

1. Hover the mouse cursor over the left edge of the *Biography Total* label in cell B9.

2. Make sure you see the black arrow cursor shape and then click to select.

	A	B	C
9		Biography Total	
10		Thriller	Psycho

Transactions-10

Notice that, when you select the field, all *Genre subtotal* cells are selected.

3.   Click: Home→Styles→Cell Styles→Total.

4.   The *Total* style is applied to all *Genre subtotal* fields.

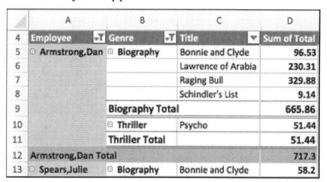

6   Remove the *Genre* subtotals.

1.   Right-click on any of the Genres in column B.

2.   Click *Field Settings* from the shortcut menu.

3.   Under *Subtotals*, click *None*.

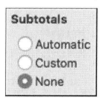

4.   Click the *OK* button.

The *Genre* subtotal fields are removed.

7   Remove the *Grand Total*.

Click:
Design→Layout→Grand Totals→Off for Rows & Columns.

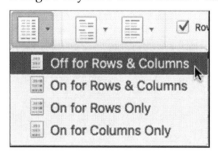

8   Save your work as *Transactions-11*.

Lesson 8-14: Display multiple summations within a single pivot table

It is possible to show the same *Value* field many times in the same pivot table.

This is useful when you need to display different summations (such as Average, Sum and Max) on a single pivot table.

1 Open *Transactions-11 from* your sample files folder (if it isn't already open).

2 Remove the *Genre* and *Title* fields from the *Rows* list.

3 Add two more *Total* fields to the *Values* list.

Drag the *Total* field from the field list to the *Values* pane twice.

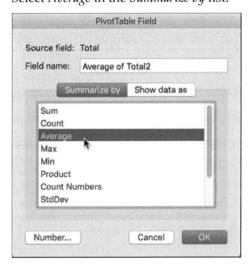

4 Change the new totals to show *Average* sales and *Maximum* sales for each employee.

1. Right-click anywhere in column C within the pivot table.

2. Click *Field Settings* from the shortcut menu.

3. Select *Average* in the *Summarize by* list.

4. Click the *OK* button.

5. Use the same technique to make the *Sum of Total3* field display the maximum (*Max*) value.

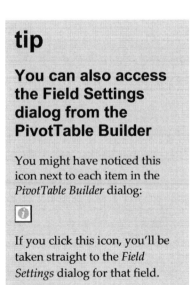
Transactions-11

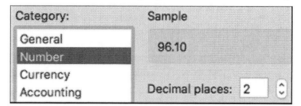

	A	B	C	D
4	Employee ⊤	Sum of Total	Average of Total2	Max of Total3
5	Armstrong,Dan	7880.51	96.10378049	248.73
6	Spears,Julie	10683.14	99.84242991	243.85
7	West,Chuck	6847.74	96.44704225	239.05

5   Format the *Average of Total2* field so that it displays two decimal places.

    1.   Right-click on any value in column C within the pivot table.

    2.   Click *Field Settings* from the shortcut menu.

    3.   Click the *Number…* button.

    4.   Select the *Number* category and set two decimal places.

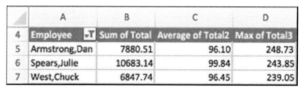

Category:	Sample
General	**96.10**
Number	
Currency	
Accounting	Decimal places: 2

    5.   Click the *OK* button twice to close both dialogs.

	A	B	C	D
4	Employee ⊤	Sum of Total	Average of Total2	Max of Total3
5	Armstrong,Dan	7880.51	96.10	248.73
6	Spears,Julie	10683.14	99.84	243.85
7	West,Chuck	6847.74	96.45	239.05

6   Add a *Grand Total*.

    Click: Design→Layout→Grand Totals→On for Columns Only.

	A	B	C	D
4	Employee ⊤	Sum of Total	Average of Total2	Max of Total3
5	Armstrong,Dan	7880.51	96.10	248.73
6	Spears,Julie	10683.14	99.84	243.85
7	West,Chuck	6847.74	96.45	239.05
8	Grand Total	25411.39	97.74	248.73

7   Save your work as *Transactions-12*.

tip

It is often easier to add calculated fields to the source data

When the data source is a worksheet (as is the case in this lesson) it is usually faster and more efficient to add the calculated field to the source data on the worksheet.

You will then see the new field appear in the field list when you refresh the pivot table.

You learned how to refresh a pivot table in: *Lesson 8-4: Understand the pivot table data cache.*

Lesson 8-15: Add a calculated field to a pivot table

1 Open *Transactions-12* from your sample files folder (if it isn't already open).

2 Remove the *Average of Total2* and *Max of Total3 Fields*.

You learned how to do this in: *Lesson 8-3: Understand pivot table rows and columns.*

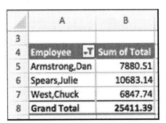

3 Format the *Sum of Total* field to show a comma thousand separator.

　1. Right-click any of the values in column B within the pivot table.

　2. Click *Field Settings* from the shortcut menu.

　3. Click the *Number...* button.

　4. Click the *Number* category.

　5. Check the *Use 1000 Separator (,)* check box.

　6. Click the *OK* button twice to close both dialogs.

4 Add a calculated field called *Bonus* that will calculate 3% of total sales.

　1. Click: PivotTable Analyze→Calculations→ Fields, Items, & Sets→Calculated Field...

　　The *Insert Calculated Field* dialog appears.

　2. Type **Bonus** into the *Name* text box.

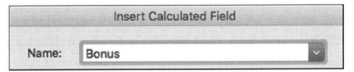

　3. Click in the *Formula* box and remove the zero, leaving only an = sign.

　4. Click *Total* in the *Fields* list and then click the *Insert Field* button.

　　The word **Total** is added to the Formula.

　5. Type ***3%** to complete the formula.

Transactions-12

Formula: = Total*3%

6. Click the *OK* button.

A new field called *Bonus* has now appeared in the field list, and a *Sum of Bonus* field has appeared in column C.

	A	B	C
4	Employee ▼	Sum of Total	Sum of Bonus
5	Armstrong,Dan	7,880.51	236.42
6	Spears,Julie	10,683.14	320.49
7	West,Chuck	6,847.74	205.43
8	Grand Total	25,411.39	762.34

5   Change the names at the top of columns B and C to *Sales* and *Bonus Due*.

1. Click cell B4.

2. Type the new name: **Sales**

3. Press the **<Tab>** key to save the value and move to cell C4.

4. Type: **Bonus Due** into cell C4.

6   Remove the *Field Header* (this is currently shown in row 4).

The pivot table looks untidy because cell A4 includes a filter button. If you wanted to print the pivot table, you would also want to remove the filter button.

	A	B	C
3			
4	Employee ▼	Sales	Bonus Due
5	Armstrong,Dan	7,880.51	236.42

Click: PivotTable Analyze→Show→Field Headers.

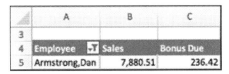

Field List

+/- Buttons

Field Headers

Show

The three items in the *Show* group are toggle buttons which allow you to show and hide different pivot table artefacts.

The pivot table is now well formatted.

	A	B	C
3			
4		Sales	Bonus Due
5	Armstrong,Dan	7,880.51	236.42
6	Spears,Julie	10,683.14	320.49
7	West,Chuck	6,847.74	205.43
8	Grand Total	25,411.39	762.34

The *Values* label has disappeared, but so has the *Employee* label.

It is possible to show the *Employee* label without the filter icon. See sidebar for a special technique you can use to make this possible.

7   Save your work as *Transactions-13*.

tip

Creating a custom header row

In this lesson, you switched off the field headers in order to remove the filter button from cell A4.

This had the side-effect of also removing the word *Employee* from cell A4. It isn't then possible to type any text into cell A4.

If you wanted to keep the *Employee* label but suppress the filter button, you would need to hide row 4 and then re-create the headers in row 3. Here's how you could do this:

1. Copy cells A4:C4 into cells A3:C3.

2. To hide row 4, right-click the row header (the number 4 on the left of the row) and then click *Hide* from the shortcut menu.

3. Type: **Employee** into cell A3.

	A	B
2		
3	Employee	Sales
5	Armstrong,Dan	7,880.51
6	Spears,Julie	10,683.14
7	West,Chuck	6,847.74
8	Grand Total	25,411.39

Lesson 8-16: Add a calculated item to a pivot table

One *field* will usually consist of several *items*. For example, the *Genre* field consists of items such as *Drama, Comedy, Action, Biography* etc.

If you wanted to show a sales target of **Sales + 10%,** you'd simply create a calculated field (as described in: *Lesson 8-15: Add a calculated field to a pivot table*).

Sometimes you will want to perform a calculation upon an arbitrary group of items. In this lesson's example, you are interested in combined sales for the *Drama, Comedy* and *Action* genres, as they are your top sellers.

Calculated items provide a solution to this problem. In this lesson, you'll add a calculated item to find the total sales in these genres.

1   Open *Transactions-13* from your sample files folder (if it isn't already open).

2   Clear all filters and fields from the pivot table.

Click: PivotTable Analyze→Actions→Clear→Clear All.

3   Add the following fields to the pivot table:

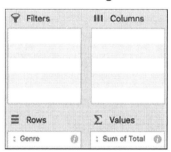

4   Format the *Sum of Total* field to show two decimal places with a thousand comma separator.

1.   Right-click on any of the values in column B within the pivot table.

2.   Click *Field Settings* from the shortcut menu.

3.   Click the *Number…* button.

4.   Click the *Number* category.

5.   Check the *Use 1000 Separator (,)* check box.

6.   Click the *OK* button twice to close both dialogs.

Your pivot table now looks like the one shown in the sidebar.

	A	B
4		Sum of Total
5	Action	37,411.40
6	Adventure	8,588.03
7	Animation	5,098.87
8	Biography	17,174.78
9	Comedy	37,614.16
10	Crime	25,212.68
11	Drama	67,097.47
12	Fantasy	11,785.28
13	Sci Fi	7,289.18
14	Thriller	5,514.95
15	Grand Total	222,786.80

5   Add a calculated item to show total sales for the genres: *Drama, Comedy* and *Action*.

1.   Click any pivot table cell in column A.

2.   Click: PivotTable Analyze→Calculations→ Fields, Items, & Sets→Calculated Item…

The *Insert Calculated Item* dialog appears.

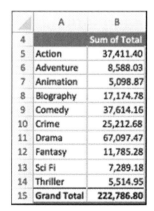

Transactions-13

This is very similar to the *Insert Calculated Field* dialog. The dialog can be confusing because it shows many fields and items that would not be valid for the *Genre* field. They are not grayed out as you would expect.

3. Name the calculated item: **Drama, Comedy & Action**

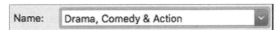

4. Select the *Genre* field and the *Drama* item and then click the *Insert Item* button.

    The formula changes to include the *Drama* item.

5. Type a + operator into the formula.

6. Add the *Comedy* and *Action* items in the same way so that your formula is the same as the following:

7. Click the *OK* button.

    A total for *Drama, Comedy & Action* appears at the bottom of the pivot table.

	A	B
14	Thriller	5,514.95
15	Drama, Comedy & Action	142,123.03
16	Grand Total	364,909.83

    Notice that this addition has corrupted the *Grand Total,* as *Drama, Comedy & Action* are now included in the *Grand Total* twice.

6   Filter the individual *Drama, Comedy* and *Action* fields so that they are no longer shown or included in the *Grand Total.*

    Because the *Field Headers* are currently switched off, you cannot apply a filter.

    1. Click: PivotTable Analyze→Show→Field Headers.

    2. The *Genre* field header appears in cell A4.

	A	B
4	Genre ▼	Sum of Total
5	Action	37,411.40

    3. Click the drop-down arrow to the right of cell A4.

    4. Remove the individual *Drama, Comedy* and *Action* items by un-checking their check boxes.

    5. The *Grand Total* is now correct.

	A	B
11	Thriller	5,514.95
12	Drama, Comedy & Action	142,123.03
13	Grand Total	222,786.80

7   Save your work as *Transactions-14.*

Lesson 8-17: Group by text

In *Lesson 8-16: Add a calculated item to a pivot table,* you used a calculated item to show a group total for the *Action, Comedy & Drama* genres.

Another solution to this requirement would be to create a *group* for these three genres. The pivot table could then show group totals.

You'll push things a little further in this lesson by placing each of the genres into three groups:

- Action, Comedy & Drama
- Crime, Biography & Fantasy
- Adventure, Sci Fi, Thriller & Animation

1   Open *Transactions-14* from your sample files folder (if it isn't already open).

2   Remove all of the existing fields and filters from the pivot table (including the calculated item added in the last lesson).

You'll often want to remove all items from your pivot table to start again. To do this, click:

PivotTable Analyze→Actions→Clear→Clear All

3   Add the following fields to the pivot table.

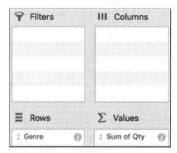

4   Format the *Sum of Qty* field so that it shows 0 decimal places and a comma separator for thousands.

1.   Right-click anywhere in column B within the pivot table.

2.   Click *Field Settings* from the shortcut menu.

3.   Click the *Number...* button.

4.   Click the *Number* category.

5.   Set 0 decimal places with a thousand separator.

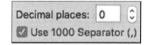

6.   Click the *OK* button twice to close both dialogs.

5   Add a group for the *Action, Comedy* and *Drama* genres.

1.   Click on the *Drama* field in column A (cell A11).

2.   Hold down the **<Cmd>** key and then click on the *Comedy* (A9) and *Action* (A5) fields in column A.

Cells A11, A9 and A5 are now selected.

Transactions-14

3. Right-click on any of the selected cells and click:
Group and Outline→Group...

The fields are grouped:

6 Change the *Genre2* label to *Category* and the *Group1* label to *Action, Comedy & Drama*.

The default names are not very descriptive. Single-click (be careful not to double-click) on each field (cells A4 and A5) and then type in the new labels.

Category	Genre	Sum of Qty
Action, Comedy & Drama	Action	4,699
	Comedy	4,747

7 Create the *Crime, Biography & Fantasy* group and the *Adventure, Sci Fi, Thriller & Animation* group.

Do this in exactly the same way (this time you will select the *Genres* in column B).

8 Resize column A and collapse all categories.

This was covered in: *Lesson 8-2: Create a grouped pivot table report.*

Your pivot table should now look like this:

Category	Genre	Sum of Qty
Action, Comedy & Drama		17,885
Adventure, Sci Fi, Thriller & Animation		3,477
Crime, Biography & Fantasy		6,441
Grand Total		27,803

9 Add subtotals for each group.

1. Right-click anywhere in column A within the pivot table.

2. Click *Field Settings* from the shortcut menu.

The *Field Settings* dialog appears.

3. Click the *Automatic* option button in the *Subtotals* section.

4. Click the *OK* button.

5. Expand the category groups (if they are not already expanded).

Subtotals are now shown for each defined group.

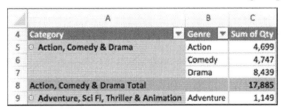

10 Save your work as *Transactions-15*.

Lesson 8-18: Group by date

Out of all of the skills covered in my classroom *Expert Skills* course, this is surely the star of the show.

Excel's ability to summarize transactional data by monthly totals is extremely difficult to achieve without a pivot table.

In versions of Excel prior to Excel 2007, this feature was so well hidden that most Excel users didn't even know it was there. Things are a little better with the new ribbon interface.

1   Open *Transactions-15* from your sample files folder (if it isn't already open).

2   Remove all of the existing fields from the pivot table.

You'll often want to remove all fields and filters from your pivot table to start again. To do this, click:

PivotTable Analyze→Actions→Clear→Clear All

3   Add the following fields to the pivot table.

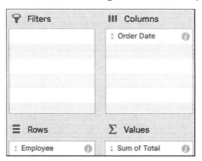

Sales are now shown for every employee and for every date.

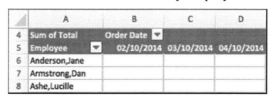

	A	B	C	D
4	Sum of Total	Order Date		
5	Employee	02/10/2014	03/10/2014	04/10/2014
6	Anderson,Jane			
7	Armstrong,Dan			
8	Ashe,Lucille			

Sales are summarized by day but it is more likely that you will want to show sales by week, month, quarter or year.

4   Show monthly sales for each employee.

1.   Right-click on any of the dates in row 5.

2.   Click: Group and Outline→Group…

The *Grouping* dialog appears.

3.   Click *Months*.

4.   Hold down **<Cmd>** and click *Years*.

Both *Months* and *Years* are selected.

When you group by months, be very careful that you also group by years. If you don't, you'll get October 2007, 2008 and 2009 grouped into a single total!

note

Grouping using the ribbon

In this lesson, you use the right-click method to display the *Grouping* dialog in order to group fields.

It is also possible to do this using the ribbon but it is a little more involved and requires more clicks.

1. Click the *Order Date* field to make it the Active Field.

2. Click: PivotTable Analyze→ Group→ Group Selection→Group.

The *Grouping* dialog is then displayed.

Transactions-15

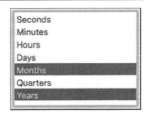

5. Click the *OK* button.

The pivot table is now grouped by year and by month.

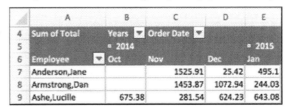

5 Collapse the pivot table to show sales by year.

1. Right-click cell B5 to display the shortcut menu for the *Years* field.

2. Click: Group and Outline→Hide Detail.

Sales are now shown by year.

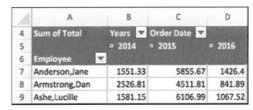

6 Expand the pivot table to show sales by month and year.

1. Right-click cell B5 to display the shortcut menu for the *Years* field.

2. Click: Group and Outline→Show Detail.

Sales are now shown by month and year.

7 Apply a filter to show sales for 2016.

1. Click the drop-down arrow next to *Years* in cell B4.

The filter dialog appears.

2. Uncheck *(Select All)* and check the *2016* box.

3. Click away from the dialog to close it.

Only sales for 2016 are now shown.

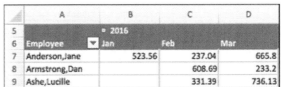

8 Save your work as *Transactions-16*.

Lesson 8-19: Group by numeric value ranges

1   Open *Employee Age Profile-1* from your sample files folder.

2   Convert the range A3:C27 into a table named **Data**.

In Excel 2016, it is best practice to base pivot tables upon tables (you would have used a named range in pre 2007 Excel versions).

1. Click anywhere in the range A3:C27.

2. Click: Insert→Tables→Table.

3. Click the *OK* button.

4. Type the name **Data** into:

   Table→Properties→Table Name

3   Rename the worksheet tab from *Sheet1* to *Data*.

4   Create a pivot table from the Data table.

1. Click anywhere inside the table.

2. Click: Insert→Tables→PivotTable.

3. Click the *OK* button.

5   Rename the pivot table worksheet tab to: **Age Profile**

6   Add the following fields to the pivot table:

(The order is important. *Age* must come before *Name*).

The pivot table now groups employees by age.

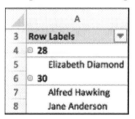

Note that some of the employees may have got a little older by the time you read this book.

Where two or more employees are of the same age, they are grouped together.

The challenge for this lesson will be to group employees into different age bands.

Employee Age Profile-1

7 Group the pivot table into the age bands: *Under 40, 40-49, 50-60* and *Over 60.*

1. Right-click any of the ages in column A (for example: cell A6).

2. Click: Group and Outline→Group...

   The *Grouping* dialog is displayed.

3. Type the following values into the dialog:

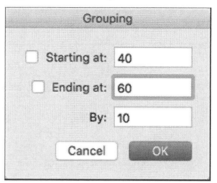

This tells Excel to group into the ages:

- Less than 40

- Between 40 and 60 in bands of 10 years

- Over 60

4. Click the *OK* button.

   Ages are now grouped as defined:

When data is grouped in this way it is sometimes referred to as a *frequency distribution.*

8 Change the *Row Labels* label in cell A3 to: **Age Group**

1. Click once on cell A3.

2. Type **Age Group** into the cell.

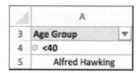

3. Press the **<Enter>** key.

9 Save your work as *Employee Age Profile-2.*

Lesson 8-20: Show row data by percentage of total rather than value

In this lesson, you will discover which genres each employee is best at selling. This will enable the company to allocate sales leads for each genre to the most competent salesperson in that genre.

This time you're not interested in total sales, but the percentage of sales by genre for each employee.

As a bonus, you'll see the percentage market share of each genre.

1   Open *Transactions-16* from your sample files folder.

2   Remove all of the existing fields and filters from the pivot table.

> You'll often want to remove all fields and filters from your pivot table to start again. To do this, click:
>
> PivotTable Analyze→Actions→Clear→Clear All

3   Add the following fields to the pivot table.

4   Format the *Sum of Total* field to show two decimal places and thousand separators.

> This was covered in: *Lesson 8-1: Create a one dimensional pivot table report from a table.*
>
> Sales are now shown for every employee and for every genre.

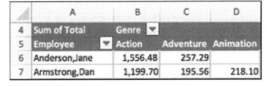

	A	B	C	D
4	Sum of Total	Genre ▼		
5	Employee ▼	Action	Adventure	Animation
6	Anderson,Jane	1,556.48	257.29	
7	Armstrong,Dan	1,199.70	195.56	218.10

5   Show sales values as a percentage of each row's total.

1.   Right-click on any of the numerical values in the pivot table.

2.   Click *Field Settings* from the shortcut menu.

> The *Field Settings* dialog is displayed.

Transactions-16

3. Click the *Show data as* tab.

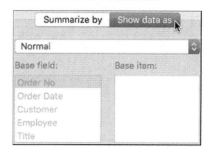

4. Select *% of row* from the *Show data as* drop down list.

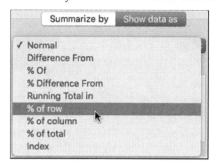

5. Click the *OK* button.

   Values are now shown as a percentage of each employee's sales:

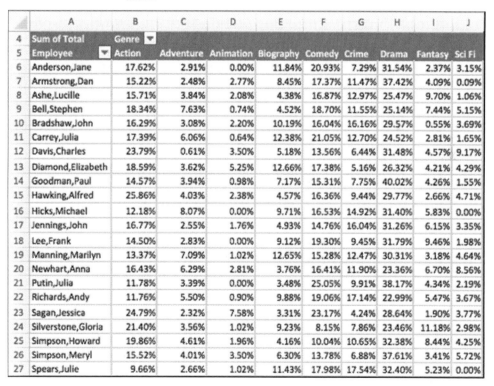

Employee	Action	Adventure	Animation	Biography	Comedy	Crime	Drama	Fantasy	Sci Fi
Anderson,Jane	17.62%	2.91%	0.00%	11.84%	20.93%	7.29%	31.54%	2.37%	3.15%
Armstrong,Dan	15.22%	2.48%	2.77%	8.45%	17.37%	11.47%	37.42%	4.09%	0.09%
Ashe,Lucille	15.71%	3.84%	2.08%	4.38%	16.87%	12.97%	25.47%	9.70%	1.06%
Bell,Stephen	18.34%	7.63%	0.74%	4.52%	18.70%	11.55%	25.14%	7.44%	5.15%
Bradshaw,John	16.29%	3.08%	2.20%	10.19%	16.04%	16.16%	29.57%	0.55%	3.69%
Carrey,Julia	17.39%	6.06%	0.64%	12.38%	21.05%	12.70%	24.52%	2.81%	1.65%
Davis,Charles	23.79%	0.61%	3.50%	5.18%	13.56%	6.44%	31.48%	4.57%	9.17%
Diamond,Elizabeth	18.59%	3.62%	5.25%	12.66%	17.38%	5.16%	26.32%	4.21%	4.29%
Goodman,Paul	14.57%	3.94%	0.98%	7.17%	15.31%	7.75%	40.02%	4.26%	1.55%
Hawking,Alfred	25.86%	4.03%	2.38%	4.57%	16.36%	9.44%	29.77%	2.66%	4.71%
Hicks,Michael	12.18%	8.07%	0.00%	9.71%	16.53%	14.92%	31.40%	5.83%	0.00%
Jennings,John	16.77%	2.55%	1.76%	4.93%	14.76%	16.04%	31.26%	6.15%	3.35%
Lee,Frank	14.50%	2.83%	0.00%	9.12%	19.30%	9.45%	31.79%	9.46%	1.98%
Manning,Marilyn	13.37%	7.09%	1.02%	12.65%	15.28%	12.47%	30.31%	3.18%	4.64%
Newhart,Anna	16.43%	6.29%	2.81%	3.76%	16.41%	11.90%	23.36%	6.70%	8.56%
Putin,Julia	11.78%	3.39%	0.00%	3.48%	25.05%	9.91%	38.17%	4.34%	2.19%
Richards,Andy	11.76%	5.50%	0.90%	9.88%	19.06%	17.14%	22.99%	5.47%	3.67%
Sagan,Jessica	24.79%	2.32%	7.58%	3.31%	23.17%	4.24%	28.64%	1.90%	3.77%
Silverstone,Gloria	21.40%	3.56%	1.02%	9.23%	8.15%	7.86%	23.46%	11.18%	2.98%
Simpson,Howard	19.86%	4.61%	1.96%	4.16%	10.04%	10.65%	32.38%	8.44%	4.25%
Simpson,Meryl	15.52%	4.01%	3.50%	6.30%	13.78%	6.88%	37.61%	3.41%	5.72%
Spears,Julie	9.66%	2.66%	1.02%	11.43%	17.98%	17.54%	32.40%	5.23%	0.00%

You can see at a glance that *Alfred Hawking* does very well with sales in the *Action* genre, and that *Paul Goodman* is our star performer in the *Drama* genre.

You should keep *Michael Hicks* and *Julie Spears* away from *Science Fiction* sales.

6 Save your work as *Transactions-17*.

note

Produce a well formatted report from a pivot table using paste values

Many users work around the formatting limitations of pivot tables like this:

1. Select and copy the cells that you need from the pivot table.

2. Select the destination cell.

3. Click: Home→Clipboard→ Paste→Paste Special→ Values and number formats.

4. Format the pasted values in any way you wish.

This works, but makes it impossible to refresh the well formatted version.

Lesson 8-21: Use pivot table values in simple formulas

1   Open *Central Park Temperature-1* from your sample files folder (if it isn't already open).

This file contains the average monthly temperatures recorded in New York's Central Park between 2010 and 2015 along with a pivot table that shows the temperatures for April, May and June side by side for the years 2014 and 2015:

	A	B	C
3	Sum of Avg Temp F	Column Labels ▾T	
4	Row Labels ▾T	2014	2015
5	Apr		52.3 54.3
6	May		64 68.5
7	Jun		72.5 71.2

With the skills you have learned in this session so far, you should have no difficulty understanding how this pivot table was created.

It took me less than 30 seconds to create this pivot table and demonstrates the amazing ability of pivot tables to quickly summarize data. It will not, however, win any design competitions.

2   Type: **increase/Decrease** into cell D4.

3   Add a formula to cell D5 to show the increase/decrease in temperature for each month.

The automatic insertion of GETPIVOTDATA functions confuses and irritates many Excel users, because most Excel users would do this:

1.   Click in cell D5.

2.   Press the equals key: <=>

3.   Click on cell C5.

4.   Press the minus key <->.

5.   Click on cell B5.

6.   Press the **<Enter>** key.

7.   Autofill cell D5 down to cell D7.

Here's the result of the above actions:

	A	B	C	D
3	Sum of Avg Temp F	Column Labels ▾T		
4	Row Labels ▾T	2014	2015	Increase/Decrease
5	Apr		52.3 54.3	2
6	May		64 68.5	2
7	Jun		72.5 71.2	2

If you examine the formula in cell D5 you'll understand why the calculations return incorrect values. You thought you were asking Excel to create the very simple formula:

=C5-B5

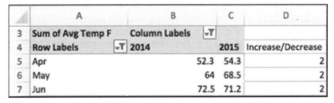

Central Park Temperature-1

Instead, Excel has created the complex formula:

=GETPIVOTDATA("Avg Temp F",$A$3,"Month",4,"Years",2015)-GETPIVOTDATA("Avg Temp F",$A$3,"Month",4,"Years",2014)

This is an odd thing for Excel to do, as it is inconsistent with the way that Excel normally behaves when creating a formula.

Unfortunately, you can't switch off this feature in Excel 2016 for Mac (see sidebar).

In: *Lesson 8-21: Use pivot table values in simple formulas,* you'll discover that you can make good use of the GETPIVOTDATA function to make your formulas more resilient to changes in the pivot table layout.

Here's how you can use simple formulas in the above scenario:

1. Delete the formulas from cells D5:D7.

2. Type **=C5-B5** (using the keyboard and not the mouse) into cell D5 (or the formula bar).

3. Autofill cell D5 down to cell D7.

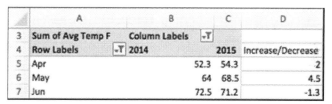

4   Use simple formulas to populate the *Simple Formula Method* range on the *Formatted Report worksheet.*

1. Delete column D from the *TemperaturePivotTable* worksheet.

2. Select the *Formatted Report* worksheet.

3. Enter this formula into cell C7:

    =TemperaturePivotTable!B5

    This formula retrieves the value of cell B5 from the *TemperaturePivotTable* worksheet.

4. Autofill this formula across to cell D7 and down to cells C8:D9.

    The values from the pivot table are displayed:

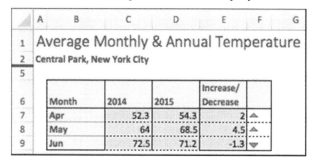

The table's cells now reference the cell addresses of the relevant pivot table's cells. It you refresh the pivot table, the values in the formatted report will also update.

5   Save your work as *Central Park Temperature-2.*

note

A value must be visible on the screen for GETPIVOTDATA to work

If you filter a pivot table, or change it in some other way so that a value is no longer visible, the GETPIVOTDATA function will return an error.

Lesson 8-22: Use the GETPIVOTDATA function

In: *Lesson 8-21: Use pivot table values in simple formulas*, you worked with this pivot table:

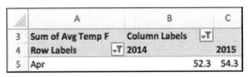

In the previous lesson you used simple formulas to reference the correct cell addresses in the pivot table (for example =B5 was used to return the temperature in April 2014).

Unfortunately, there's a problem with this approach. When a pivot table is filtered, cell addresses move. For example, if I were to change the filter to also show 2013 temperatures in the pivot table, the pivot table would look like this:

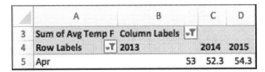

Cell B5 now points to the temperature in April 2013 instead of April 2014, making my formatted report invalid.

To avoid this type of error, you can use the GETPIVOTDATA function to make the formulas resilient to pivot table layout changes.

1   Open *Central Park Temperature-2* from your sample files folder.

2   Automatically create a GETPIVOTDATA function that will return the correct pivot table value to cell C14 in the *Formatted Report* worksheet.

   1.   Click in cell C14 on the *Formatted Report* worksheet and press the equals key: <=>

   2.   Select the *TemperaturePivotTable* worksheet.

   3.   Click in cell B5 and press the <Enter> key.

        A GETPIVOTDATA function is created in cell C14 on the *FormattedReport* worksheet.

=GETPIVOTDATA("Avg Temp F",TemperaturePivotTable!$A$3,"Month",4,"Years",2014)

3   Adjust the GETPIVOTDATA arguments so that they will autofill correctly.

   The GETPIVOTDATA function created by Excel is quite difficult to understand. As with all complex functions, things become a lot easier if you launch the *Formula Builder* task pane.

   1.   Click in cell C14 on the *FormattedReport* worksheet to make it the active cell.

   2.   Click the *Insert Function* button on the left of the formula bar. f_x

Central Park Temperature-2

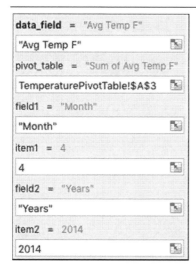

3. The *Formula Builder* task pane appears (see sidebar).

Things are now very easy to understand. The function is returning the *Avg Temp F* value displayed at the intersection of month 4 (April) in the *Month* column and 2014 in the *Years* row displayed in the pivot table.

The pivot table as a whole is identified by any cell within the pivot table (in this case cell A3 is used, but any cell within the pivot table would work).

It should be clear that, no matter how the pivot table layout is changed, the correct result will always be returned. It is vital, however, that the values are always displayed somewhere on the pivot table, otherwise the function will return an error.

4. Fix the formula so that it will autofill correctly.

There's a small problem with the *item1* and *item2* values. They will not autofill correctly. Make the following small changes:

$B14 and C$13 are mixed cell references (mixed cell references are covered in depth in the *Essential Skills* book in this series). They mean "always look in column B but adjust the row" and "always look in row 13 but adjust the column".

The month value (the *item1* argument) is returned using the MONTH function (using the month shown in column B as the function's argument).

The MONTH function works because the months shown in column B are actually date serial numbers formatted as months (you learned about date serial numbers in: *Lesson 3-7: Understand date serial numbers*). The year value (the *item2* argument) is simply obtained from the year value in row 13.

5. Click the *Done* button.

4 Autofill the GETPIVOTDATA function across to cell D14 and down to cells C15:D16.

5 Test the formatted reports for resilience when the *Year* filter is changed.

Click the *Column Labels* filter button on the pivot table and change the filter to also display 2013 temperatures. Notice that the *GETPIVOTDATA method* formatted report still shows the correct values, while the *Simple Formula method* formatted report now shows incorrect values.

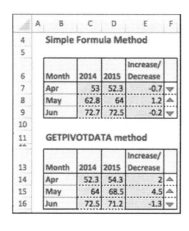

6 Save your work as *Central Park Temperature-3*.

Lesson 8-23: Embed multiple pivot tables into a worksheet

In this lesson, you'll create the following *Sales Summary* worksheet containing three embedded pivot tables:

	A	B		C	D	E		F	
1		Sales Summary							
2									
3		**Customer**	▼	**Sales**		**Employee**	▼	**Sales**	
4		Addison-Freelander Screen Agency		17,135.23		Anderson,Jane		8,833.40	
5		AV Supplies		15,199.30		Armstrong,Dan		7,880.51	
6		Box Office Supplies		22,923.09		Ashe,Lucille		8,755.66	
7		Cheapo Cheap DVD's Ltd		20,145.10		Bell,Stephen		11,649.76	
8		Cinefocus DVD		22,277.45		Bradshaw,John		9,329.37	
9		Classic Films		17,549.80		Carrey,Julia		6,091.91	
10		Creative Films		14,637.39		Davis,Charles		6,800.56	
11		Lights-Camera-Action Ltd		18,106.20		Diamond,Elizabeth		8,965.29	
12		Magic Lantern Classic Film Rental		20,055.78		Goodman,Paul		9,578.01	
13		Silver Screen Video		20,757.07		Hawking,Alfred		10,946.28	
14		Soft Focus Video Rental		17,870.60		Hicks,Michael		7,091.10	
15		Video Flicks International		16,129.79		Jennings,John		11,190.73	
16		**Grand Total**		**222,786.80**		Lee,Frank		13,488.16	
17						Manning,Marilyn		9,064.16	
18		**Genre**	▼	**Sales**		Newhart,Anna		8,937.66	
19		Action		37,411.40		Putin,Julia		8,590.69	
20		Adventure		8,588.03		Richards,Andy		8,302.17	
21		Animation		5,098.87		Sagan,Jessica		11,004.66	
22		Biography		17,174.78		Silverstone,Gloria		8,349.05	
23		Comedy		37,614.16		Simpson,Howard		9,370.30	
24		Crime		25,212.68		Simpson,Meryl		6,522.80	
25		Drama		67,097.47		Spears,Julie		10,683.14	
26		Fantasy		11,785.28		Streep,Margaret		14,513.69	
27		Sci Fi		7,289.18		West,Chuck		6,847.74	
28		Thriller		5,514.95		**Grand Total**		**222,786.80**	
29		**Grand Total**		**222,786.80**					

When several key performance indicators are combined to produce an overview of a business process (in this case Sales) the worksheet is sometimes called a *Dashboard* or *Executive Information System*.

This lesson will also confirm your understanding of many of the skills learned in this session.

1 Open *Transactions-17* from your sample files folder.

2 Add a new worksheet and name it: **Summary**

3 Type **Sales Summary** into cell B1.

Transactions-17

4 Apply the *Title* style to cell B1.

Click: Home→Styles→Cell Styles→Titles and Headings→Title.

5 Embed a pivot table starting at cell B3 to show sales value by *Customer*.

1. Click in cell B3.

2. Click: Insert→Tables→PivotTable.

3. Type **Data** into the *Table/Range* box.

4. Click the *Existing worksheet* option button.

5. Click the *OK* button.

6. In the *PivotTable Builder* dialog, drag the *Customer* field into the *Rows* box and the *Total* field into the *Values* box.

6 Embed a pivot table starting at cell B18 to show sales value by *Genre*.

7 Embed a pivot table starting at cell E3 to show sales value by *Employee*.

8 Format all values to show two decimal places and thousand separators.

This was first covered in: *Lesson 8-15: Add a calculated field to a pivot table.*

9 Change the *Row Labels* text in cells B3, B18 and E3 to read: **Customer**, **Genre** and **Employee**

This was first covered in: *Lesson 8-15: Add a calculated field to a pivot table.*

10 Change the *Sum of Total* labels in cells C3, C18 and F3 to read: **Sales**

11 Add a *3 Traffic Lights (Unrimmed)* conditional format to cells C4:C15.

Conditional formatting is covered in depth in the *Essential Skills* book in this series.

1. Select cells C4:C15.

2. Click: Home→Styles→Conditional Formatting→ Icon Sets→3 Traffic Lights (Unrimmed).

12 Add a *Light Blue Data Bar* conditional format to cells C19:C28.

13 Add a *5 Ratings (Icon Set)* conditional format to cells F4:F27.

14 Re-size the column widths to enhance visual appearance.

15 Save your work as *Transactions-18*.

Lesson 8-24: Use slicers to filter multiple pivot tables

Earlier in this session you learned how to use slicers to provide an elegant user interface when filtering pivot tables.

Slicers become even more powerful when used to filter multiple pivot tables (such as the worksheet created in: *Lesson 8-23: Embed multiple pivot tables into a worksheet*).

In this lesson you'll refine this worksheet to create an overview of sales using slicers to enable the user to filter all of the pivot tables at the same time.

This is a feat that can only be accomplished using slicers. The filter fields that you learned about in: *Lesson 8-6: Use report filter fields* are only capable of filtering a single pivot table.

1 Open *Transactions-18 from* your sample files folder (if it isn't already open).

2 Name the pivot tables: **Customer**, **Employee** and **Genre**

When working with multiple pivot tables it is useful to give each an intuitive name.

1. Click on the *Customer* pivot table to activate it.

2. Click: PivotTable Analyze→PivotTable→PivotTable Name.

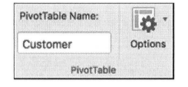

3. Type **Customer** in the *PivotTable Name* box and press the **<Enter>** key.

4. Repeat the process to name the *Employee* and *Genre* pivot tables.

3 Add three slicers that will filter the *Customer* pivot table by *Employee, Customer* and *Genre.*

You learned how to do this in: *Lesson 8-7: Filter a pivot table visually using slicers.*

4 Size and format the slicers so that they provide a compact and attractive user interface.

You learned how to do this in: *Lesson 8-7: Filter a pivot table visually using slicers.*

When you have finished, your user interface should be similar to the screen grab on the facing page.

5 Test your slicers.

Notice that the slicers only affect the *Customer* pivot table. No matter what filter condition you set in the slicers, the values in the *Genre* and *Employee* pivot tables remain unaffected.

6 Connect the slicers to all three pivot tables.

1. Click the *Genre* slicer to select it.

2. Click: Slicer→Slicer→Report Connections.

The *Report Connections* dialog appears.

Transactions-18

note

How can I stop Excel changing pivot table column widths?

This is caused by a glitch in Excel's *Autofit* feature.

The easy solution is to switch off Autofit and size the column widths manually.

To switch off Autofit:

1. Right-click on each pivot table in turn.

2. Select *PivotTable Options* from the shortcut menu.

3. Click the *Layout* tab.

4. Clear the *Autofit column widths on update* check box.

5. Manually resize each column so that they are wide enough to display their contents correctly.

3. Check the *Employee* and *Genre* check boxes to connect this slicer to all three pivot tables on the *Summary* worksheet.

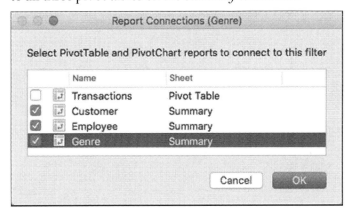

4. Click the *OK* button.

5. Repeat this process for the *Customer* and *Employee* slicers.

7   Test your slicers.

Notice that the slicers now work the way you want them to. All three pivot tables are filtered in accordance with the slicer filters that you select.

You may find that the columns are not wide enough to display their values when a filter is applied. See sidebar for a solution to this problem.

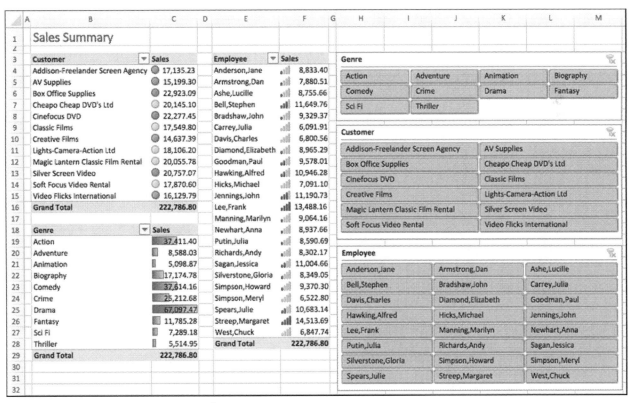

8   Save your work as *Transactions-19*.

Session 8: Exercise

1   Open *Film Sales-1* from your sample files folder.

2   Convert the range into a table named *Data*.

3   Create a pivot table from the *Data* table.

4   Add *Row Labels* and *Values* so that your pivot table looks like this:

	A	B	C
3	Row Labels ▼	Sum of Qty	Sum of Total
4	Fedex	6929	55793.38
5	Royal Mail	6606	52965.68
6	TNT	7366	58884.38
7	UPS	6902	55143.36
8	Grand Total	27803	222786.8

5   Re-format the values in the pivot table and change the text in the headers, so that your pivot table looks like this:

	A	B	C
3	Carrier ▼	Units	Cost
4	Fedex	6,929	55,793.38
5	Royal Mail	6,606	52,965.68
6	TNT	7,366	58,884.38
7	UPS	6,902	55,143.36
8	Grand Total	27,803	222,786.80

6   Add a calculated field to calculate the average cost per unit for each carrier formatted to two decimal places with a 1000 comma separator.

	A	B	C	D
3	Carrier ▼	Units	Cost	Cost per Unit
4	Fedex	6,929	55,793.38	8.05
5	Royal Mail	6,606	52,965.68	8.02
6	TNT	7,366	58,884.38	7.99
7	UPS	6,902	55,143.36	7.99
8	Grand Total	27,803	222,786.80	8.01

7   Embed a second pivot table starting in cell A10 of the same worksheet that will display sales by studio in an attractive format.

	A	B
10	Studio ▼	Sales
11	20th Century Fox	12,819.76
12	BBC TV	2,891.99
13	Columbia Pictures	11,007.66

8   Save your work as *Film Sales-2*.

Film Sales-1

If you need help slide the page to the left ▶

Session 8: Exercise Answers

These are the four questions that students find the most difficult to answer:

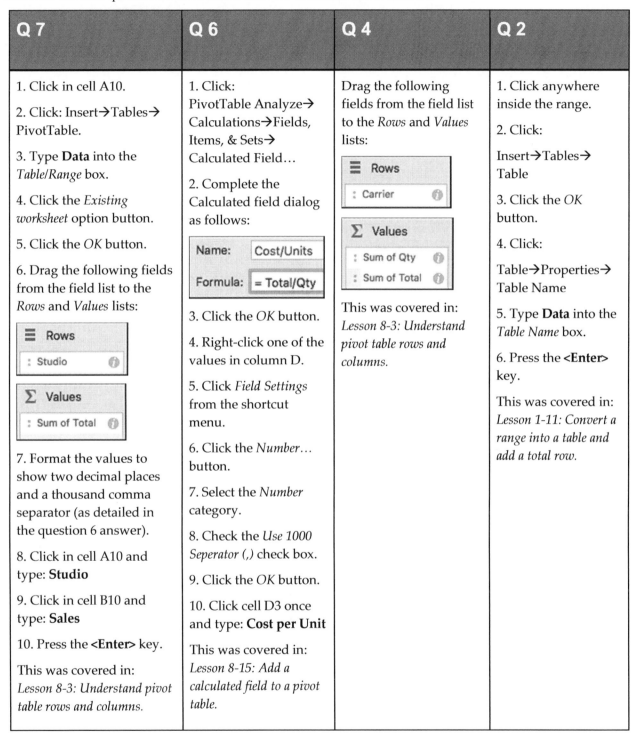

Q 7	Q 6	Q 4	Q 2
1. Click in cell A10. 2. Click: Insert→Tables→PivotTable. 3. Type **Data** into the *Table/Range* box. 4. Click the *Existing worksheet* option button. 5. Click the *OK* button. 6. Drag the following fields from the field list to the *Rows* and *Values* lists: **☰ Rows** : Studio **Σ Values** : Sum of Total 7. Format the values to show two decimal places and a thousand comma separator (as detailed in the question 6 answer). 8. Click in cell A10 and type: **Studio** 9. Click in cell B10 and type: **Sales** 10. Press the **<Enter>** key. This was covered in: *Lesson 8-3: Understand pivot table rows and columns.*	1. Click: PivotTable Analyze→Calculations→Fields, Items, & Sets→Calculated Field... 2. Complete the Calculated field dialog as follows: Name: Cost/Units Formula: = Total/Qty 3. Click the *OK* button. 4. Right-click one of the values in column D. 5. Click *Field Settings* from the shortcut menu. 6. Click the *Number...* button. 7. Select the *Number* category. 8. Check the *Use 1000 Seperator (,)* check box. 9. Click the *OK* button. 10. Click cell D3 once and type: **Cost per Unit** This was covered in: *Lesson 8-15: Add a calculated field to a pivot table.*	Drag the following fields from the field list to the *Rows* and *Values* lists: **☰ Rows** : Carrier **Σ Values** : Sum of Qty : Sum of Total This was covered in: *Lesson 8-3: Understand pivot table rows and columns.*	1. Click anywhere inside the range. 2. Click: Insert→Tables→Table 3. Click the *OK* button. 4. Click: Table→Properties→Table Name 5. Type **Data** into the *Table Name* box. 6. Press the **<Enter>** key. This was covered in: *Lesson 1-11: Convert a range into a table and add a total row.*

If you have difficulty with the other questions, here are the lessons that cover the relevant skills:

3   Refer to: *Lesson 8-1: Create a one dimensional pivot table report from a table.*

5   Refer to: *Lesson 8-1: Create a one dimensional pivot table report from a table* and *Lesson 8-7: Filter a pivot table visually using slicers.*

Appendix A: Differences between the Windows and Mac versions of Excel 2016

Excel 2016 for Mac and *Excel 2016 for Windows* are not identical products, and there are many differences between the two.

The skills taught in this course will still be useful if you apply them to the Windows version of Excel 2016, but you may find that some features behave differently.

This appendix does not list every difference between the Windows and Mac versions. Instead, it only lists the differences that apply to this *Expert Skills* course.

If any of the features listed in this appendix are of vital importance to you, you can discover how to use them in the Windows version of this course.

Important:

Microsoft release regular updates that may implement missing features or change the way that Excel 2016 behaves.

This information was true as of February 2016, but the product may have changed since this book was published.

Additional features available in Excel 2016 for Windows

■ Quick Analysis

The Windows version of Excel 2016 shows a 'smart tag' below selected cells that enables you to quickly create totals, charts, tables and sparklines. The Mac version does not include this feature.

■ Flash Fill

Flash Fill is a feature of Excel 2016 for Windows that enables Excel to automatically split text and carry out calculations by intelligently guessing what the user is trying to do. This feature is not included with the Mac version.

■ Evaluate Formula

The Windows version of Excel 2016 includes an *Evaluate Formula* dialog that allows you to see how formulas are calculated step by step. This feature does not exist in Excel 2016 for Mac.

■ External data source drivers

The Windows version of Excel 2016 is able to connect to any ODBC data source. The Mac version can only connect to SQL Server data sources by default, but 3rd party drivers are available that enable other data sources to be used.

■ Watch Window

The Watch Window is a feature of Excel 2016 for Windows that enables you to monitor the values of cells anywhere in the workbook. This can be useful in complex workbooks with many interconnected worksheets.

The Watch Window is not available in the Mac version of Excel 2016.

■ Ribbon customization

Excel 2016 for Windows allows the ribbon to be fully customized. This enables you to change the commands shown on the default ribbon tabs and to create entirely new ribbon tabs.

The ribbon cannot be customized in Excel 2016 for Mac.

■ Commands not in the Ribbon

Excel 2016 for Windows contains many 'hidden' features that are not shown on the ribbon. These include the *Speak Cells* features that enable Excel to audibly read the values from cells, as well as many other special features.

Excel 2016 for Mac does not have any additional features that are not shown on the ribbon or Menu Bar.

■ Allow Users to Edit Ranges

In the Windows version of Excel 2016, it's possible to add multiple passwords to a workbook that each have access to different cells. This can be useful if a workbook has several users that should be given different access rights.

Excel 2016 for Mac only allows a single password to be created for each workbook.

■ Digital Signatures

Excel 2016 for Windows has the ability to apply a *digital signature* to a workbook. These are used to prove the identity of the author and certify that a document can be trusted.

It is not possible to apply a digital signature to a workbook using Excel 2016 for Mac.

■ ActiveX Controls

ActiveX controls are alternative versions of the form controls that are shown in: *Lesson 7-1: Add group box and option button controls to a worksheet form*. They are rarely used, and are intended to be used with the VBA programming language.

ActiveX controls are not available in the Mac version of Excel 2016.

■ Trusted files and folders

The Windows version of Excel 2016 allows you to define a list of trusted files and folders. Files that are trusted or saved to a trusted folder can be opened without any warnings, even if they contain macros.

It isn't possible to define trusted files and folders in Excel 2016 for Mac, so a warning will be shown every time any macro-enabled workbooks are opened.

■ Macro security settings

Excel 2016 for Windows allows you to choose between several settings for macro security. Macros can be completely disabled, enabled after showing a warning message, only enabled for digitally signed workbooks, or always enabled.

Excel 2016 for Mac only allows the warning message to be either switched on or switched off.

■ Relative references in macros

In the Windows version of Excel 2016, it's possible to record macros using either *absolute* or *relative* references. Absolute references mean that the macro will always affect the same cells every time it runs. Relative references mean that it will affect cells relative to the position of the active cell when the macro runs. Relative macros are very useful when you need a macro to affect different cells each time the user runs it, instead of always affecting the same cells.

It isn't possible to record a macro with relative references in Excel 2016 for Mac, so all macros use absolute references.

■ Slicer table filtering

Excel 2016 for Windows enables you to filter a table with a slicer. This is not possible in the Mac version of Excel 2016, where slicers can only be used to filter pivot tables.

■ Timelines

A timeline is a special type of slicer that is specifically used to filter data by date and time.

Timelines aren't available in Excel 2016 for Mac, but you can replicate their functionality using slicers, as shown in: *Lesson 8-8: Use slicers to create a custom timeline*.

■ OLAP pivot tables and relationships

Standard Excel pivot tables can only summarize data from a single table, while OLAP pivot tables can draw their data from multiple tables. To make this possible, *relationships* must be created between the data tables, creating what is known as a *data model*.

OLAP features are only available in Excel 2016 for Windows, so none of these features can be used in the Mac version of Excel.

■ Automatic date grouping in pivot tables

When a field containing date information is added to a pivot table in Excel 2016 for Windows, it is automatically split into appropriate groups (usually *Year, Quarter, Month* and *Day*).

This does not happen in the Mac version of Excel 2016, but the same result can be achieved by using the *Group* feature, as shown in: *Lesson 8-18: Group by date*.

■ Automatic insertion of GETPIVOTDATA functions setting

When you create a formula that references cells within a pivot table, Excel automatically inserts a GETPIVOTDATA function. This feature can be disabled in the Windows version of Excel 2016, but is always enabled in the Mac version.

■ PivotCharts

Excel 2016 for Windows enables you to create PivotCharts. These are charts that have the same features as pivot tables, including the ability to filter data within the chart.

PivotCharts cannot be created in Excel 2016 for Mac.

■ 3D Maps

Excel 2016 for Windows has the ability to display data on a 3D map of the world. This is useful for presenting data that is tied to geographical locations.

3D Maps cannot be created in Excel 2016 for Mac.

■ Get & Transform

Get & Transform (previously known as PowerQuery) is now included in Excel 2016 for Windows.

Get & Transform allows you to connect to external data sources and perform many different transformations upon them, including unpivoting summarized data, appending several data sources together and setting data types.

Get & Transform is not available in Excel 2016 for Mac.

■ <Alt>+<;> keyboard shortcut

In the Windows version of Excel 2016, you can use the **<Alt>+<;>** keyboard shortcut to quickly select visible cells.

This keyboard shortcut is not available in the Mac version of Excel 2016.

■ Range name scope

Excel 2016 for Windows allows range names to have either *worksheet* or *workbook scope*. Range names with *worksheet scope* can only be referenced within a single worksheet, while *workbook scope* allows them to be referenced anywhere in the workbook.

In Excel 2016 for Mac, all range names have workbook scope, so you cannot define a range name that only resides in a single worksheet.

Range names are covered in: *Lesson 4-1: Automatically create single-cell range names.*

■ Paste names in dialogs

The *Paste Names* feature enables quick insertion of range names. This is shown in: *Lesson 4-1: Automatically create single-cell range names.*

Excel 2016 for Mac does not allow this feature to be used within dialogs. It can only be used to insert range names into cells and formulas.

In Excel 2016 for Windows, this feature can also be used to insert range names into dialogs and task panes.

■ 'Data entered in a table is invalid' error checking rule

Excel 2016 for Mac's eight error checking rules are shown in: *Lesson 4-11: Understand background error checking and error checking rules.*

Excel 2016 for Windows offers one additional error checking rule, called: *Data entered in a table is invalid.* This rule is only relevant when connecting to data that is stored on a SharePoint server.

■ Pivot table Defer Layout Update option

Excel 2016 for Windows offers a *Defer Layout Update* option when editing pivot tables. This allows you to fully configure a pivot table without anything appearing on the worksheet, and without any calculations being performed. This is useful when working with very large data sets that could take a long time to calculate.

The *Defer Layout Update* option is not available in Excel 2016 for Mac.

■ Fn+F4 shortcut key in Formula Builder

The **Fn+F4** keyboard shortcut is used to quickly define absolute cell references. Unfortunately, this keyboard shortcut cannot be used within the *Formula Builder* task pane. This limitation can be worked around by using the technique shown in: *Lesson 3-6: Use the SUMIF and COUNTIF functions to create conditional totals*.

The Fn+F4 keyboard shortcut works without problems in the equivalent dialog in Excel 2016 for Windows (the *Insert Function* dialog).

■ 'Always create backup' save option

When saving a workbook, Excel 2016 for Windows offers the *Always create backup* option. If this option is enabled, a separate backup version of the workbook is created whenever the workbook is saved.

This option is not available in the Mac version of Excel 2016.

■ Embedded object resizing

Excel workbooks embedded into other document types cannot be resized in the Mac version of Office 2016. This can be worked around by embedding the workbook from a linked file, as shown in: *Lesson 6-4: Link an Excel worksheet to a Word document*.

■ Merging multiple workbooks simultaneously

Excel 2016 for Mac only allows you to merge two workbooks at a time when sharing a workbook using the *merge method*. You can merge as many workbooks as necessary, but you must merge them one at a time.

Excel 2016 for Windows allows you to merge multiple workbooks simultaneously.

Sharing using the merge method is covered in: *Lesson 6-8: Share a workbook using the merge method*.

■ Multi-Select button in slicers

Excel 2016 for Mac allows you to select multiple items in a slicer by holding down the **Cmd** key.

Excel 2016 for Windows adds an additional *Multi-Select* button to slicers, which allows you to select multiple items without holding down any keys.

Selecting multiple items in slicers is shown in: *Lesson 8-8: Use slicers to create a custom timeline*.

■ Select all search results in pivot table filters

Excel 2016 for Mac offers the ability to perform a search within a pivot table filter. However, it does not offer an option to select all search results, so they must be selected individually. This is shown in: *Lesson 8-6: Use report filter fields*.

Note that this feature *is* available in standard filters; it is only missing from pivot table filters.

Excel 2016 for Windows offers this option in all filters, including pivot tables.

▓ Pivot table filter by selection

Excel 2016 for Mac enables you to filter an ordinary range of data by selecting a range of cells and then filtering to show only records that match the selected values. However, this option is not available when working with pivot tables.

This feature is demonstrated in: *Lesson 1-5: Apply a simple filter to a range.*

Excel 2016 for Windows allows this option to be used within pivot tables.

Features that behave differently in Excel 2016 for Windows

■ **Formula Builder task pane**

In the Windows version of Excel 2016, the Formula Builder task pane is replaced by the Insert Function dialog.

The Insert Function dialog has the same purpose and features of the Formula Builder, but appears as a floating dialog instead of a task pane.

■ **Insert Name feature**

In the Mac version of Excel, you can quickly insert a range name by clicking:

➲→Insert→Name→Paste, as shown in: *Lesson 4-1: Automatically create single-cell range names*.

In the Windows version of Excel, this feature is accessed using the Ribbon command:

Formulas→Defined Names→Use in Formula.

■ **Name Manager**

Excel 2016 for Windows offers a separate *Name Manager* dialog that enables you to view and edit all of the range names that have been defined within a workbook.

In the Mac version of Excel 2016, these features have been included in the *Define Name* dialog. This is demonstrated in: *Lesson 4-4: Automatically create range names in two dimensions*.

■ **Error checking dialog modality**

The *Error Checking* dialog is shown in: *Lesson 4-12: Manually check a worksheet for errors*. The Mac version of Excel 2016 does not allow you to interact with the workbook as long as the dialog is open (in other words, it is a *modal* dialog).

Excel 2016 for Windows allows you to make changes to the workbook while the *Error Checking* dialog is on-screen. This will pause error checking, requiring you to click a *Resume* button when returning to the dialog.

■ **Scenario summary report formatting**

A scenario summary report is shown in: *Lesson 5-4: Create a scenario summary report*.

Scenario summary reports created in Excel 2016 for Windows have different formatting to summary reports created in Excel 2016 for Mac. The differences are only cosmetic, so the same values will be displayed in both versions.

■ **Custom views and tables**

Excel 2016 for Windows does not allow custom views to be created if a table is present anywhere in the workbook.

The Mac version allows custom views and tables to coexist.

■ **Protect Windows**

The *Protect Windows* option does not work in Excel 2016 for Windows, but will work without problems in Excel 2016 for Mac.

Protect Windows was shown in: *Lesson 5-10: Control the changes users can make to workbooks*.

■ Editing embedded Excel objects

In Office 2016 for Windows, it's possible to edit an embedded Excel object within a Word document without leaving Word.

In Office 2016 for Mac, editing an embedded Excel object always launches a separate Excel window.

■ PivotTable Builder dialog

Excel 2016 for Mac uses the *PivotTable Builder* dialog to configure pivot tables.

Excel 2016 for Windows replaces this with a *PivotTable Fields* task pane.

The dialog and task pane have the same purpose and features.

■ Locked workbook notifications

When a workbook is locked for editing by another user, you are prompted to open the workbook in read-only mode. This is shown in: *Lesson 6-7: Share a workbook using the lock method*.

The Windows version of Excel 2016 allows you to choose whether you want to be notified when the other user closes the workbook. Excel 2016 for Mac defaults to this option, so you will always be notified when a locked workbook becomes available for editing.

■ Manual pivot table sorting

Manual pivot table sorting is shown in: *Lesson 8-5: Apply a simple filter and sort to a pivot table*.

The same thing is possible in Excel 2016 for Windows, but it must be specifically enabled. Manual sorting is always enabled in Excel 2016 for Mac.

■ Range name bug

Excel 2016 for Windows contains a bug where the Apply Names feature (shown in: *Lesson 4-3: Use range names to make formulas more readable*) does not always work correctly.

This bug is not present in Excel 2016 for Mac, so range names should always be applied to formulas without problems.

■ Filtering pivot tables by multiple values

Excel 2016 for Windows defaults to only allow a single value to be selected in a pivot table filter. To select more than one value, the *Select Mutiple Items* option must be enabled.

Excel 2016 for Mac always allows multiple items to be selected in pivot table filters.

Pivot table filters are covered in: *Lesson 8-6: Use report filter fields*.

■ Pivot table Group and Outline options

Excel 2016 for Mac allows the pivot table outline to be expanded and collapsed by using the commands: Group and Outline→Show Detail and Group and Outline→Hide Detail.

This is shown in: *Lesson 8-2: Create a grouped pivot table report*.

Excel 2016 for Windows uses an *Expand/Collapse* menu in place of the *Group and Outline* menu and uses the commands *Expand* and *Collapse* in place of *Show Detail* and *Hide Detail*.

■ Recommended PivotTables

When creating a pivot table, Excel 2016 for Mac offers the *Recommended PivotTables* option. This option automatically creates a pivot table based upon your data that should be useful for general purposes, but it will create the same generic pivot table each time.

Excel 2016 for Windows offers a choice of several different recommended pivot tables when this option is used, instead of always using the same template.

Appendix B: Skills Covered in the Essential Skills Course

In order to get the most out of this book you should already be very comfortable with Excel's main features. We also have an *Essential Skills* course for absolute beginners.

ISBN: 978-1-909253-11-7
342 pages.

ISBN: 978-1-909253-12-4
(This book).

This (Expert Skills) book assumes that you have already mastered the skills taught in the *Essential Skills* book.

So how do you know if your skills are already advanced enough to tackle this book?

This appendix lists the objectives for each of the eight sessions in the *Essential Skills* course.

If you already have all (or at least most) of the skills taught in the *Essential Skills* course you are ready to upgrade your skills to Expert level with this course.

Essential skills course outline

Session 1

- Configure your mouse and understand right clicking
- Start Excel and open a new blank workbook
- Understand update models
- Check that your Excel version is up to date
- Change the Office Theme
- Maximize, minimize, re-size, move and close the Excel window
- Understand Full Screen view
- Download the sample files and open/navigate a workbook
- Save a workbook to a local file
- Understand common file formats
- Pin a workbook and understand file organization
- View, move, add, rename, delete and navigate worksheet tabs
- Use the ribbon
- Understand ribbon components
- Understand views
- Hide and show the Formula Bar and ribbon
- Use the help search system

Session 2

- Enter text and numbers into a worksheet
- Create a new workbook and view two workbooks at the same time
- Use AutoSum to quickly calculate totals
- Select a range of cells and understand Smart Tags
- Enter data into a range and copy data across a range
- Select adjacent and non-adjacent rows and columns
- Select non-contiguous cell ranges and view summary information
- AutoSelect a range of cells
- Re-size rows and columns
- Use AutoSum to sum a non-contiguous range
- Use AutoSum to quickly calculate averages
- Create your own formulas
- Create functions using Formula AutoComplete
- Use AutoFill for text and numeric series

- Use AutoFill to adjust formulas
- Use AutoFill Options
- Speed up your AutoFills and create a custom fill series
- Use the zoom control
- Print out a worksheet

Session 3

- Insert and delete rows and columns
- Use AutoComplete and fill data from adjacent cells
- Cut, copy and paste
- Cut, copy and paste using drag and drop
- Use Paste Values and increase/decrease decimal places displayed
- Transpose a range
- Use Undo and Redo
- Insert, View and Print cell comments
- Understand absolute, relative and mixed cell references
- Understand templates
- Create a template
- Use a template
- Freeze columns and rows
- Split the window into multiple panes
- Check spelling

Session 4

- Format dates
- Understand date serial numbers
- Format numbers using built-in number formats
- Create custom number formats
- Horizontally and Vertically align the contents of cells
- Merge cells, wrap text and expand/collapse the formula bar
- Understand themes
- Use cell styles and change themes
- Add borders and lines
- Create your own custom theme
- Create your own custom cell styles
- Use a master style book to merge styles
- Use simple conditional formatting

- Manage multiple conditional formats using the Rules Manager
- Bring data alive with visualizations
- Create a formula driven conditional format
- Insert a Sparkline into a range of cells
- Apply a common vertical axis and formatting to a Sparkline group
- Apply a date axis to a Sparkline group and format a single Sparkline
- Use the Format Painter
- Rotate text

Session 5

- Understand chart types, layouts and styles
- Create a simple chart with two clicks
- Move, re-size, copy and delete a chart
- Create a chart using the Recommended Charts feature
- Add and remove chart elements using Quick Layout
- Apply a pre-defined chart style and color set
- Manually format a chart element
- Format 3-D elements and add drop shadows
- Move, re-size, add, position and delete chart elements
- Change a chart's source data
- Assign non-contiguous source data to a chart
- Understand data series and categories
- Change source data using the Select Data Source dialog tools
- Chart non-contiguous source data by hiding rows and columns
- Create a chart with numerical axes
- Deal with empty data points
- Add data labels to a chart
- Highlight specific data points with color and annotations
- Add gridlines and scale axes
- Emphasize data by manipulating pie charts
- Create a chart with two vertical axes
- Create a combination chart containing different chart types
- Add a trend line
- Add a gradient fill to a chart background
- Create your own chart templates

Session 6

- View the same workbook in different windows
- Duplicate worksheets within a workbook
- Move and copy worksheets from one workbook to another
- Hide and unhide a worksheet
- Create cross worksheet formulas
- Understand worksheet groups
- Use find and replace

Session 7

- Print Preview and change paper orientation
- Use Page Layout view to adjust margins
- Use Page Setup to set margins more precisely and center the worksheet
- Set paper size and scale
- Insert, delete and preview page breaks
- Add auto-headers and auto-footers and set the starting page number
- Add custom headers and footers
- Specify different headers and footers for the first, odd and even pages
- Print only part of a worksheet
- Add row and column data labels and grid lines to printed output
- Print several selected worksheets and change the page order

Session 8

- Save a workbook to a OneDrive
- Open a workbook from a OneDrive
- Understand operating systems and devices
- Understand Office versions
- Understand Excel Online
- Open a workbook using Excel Online
- Share a link to a workbook
- Edit a workbook simultaneously with other users using Excel Online

Index

The Essential Skills book isn't only for beginners! Experts find it useful too.

Many purchasers of *Expert Skills* decide to also purchase the *Essential Skills* book (the first book in this series). *Essential Skills* isn't only for Excel beginners. I often teach this course (as a classroom course) to professionals that have used Excel for over ten years and they *always* gain some fantastically useful skills from the course.

While *Expert Skills* is aimed at users that are already comfortable with Excel, *Essential Skills* assumes no previous exposure to Excel and teaches all of the core skills. This is usually enough for the average office worker.

Turn back a few pages to *Appendix B* and you'll find a summary of all lessons taught in the *Essential Skills* book.

Search for it at **Amazon.com** or **Amazon.co.uk.**

You can also find links to book resellers stocking this title at the **ExcelCentral.com** web site (click *Books* on the top menu bar).

Use your new Excel skills to teach your own classroom courses.

If you've worked through the Essential Skills and Expert Skills books carefully you are now a true Excel expert.

There is a huge demand, everywhere in the world, for Excel training at all levels. The skills you have learned in the books will enable you to teach both introductory Excel courses (providing all of the skills needed by most office workers) and expert-level Excel courses.

We can directly and rapidly supply books, at educational discount prices, to Excel instructors, corporate clients, schools, colleges and universities from our warehouses in the USA (also serving Canada), UK (also serving Europe) and Australia (also serving New Zealand).

Our books are also printed in the USA, UK, Australia, Germany, Brazil, Poland, South Korea and Russia, so are instantly available in almost every country by simply quoting the ISBN number (shown below) to any bookseller or wholesaler.

Use our books to teach all Excel versions.

This book is available for Excel 2016 for Mac along with all Excel for Windows versions in common use today (Excel 2007, 2010, 2013 and 2016). This means that you'll be able to teach Excel classes even if the client uses an earlier version. You can use the books as courseware during your classes and then give each student a copy of the book to take home as reference material when the course is over.

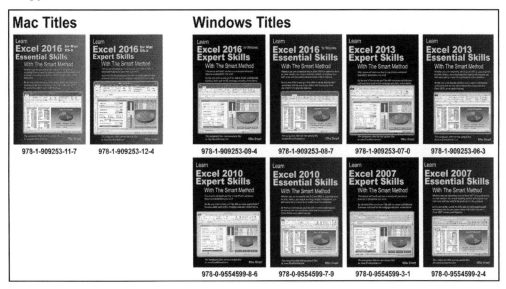

You can quote the ISBN numbers shown above to any book retailer or wholesaler. All major distributors have our books in stock for immediate delivery.

Order 5+ books and we'll offer you an educational discount!

If you live in the USA, Canada, UK, Europe, Australia or New Zealand we can rapidly deliver books to your doorstep at a discount price. You only need to order five books or more (you can mix titles if you wish).

To place a wholesale order fill in our online form here:

http://www.excelcentral.com/discounts

Obtain a fast solution to any Excel issue using our support forum

Now that you have mastered Excel you will need to apply your skills to real-world business problems.

Sometimes the correct solution to a specific Excel-related problem is not immediately apparent. Our online support forum enables you to ask our consultants any Excel-related question. One of our staff members will solve the problem – usually within 24 hours of posting.

Here's an example of a support request and reply:

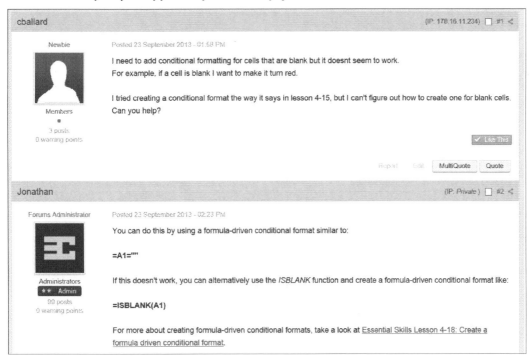

You need to be a member to post questions but you can view all previously asked questions and answers completely free of charge at:

http://forums.excelcentral.com/

Made in the USA
San Bernardino, CA
03 July 2017